Müllenbrock · *The Culture of Contention*

Monographs on Eighteenth-Century English Literature and Culture

edited by
Heinz-Joachim Müllenbrock (Göttingen)
and Hermann Josef Real (Münster)

Forschungen zur englischen Literatur und Kultur des 18. Jahrhunderts

herausgegeben von
Heinz-Joachim Müllenbrock (Göttingen)
und Hermann Josef Real (Münster)

Heinz-Joachim Müllenbrock

The Culture of Contention

A Rhetorical Analysis of the Public Controversy about the Ending of the War of the Spanish Succession, 1710-1713

1997

Wilhelm Fink Verlag

Gedruckt mit Unterstützung des Förderungs- und Beihilfefonds
Wissenschaft der VG Wort

Die Deutsche Bibliothek - CIP-Einheitsaufnahme

Müllenbrock, Heinz-Joachim:
The culture of contention : a rhetorical analysis of the public controversy about the ending of the war of the Spanish succession, 1710 - 1713 / Heinz-Joachim Müllenbrock. - München : Fink, 1997
(Monographs on eighteenth-century English literature and culture)
ISBN 3-7705-3208-2

ISBN 3-7705-3208-2

Herstellung: Ferdinand Schöningh GmbH, Paderborn

To my daughter
Maren

Unhappy Nation! What End can these Things lead us to? Not a Publick Society, not a Coffee-house, not a Meeting of Friends, not a Visit; but like *Jehu to Jezabel, who is on my Side?* Who? Who is for Peace? Who is for carrying on the War? Society is converted into Cabal, all Publick Meetings appear sorted into Committees, or bandyed into Sides as their Notions of Peace or War encline them.

(Defoe, *An Essay at a Plain Exposition of that Difficult Phrase a Good Peace*)

CONTENTS

Preface and Acknowledgements

During the years of researching for this book and also while writing it I have received considerable support from a number of people and institutions.

The University of Göttingen provided generous aid in setting up a comprehensive corpus of primary texts in the English Department.

For his help with the computer-management of this archive I want to thank Prof. Fritz-Wilhelm Neumann of Erfurt University, formerly of the Göttingen English Department.

I should like to express my thanks to several institutions for the encouragement I received in my work: I am grateful to the British Council for a research grant, to the Deutsche Forschungsgemeinschaft for providing funds for materials and personnel, and to the Volkswagen-Stiftung for awarding me an Akademie-Stipendium.

I also wish to thank the librarians of the British Library, the Bodleian Library and the Göttingen University Library for their untiring help.

I received valuable impulses for my work from graduate classes I conducted together with Prof. Hermann Wellenreuther of the History Department of Göttingen University on the public controversies surrounding the termination of the War of the Spanish Succession and the Seven Years' War.

I want to thank Dr. Hans E. Bödeker of the Max-Planck-Institut für Geschichte in Göttingen for his critical review of the introductory chapter.

In my attempt to produce a book in English I received the unfailing support of Dr. Wolfgang Riebe and Dr. James Howard Shaw.

I am grateful to my secretary, Mrs. Sabine Imse, for the pains she has taken with the typescript.

My thanks are also due to my research assistant, Miss Christine Lerche, for checking the typescript and compiling the index.

Introduction: Aims and Method

After some preliminaries in the seventeenth century, the controversy over the termination of the War of the Spanish Succession was the first example in England of a public debate of a great national issue with full media participation. Aspects of foreign, military, domestic and social policy combined to form a set of complex issues of the utmost significance. The debate about the Peace of Utrecht - with its intertwinement of domestic and foreign policy - is the prototype of political contention conducted in public. The significance and impact of the debate attracted a wide range of writers. They made known their stance on the issue of war and peace, which virtually divided the nation, with unprecedented completeness and clarity. This important debate may therefore be regarded as the focal point of a public political culture as it developed in early eighteenth-century England and was eventually to have a lasting impact even abroad.

The present monograph is the first attempt at a detailed account of the debate with special emphasis on its rhetorical features. We want to describe the process of public political communication, in particular its linguistic features. In what manner was language utilized in the attempt to shape politics by appealing to public opinion? First the chronological rhythm of the debate with its sequence of shifts in public consciousness is outlined in order to assess its rhetorical macrostructure. A chapter focusing on the polemical interaction of the turning-point debate, the climax of public altercation, forms the link between those chapters that deal with aspects of macrostructure and those describing its microstructure. Subsequently, microstructural analyses assess the potential of the different forms of political rhetoric and how they interacted in the polemical context of the debate. What was each individual genre's specific function in the dissemination of propaganda? After describing the rhetorical profile of the full scope of political literature, attention focuses on the language of politics, with special reference to the contrast between Whigs and Tories. The general characteristics of political discourse - techniques of argumentation, terminology, imagery - are dealt with. Some observations on aspects of authorship and readership will complete the picture of the public scene.

The book concludes with remarks on the relationship between the public political culture as it had developed and the understanding of politics still prevailing among the political class; this may also throw further light on the historical significance of the Utrecht controversy.

Preliminary Methodological Considerations

The debate about the Peace of Utrecht, which was the first full-fledged manifestation in eighteenth-century England of an emerging 'public political culture' - a term which will be explained more fully in the course of this introduction - and in the long term also set an example for the rest of the world, has for quite some time been of increasing interest as an object of research. The following survey briefly sketches some historiographical approaches to the early eighteenth century in so far as they have proved useful for the present study. Our own research draws on this material, which therefore deserves to be mentioned at least in outline.

Especially valuable have been the investigations since the nineteen-sixties which attempt a reappraisal of late seventeenth and early eighteenth-century English political history. After Walcott's hapless attempt to apply Namierean categories to early eighteenth-century England[1] had been fended off, there was an adequate assessment of the political conditions which did justice to the special characteristics of the period. The crucial fact that the opposing views of Whigs and Tories manifested themselves strictly along party lines with rather clear-cut ideological divisions, which is so typical of the political debate under Queen Anne, was analysed ever more thoroughly. Although political parties were a familiar phenomenon, they were still regarded with suspicion - Shaftesbury, for example, condemned them as an abuse of social impulses[2] - and were unequivocally approved of by only a few contemporaries such as Shute Barrington[3]. But this did not weaken the parties' actual impact on the political life of the period. The factual evidence showing the ideological differences between the parties, which historiography has so amply provided, is an indispensable prerequisite for our own approach. In this context one thinks of the combined efforts of such distinguished historians as Geoffrey Holmes[4], J.H. Plumb[5], W.A. Speck[6] and Henry Horwitz[7], whose work opened the way to an adequate evaluation of early eighteenth-century political life in England.

---

1 See Robert Walcott, *English Politics in the Early Eighteenth Century* (Oxford, 1956). - Cf. on the one-sidedness of the Namier approach H.T. Dickinson, "Party, Principle and Public Opinion in Eighteenth Century Politics", *History* 60 (1975), p. 237.

2 See *Sensus Communis; an Essay on the Freedom of Wit and Humour* (1709): Anthony Earl of Shaftesbury, *Characteristics of Men, Manners, Opinions, Times, etc.*, ed. John M. Robertson, 2 vols. (Gloucester, Mass., 1963), I, 77.

3 See J.A.W. Gunn, "Party before Burke: Shute Barrington", *Government and Opposition* III, no. 2 (Spring 1968), pp. 223-240.

4 See Geoffrey Holmes, *British Politics in the Age of Anne* (London and New York, 1967; rev. ed. 1987); *id.* and W.A. Speck (Eds.), *The Divided Society: Party Conflict in England 1694-1716* (London, 1967, repr. 1970); *id.* (Ed.), *Britain after the Glorious Revolution 1689-1714* (London and Basingstoke, 1969); *id.*, *Politics, Religion and Society in England 1679-1742* (London and Ronceverte, 1986).

5 See J.H. Plumb, *The Growth of Political Stability in England, 1675-1725* (London, Melbourne, Toronto, 1967).

6 See W.A. Speck, *Tory and Whig: The Struggle in the Constituencies, 1701-1715* (London, 1970); *id.* and Holmes (Eds.), *The Divided Society: Party Conflict in England 1694-1716.*

7 See Henry Horwitz, "Parties, Connections, and Parliamentary Politics, 1689-1714: Review and Revision", *Journal of British Studies* 6, No. 1 (November 1966), pp. 45-69; *id.*, *Parliament, Policy and Politics in the Reign of William III* (Newark, 1977).

One aim of the renewed historiographical interest in the early eighteenth century is to shed some light on the interdependence between high politics - both government and opposition - and propaganda. It has been shown that political decisions were increasingly underpinned by laying open their rationale. Already in Queen Anne's reign a decisive breakthrough occurred when senior politicians accepted the fact that publicly debating political decisions - whether still pending or already implemented - and subjecting them to media scrutiny had become an irreversible ingredient of contemporary politics. Henry L. Snyder has shown in several articles how the process of political decision making was increasingly accompanied by propaganda activities[1]. It was then J.A. Downie, who, in his monograph of 1979[2], provided detailed insight into the way in which Harley deliberately encouraged propaganda, which proves that those engaged in the decision making process saw the necessity to seek public approval. Harley's systematic use of propaganda shows that the need to publicly justify political action was regarded as irrevocable and had thus become a permanent feature of national politics.

Historiography's new and more extensive approach to the early eighteenth century, which has set important guidelines for the present book as well, has also increased our knowledge of the general environment in which British journalism developed since the turn of the eighteenth century. In this context the detailed analysis of the legal conditions of the period, first undertaken by Laurence Hanson in his standard work[3] and pursued further with more precise results especially by John Feather[4], must be mentioned. Commercial and technological factors, too, influenced the process of transformation of English journalism especially after 1695. This occupation with the setting of expanding journalism also includes a precise account of the circumstances which proved relevant to the development of the book market and the publishing trade. The findings of Michael Treadwell[5] deserve special mention in this connection.

---

1 Among the many contributions see e.g. Henry L. Snyder, "The Reports of a Press Spy for Robert Harley: New Bibliographical Data for the Reign of Queen Anne", *The Library*, Fifth Series, 22, no. 4 (December 1967), pp. 326-345.

2 See J.A. Downie, *Robert Harley and the Press. Propaganda and Public Opinion in the Age of Swift and Defoe* (Cambridge, 1979).

3 See Laurence Hanson, *Government and the Press, 1695-1763* (Oxford U.P., 1936). Cf. also the later publication by Frederick Seaton Siebert, *Freedom of the Press in England 1476-1776. The Rise and Decline of Government Controls* (Urbana, Ill., 1952).

4 See John Feather, "The Book Trade in Politics: The Making of the Copyright Act of 1710", *Publishing History* 8 (1980), pp. 19-44; *id.*, "The English Book Trade and the Law 1695-1799", *Publishing History* 12 (1982), pp. 51-75; *id.*, "From Censorship to Copyright: Aspects of the Government's Role in the English Book Trade 1695-1775", *Books and Society in History. Papers of the Association of College and Research Libraries, Rare Books and Manuscripts Preconference, 24-28 June, 1980, Boston, Massachusetts*, ed. Kenneth E. Carpenter (New York and London, 1983), pp. 173-198; *id.*, *A History of British Publishing* (London and New York, 1988).

5 See Michael Treadwell, "London Trade Publishers 1675-1750", *The Library*, Sixth Series, 4, No. 2 (June 1982), pp. 99-134; *id.*, "Swift's Relations with the London Book Trade to 1714", *Author/Publisher Relations during the Eighteenth and Nineteenth Cen-*

Establishing the authorship of relevant texts and dating them are further objectives of research on the early eighteenth century relevant to this study. In spite of the present author's acute awareness of these problems he has little to contribute to their solution. Furbank's and Owens' book on Daniel Defoe[1] illustrates the often insurmountable difficulties besetting any attempt to establish with certainty the authorship of texts. The same is true with regard to the dates of texts. This is why one is particularly grateful if there is as firm a basis to build on as that provided by David Woolley with regard to Jonathan Swift's political prose towards the end of Queen Anne's reign[2]. Repeatedly faced with pragmatic considerations, the present author could not but date certain texts simply according to likelihood. The reader should therefore be prepared to tolerate a degree of uncertainty in this respect.

Excellent work has been done, with ever more thorough studies on the public political culture of the early eighteenth century. These enable us to form a detailed picture of the period. However, so far there is no systematic study of the rhetorical implementation of the controversy over the termination of the War of the Spanish Succession. At the end of this admittedly brief survey, I want to define my own objective more closely by setting it against some outstanding monographs that have already cast some light on important aspects of the subject. In his pioneering study of 1881 Alexandre Beljame[3] had shown that in an atmosphere of party-political strife a particular brand of journalism had developed which provided authors of otherwise modest means with a profitable source of income; and D.H. Stevens in his book of 1916[4], in which he concentrated mainly on the journals and periodicals of the time, showed how under Queen Anne writers and their work had become politicised, a development which, however, he referred to somewhat inadequately as a perversion of literary standards through political constraints[5]. But otherwise he saw quite clearly the consequences of conducting political controversies in public, namely that writers were drawn into the maelstrom of political propaganda.

---

turies, ed. Robin Myers and Michael Harris (Oxford Polytechnic Press, 1983), pp. 1-36; *id.*, "On False and Misleading Imprints in the London Book Trade, 1660-1750", *Fakes and Frauds: Varieties of Deception in Print and Manuscript*, ed. Robin Myers and Michael Harris (Winchester: St. Paul's Bibliographies, 1989), pp. 29-46.

1 See P.N. Furbank and W.R. Owens, *The Canonisation of Daniel Defoe* (New Haven and London, 1988). On the problem of attribution of authorship in Defoe's case cf. also J.A. Downie, "Defoe's Early Writings", *The Review of English Studies*, N.S., XLVI (1995), pp. 225-230.

2 See David Woolley, "The Canon of Swift's Prose Pamphleteering, 1710-1714, and *The New Way of Selling Places at Court*", *Swift Studies* 3 (1988), pp. 96-117.

3 See Alexandre Beljame, *Le Public et les Hommes de Lettres en Angleterre au Dix-Huitième Siècle, 1660-1744* (Paris, 1881).

4 See David Harrison Stevens, *Party Politics and English Journalism, 1702-1742* (Menasha, Wisconsin, 1916).

5 See *ibid.*, p. 80.

Then, in 1958, after a lapse of time owing perhaps to historiography's changed priorities over the years, Douglas S. Coombs in a substantial monograph[1] showed from a primarily Dutch, and naturally slanted perspective, how party-political disputes were conducted both intensively and extensively to support foreign-policy goals. Our own study follows Coombs' approach of using the largest possible corpus of texts and is based on a comprehensive examination of all available material with due emphasis on representative samples in order to highlight particular features. With regard to the time pattern of the debate, its internal rhythm, on which Coombs sometimes remains somewhat vague, we aim at greater precision. In particular, for all the impressive documentary evidence of the political parties' fierce public exchanges, there is practically nothing in Coombs on h o w rhetoric was made to serve propagandistic ends, no close analysis of the forms of propaganda and the techniques of polemical interaction.

Finally, Downie's monograph of 1979, *Robert Harley and the Press. Propaganda and Public Opinion in the Age of Swift and Defoe*, provided convincing proof that public political debate was an indispensable element of the political system, that the strategies for influencing public opinion were closely connected with the political Establishment. After early attempts by Lord Somers at the beginning of the century, Harley's circumspect use of propaganda marked the irreversible integration of public political controversy into the political process of the time. In his book Downie shows that this development was particularly strong in the years after 1710 and eventually resulted in subjecting every significant political issue to the scrutiny of public opinion, which was polarised along the dividing lines of an antagonistic two-party system. The proof that Downie furnishes in his book of the interlinking of politics and propaganda, and the insight he offers into the sophisticated ways in which journalism was made to serve as a backup for the political process, have further encouraged the present writer to analyse the entire range of rhetorical efforts which were made to secure a favourable reaction from the public, and to describe how the will to exercise political power translated into diverse forms of polemics. In other words, we are trying to provide the 'rhetorical correlative' to the culture of political contention as it was firmly established towards the end of Queen Anne's reign.

This interdisciplinary[2] study, which has also benefited greatly from the substantial analyses of the interrelationship between politics and journalism in Frances Harris' unpublished dissertation[3], focuses on how the political debate unfolded in the years 1710-1713, what means and techniques of political propaganda were employed and what forms of political rhetoric served which particular purpose. 'Forms of political rhetoric' here means 'genres' in political literature as they ap-

---

1 See Douglas S. Coombs, *The Conduct of the Dutch: British Opinion and the Dutch Alliance during the War of the Spanish Succession* (The Hague and Achimota, 1958).

2 On the necessity of interdisciplinary research in this field cf. *inter alia* the introduction in *Culture, Politics and Society in Britain, 1660-1800*, ed. Jeremy Black and Jeremy Gregory (Manchester and New York, 1991), pp. 1-12.

3 See Frances Marjorie Harris, *A Study of the Paper War Relating to the Career of the 1st Duke of Marlborough, 1710-1712* (doctoral thesis, University of London, 1975).

peared during the political debate. 'Rhetoric' describes on the one hand any individual linguistic effort to influence the formation of public opinion and on the other hand refers in a more general sense to the sum total of such efforts. Thus, as a collective term 'rhetoric' covers the diverse forms of writing that participated in the formation of public opinion *without doors* with a possible influence on decisions taken *within doors*. 'Propaganda', a term I use - like Schwoerer[1] for example - without any implied value judgment, refers to the way in which certain rhetorical objectives were realised and also to the entire corpus of political literature in which rhetoric was thus employed; finally 'propaganda' refers to the underlying political intentions. Occasionally I use 'discourse' to refer to publicly conducted controversy; more than 'propaganda' it underlines the dependence of such public debate on historical circumstance. Our analysis of political rhetoric so defined aims to show how political notions were voiced by applying linguistic strategies which in turn reflected the specific conditions in which a public political culture was developing in early eighteenth-century England. In view of the comprehensiveness of the political debate at the time and the wide range of related genres it seems reasonable to apply the traditional categories of rhetoric to the analysis of political texts, but sufficiently fine-tune them to do justice to any particular context or situation. This less restricted approach, which makes use of categories that are universally applicable to all forms of political writing, seems more appropriate in our case than to do what Quentin Skinner and J.G.A. Pocock, for example, did so well, namely to reconstruct those variations of political language which mark the high points of political thought and then use these to elucidate the history of ideas along pragmatic lines[2]. Although Skinner, too, is concerned with establishing meaning in the intentional sense in specific contexts, the writings of the great political thinkers with their considerable historical and intellectual depth require a more complex treatment, while those genres involved in the conduct of day-to-day politics and more directly governed by the laws of rhetoric may be illuminated by bringing them briefly into sharp focus to reveal their polemical structures. As indicated above, we will at the end of our investigation come full circle, so to speak, by drawing a final conclusion as to the state of public political culture in England as mirrored in the debate on the ending of the War of the Spanish Succession.

---

1 See Lois G. Schwoerer, "Propaganda in the Revolution of 1688-89", *American Historical Review* 82 (1977), pp. 843-874.

2 On this debate, which cannot be properly documented here, see *inter alia* the following articles: Lotte Mulligan, Judith Richards and John Graham, "Intentions and Conventions: A Critique of Quentin Skinner's Method for the Study of the History of Ideas", *Political Studies* 27 (1979), pp. 84-98; James H. Tully, "Review Article: The Pen is a Mighty Sword: Quentin Skinner's Analysis of Politics", *British Journal of Political Science* 13 (1983), pp. 489-509; "What Is Intellectual History?", *History Today* 35 (1985), pp. 46-54; David Boucher, *Texts in Context. Revisionist Methods for Studying the History of Ideas* (Dordrecht/Boston, Lancaster, 1985), chapters 4 and 5; Melvin Richter, "Zur Rekonstruktion der Geschichte der Politischen Sprachen: Pocock, Skinner und die *Geschichtlichen Grundbegriffe*", Hans Erich Bödeker and Ernst Hinrichs (Eds.), *Alteuropa - Ancien Régime - Frühe Neuzeit: Probleme und Methoden der Forschung* (Stuttgart-Bad Cannstatt, 1991), pp. 134-174.

THE DEVELOPMENT OF A 'PUBLIC POLITICAL CULTURE' IN ENGLAND AFTER THE GLORIOUS REVOLUTION

As Joseph Klaits[1] has shown, the French absolutist regime, too, would not miss the opportunity to make use of the printed word for propaganda purposes, for instance in foreign-policy matters. In various ways propaganda in France was diplomacy by other means. In England, on the other hand, the political culture developing after the Revolution of 1688/89 was truly 'public' in the sense that political issues were more and more often debated in the public arena, which, though not entirely free from state interference, was far from being subjected to any rigorous control. Since the end of the seventeenth century discussion of political issues in England took place in a semi-autonomous sphere in which freedom of expression was practically guaranteed to an extent completely unknown on the European Continent. There foreign-policy issues were almost never discussed publicly[2], not even in the case of France, where a fair measure of public debate already existed, as has been maintained for example by Mona Ozouf[3]. 'Public' in this connection also describes the fact that support was not only secured - by order from above, so to speak - for government decisions, but that government and opposition alike - witness the bipartisan practice of free distribution of political literature[4] - put their conflicting views before a wider forum beyond the confines of Parliament, where they had to pass the test of public judgment and occasionally had to be revised. Moreover, the term 'public political culture'[5] refers to the need that policy makers felt to seek assent from a wider audience, to have their decisions judged by a kind of ad hoc forum which, though acting in a constitutional void, as it were, was in actual fact - at least in essence - a kind of complementary controlling institution. The political class seemed increasingly inclined to no lon-

---

1 See Joseph Klaits, *Printed Propaganda under Louis XIV. Absolute Monarchy and Public Opinion* (Princeton U.P., 1976).

2 Cf. Jeremy Black, "The British Press and Europe in the Early Eighteenth Century", *The Press in English Society from the Seventeenth to Nineteenth Centuries*, ed. Michael Harris and Alan Lee (Rutherford, London and Toronto, 1986), p. 67.

3 See Mona Ozouf, "'Public Opinion' at the End of the Old Regime", *Journal of Modern History* 60, Supplement (September 1988), pp. S1-S21.

4 See *inter alia* Michael Harris, "Newspaper Distribution during Queen Anne's Reign. Charles Delafaye and the Secretary of State's Office", *Studies in the Book Trade* (Oxford, 1975), p. 149 and Frances Harris, "Paper-Round: The Distribution of Whig Propaganda in 1710", *Factotum* No. 9 (August 1980), pp. 12-13.

5 The further development of this phenomenon is dealt with in an informative volume edited by Eckhart Hellmuth, *The Transformation of Political Culture. England and Germany in the Late Eighteenth Century* (The German Historical Institute London, 1990). The term 'public' political culture is, however, not used there.

ger ignore that the "larger political nation"[1], avid for political literature, demonstrated a growing political commitment and in its wake expected that decisions be transparent and stand the test of rational analysis. At the same time public political culture, despite its inherent, often deplored contentiousness, exercised a stabilising function by enabling a bridge to be built between the numerically inferior political class and the vast majority of the population, which demanded its share in the political debate.

The Revolution of 1688/89 may be regarded as the beginning of a public political culture in England. The focus of power shifted from the Crown to the various aristocratic factions competing in Parliament; this led to a change in the constitutional pattern which fostered the rise of English journalism[2]. In France, however, the competitive, individualistic element of public discourse never allowed the ideal of integration to disappear[3]. William III's propaganda efforts to lead the Glorious Revolution to success ushered in a new age for journalism, too, as L.G. Schwoerer has shown in great detail in one of his articles[4]. After a short period of political unity a power struggle developed from 1694 onwards in the wake of the Triennial Act. It was this struggle between the aristocratic factions dominating the political parties which turned out to be a seedbed for public political disputes. The struggle between Whigs and Tories transcended the parliamentary arena with its political in-groups and thus turned the wider public into a kind of new appellate authority. The vast majority of the population, that is all those who did not have the right to vote, were thus given a chance to participate in the process of political communication. The rivalries between the parties fostered the formation of political opinions among a pluralistic public susceptible to different forms of propaganda according to social background and wooed by government and opposition alike publicly arguing their case. Of course one must keep in mind that in most cases "it is almost impossible to assess how far it [propaganda] reflected and how far it formed opinion"[5].

When the Licensing Act expired in 1695, this was for all practical purposes also the end of state censorship. Conditions were henceforth more favourable to the development of a public political culture[6] that met the needs inherent in British politics. After the lapse of the Licensing Act printing and publishing experienced a tremendous boom. In the wake of unlicensed printing in London alone ten

---

1 Cf. Lawrence Stone, "Literacy and Education in England 1640-1900", *Past and Present* 42 (1969), p. 85.

2 See in this connection the sketch in Heinz-Joachim Müllenbrock (Ed.), *Europäische Aufklärung II*, Neues Handbuch der Literaturwissenschaft, 12 (Wiesbaden, 1984), pp. 2-7.

3 See e.g. Ozouf, "'Public Opinion' at the End of the Old Regime", pp. S5, S15-16.

4 See p. 16, note 1.

5 W.A. Speck, "Political Propaganda in Augustan England", *Transactions of the Royal Historical Society*, Fifth Series, 22 (1972), p. 28.

6 Cf. Feather, "The English Book Trade and the Law 1695-1799", p. 52 and Raymond Astbury, "The Renewal of the Licensing Act in 1693 and its Lapse in 1695", *The Library*, Fifth Series, 33, no. 4 (December 1978), p. 322.

new papers were founded within ten years[1], and of the newly founded periodicals under Queen Anne a surprisingly large number were political[2]. In 1695 there had been only one newspaper, the official *London Gazette*, and now new publications were mushrooming. *The Daily Courant*, the first daily paper, appeared in 1702, the *Evening Post*, the first evening paper, in 1706[3]. In 1704 the foundation of Defoe's *Review* marked the growing importance of periodicals; the periodical essayists were soon to become important figures in the struggle to influence public opinion. The *Review* had been preceded by the *Observator*, which catered for a certain section of the public with its dialogue format. In the *Tatler* of 21 May 1709 Joseph Addison seemed somewhat amused by the fact that so many papers were competing to meet the needs of a public hungry for political information[4]. The participation of periodicals and newspapers in the public debate - something that did not exist to any comparable degree before 1695 - created conditions in which the battle for public support could take place uninterrupted over longer periods[5]. Especially those periodicals which specialized in commentary and the formation of opinion and had apparently met with little response at first but expanded fast after 1702[6] became a measure of the growing intensity of public political controversy and the concomitant increasing polarisation of the political parties. The diversity and range of political literature can hardly be overrated. Nearly all genres were represented and almost all the well-known authors contributed to the public dispute[7], which experienced another boost after 1710[8]. Although research has not been able so far to provide reliable figures on the reading public - this applies even to the London area - there is sufficient evidence that the public debate of political issues, conducted with hitherto unknown intensity - which can be measured by the impressive number of responses to all forms of political writing -, met with a widely positive reaction, and the emergence of a public political culture may well be seen as a revolution in its own right.

It is not easy to judge the reading public in terms of sheer numbers. Some reliable figures on the circulation of periodicals do exist[9], but they say little about

---

1 Cf. Eckhart Hellmuth, *'Liberty' und 'Licentiousness'. Der Diskurs über Pressefreiheit im frühneuzeitlichen England (ca. 1660 - ca. 1800)* (Habilitationsschrift, University of Trier, 1990), p. 114.

2 Cf. Stevens, *Party Politics and English Journalism*, pp. 61 and 63.

3 Cf. Downie, *Robert Harley and the Press*, p. 9.

4 See *The Tatler*, ed. Donald F. Bond, 3 vols. (Oxford, 1987), I, 148-151.

5 Rightly pointed out by William Speck in "Politics and the Press", *The Press in English Society from the Seventeenth to Nineteenth Centuries*, ed. Harris and Lee, p. 47.

6 Cf. E.S. De Beer, "The English Newspapers from 1695 to 1702", Ragnhild Hatton and J.S. Bromley (Eds.), *Willliam III and Louis XIV. Essays 1680-1720 by and for Mark A. Thomson* (Liverpool U.P., 1968), p. 127.

7 Cf. Paula R. Backscheider, *Daniel Defoe: His Life* (Baltimore and London, 1989), p. 328.

8 Cf. Stevens, *Party Politics and English Journalism*, p. 68.

9 See James R. Sutherland, "The Circulation of Newspapers and Literary Periodicals, 1700-30", *The Library*, Fourth Series, 15 (1934-35), pp. 110-122; J.M. Price, "A Note on the Circulation of the London Press, 1704-1714", *Bulletin of the Institute of Histori-*

how many people actually read them. Addison, as we know, assumed that each issue of the *Spectator*, on display in coffee houses, was read by about twenty people[1], but optimistic guesses put this figure much higher[2]. As to the *Evening Post*, a 'partisan paper', each copy is assumed to have had ten readers[3]. But then circulation figures reveal comparatively little about a paper's or a periodical's political impact[4], Defoe's *Review* being a good case in point.

It is also difficult to quantify the potential readership of political literature. It may be assumed with some certainty that the high educational standard that prevailed in mid-seventeenth century England as compared with the European Continent continued well into Queen Anne's reign[5]. Literacy was especially widespread among the middle class[6]. However, research infers literacy from the sole fact that people were able to write their names, a method that has over and again been rightly criticised as facile[7], because the simple fact that people were able to sign documents says little about whether they actually understood particular texts[8]. Significantly, historians on the one hand and literary historians[9] on the other differ in their assessment of literacy, with the former usually being more optimistic. But even these optimistic figures need to be qualified according to whether they refer to London, other cities and towns or rural areas; similar distinctions have to be made with regard to social background.

It is probably not far from the truth to assume that just as eighteenth-century literature in the sense of belles-lettres was mainly written for the middle and upper classes - a familiar fact to any literary historian - so was political literature. Political propaganda thus followed the pattern of the reading public's expectations and abilities, which in turn depended on the educational standards of the respec-

---

cal Research 31 (1958), pp. 215-224; and especially Henry L. Snyder, "The Circulation of Newspapers in the Reign of Queen Anne", *The Library*, Fifth Series, 23, no. 3 (September 1968), pp. 206-235; *id.*, "A Further Note on the Circulation of Newspapers in the Reign of Queen Anne", *The Library*, Fifth Series, 31, no. 4 (December 1976), pp. 387-389.

1 See the programmatic tenth number of the *Spectator* (12 March 1711).

2 Cf. De Beer, "The English Newspapers from 1695 to 1702", p. 126.

3 Cf. F.P. Lock, *Swift's Tory Politics* (London, 1983), p. 5.

4 Cf. Snyder, "The Circulation of Newspapers in the Reign of Queen Anne", p. 209.

5 Cf. Stone, "Literacy and Education in England 1640-1900", p. 109.

6 See *ibid.*, p. 109 and David Cressy, *Literacy and the Social Order. Reading and Writing in Tudor and Stuart England* (Cambridge U.P., 1980), pp. 176-177.

7 See for example R.A. Houston, *Scottish Literacy and the Scottish Identity. Illiteracy and Society in Scotland and Northern England 1600-1800* (Cambridge U.P., 1985), pp. 162 and 179ff. and Ernst Hinrichs, "Wie viele Menschen konnten um 1800 lesen und schreiben?", Helmut Ottenjann and Günter Wiegelmann (Eds.), *Alte Tagebücher und Anschreibebücher* (Münster, 1982), p. 100.

8 The present author would like to warn against unfounded confidence with a confession by Sancho Panza (*Don Quijote*, part II, ch. 36): "'[...] yo no sé leer ni escribir, puesto que sé firmar'"!

9 See e.g. Ian Watt, *The Rise of the Novel. Studies in Defoe, Richardson and Fielding* (5th impr., London, 1967), p. 36. Cf. also the sceptical view of Germany in the eighteenth century in Rudolf Schenda, *Volk ohne Buch* (Frankfurt a.M., 1970), pp. 443-445.

tive social strata[1]. We do not, by the way, concern ourselves in this study with any such distinction between the metropolis and the provinces as to the production and reception of political propaganda. In fact, our study is based throughout on the conditions and circumstances as they prevailed in and around London.

Although English journalism was admired and envied on the Continent, its legal foundation was anything but solid. Not only did the "law of seditious libel", frequently invoked by political bodies[2], hang like the sword of Damocles over the heads of wayward writers[3], as Swift experienced to his cost after the publication of *The Public Spirit of the Whigs* (1714)[4], there were also attempts by Parliament towards the end of Queen Anne's reign to muzzle journalists and publishers. This was usually justified by those who were opposed to granting any freedom to the press with the latter's alleged licentiousness. In the contemporary debate on how much freedom should be granted to the press, the pendulum swung between the extreme positions of liberty and licentiousness. But in spite of efforts to turn back the clock in the development of journalism - between 1695 and 1704 there were no fewer than nine bills before Parliament to bring back censorship[5] -, it is a sign of the level which the public political culture had attained that none of these attempts got beyond the committee stage and that - as John Feather[6] remarks - there was no new licensing system. In only a few cases, moreover, were legal proceedings actually initiated[7] in connection with particular publications. And when, between 1711 and 1714, Lord Bolingbroke[8] and some High Church Tories again polemically denounced journalistic licentiousness and demanded legislative measures to curb journalism's baleful influence, it was to no avail in spite of the Queen's benevolent support[9].

In this context the Stamp Act of 1712, which was especially aimed at newspapers[10], may be regarded as a compromise measure supported in particular by Bolingbroke and intended to contain the expansion of the press through taxation. Although opinion is divided as to the motives behind the Stamp Act, whether the

---

1 Cf. Speck, "Political Propaganda in Augustan England", p. 27.

2 See e.g. *Journals of the House of Commons, 1547-1796*, XI (London, 1695), 354.

3 See in this connection Feather, "The English Book Trade and the Law 1695-1799", pp. 62-63.

4 See in this connection Maurice J. Quinlan, "The Prosecution of Swift's *Public Spirit of the Whigs*", *Texas Studies in Literature and Language* 9 (1967-68), pp. 167-184 and John Irwin Fischer, "The Legal Response to Swift's *The Public Spirit of the Whigs*", *Swift and his Contexts*, ed. John Irwin Fischer, Hermann J. Real and James Woolley (New York, 1989), pp. 21-38.

5 Cf. Hellmuth, *'Liberty' und 'Licentiousness'*, p. 117.

6 See "The Book Trade in Politics", pp. 28, 37, 39.

7 Cf. Feather, "From Censorship to Copyright", pp. 181 and 186.

8 Cf. *Letters and Correspondence, Public and Private, of the Right Honourable Henry St. John, Lord Visc. Bolingbroke*, ed. Gilbert Parke, 4 vols. (London, 1798), II, 486.

9 Cf. Feather, "The Book Trade in Politics", pp. 37-39.

10 Cf. Michael Harris, *London Newspapers in the Age of Walpole. A Study of the Origins of the Modern English Press* (Rutherford, London and Toronto, 1987), p. 19 and Price, "A Note on the Circulation of the London Press, 1704-1714", p. 219.

objectives were mainly political[1] or primarily fiscal[2], it did not - apart from some drastic short-term effect[3] - succeed in putting journalism permanently on a leash. It seems as if broadside ballads were indeed seriously affected[4], but a legal loophole allowed newspapers consisting of more than one sheet to be registered as pamphlets, and they were thus able to improve their financial situation[5]. So, in a way, the Stamp Act even facilitated certain innovative changes in the journalistic landscape.

The extent to which 'freedom of the press' had become a firmly-rooted concept in people's minds is indicated by the manifestos written by prominent authors under the threat of restraining measures. In *Reasons against Restraining the Press* (1704) Matthew Tindal, to whom freedom of the press was equal to a Protestant basic right, maintained that any suppressive measure would give one party an edge over the other[6]. Similarly, in his *Essay on the Regulation of the Press*, also published in 1704, Defoe argued in favour of a free press not least because it would give equal opportunity to both parties in their attempt to win over public opinion[7]. When towards the end of Queen Anne's reign the High Church wing of the Tory party was actually flirting with the idea of reintroducing stricter measures to control the press - clear evidence of this is provided by W. Mascall's memorandum *A Proposal for Restraining the Great Licentiousness of the Press* (ca. 1712) - Addison joined the debate and in *The Thoughts of a Tory Author, concerning the Press* (1712) weighed the pros and cons of unlicensed printing. In order to weaken the position of Bolingbroke and the High Tories, who favoured stricter press laws, he aimed his essay at the Tory moderates, appealing to them to adopt a more conciliatory stance. Addison, whose position was similar to Defoe's, reminded the Tories with pointed humour that they in particular had recently been taking advantage of the opportunities of a free press[8], thus referring to the sym-

---

1 Thus e.g. Snyder, "The Circulation of Newspapers in the Reign of Queen Anne", p. 219.

2 Thus e.g. Alan Downie, "The Growth of Government Tolerance of the Press to 1790", *Development of the English Book Trade, 1700-1899*, ed. Robin Myers and Michael Harris (3rd impr., Oxford Polytechnic Press, 1982), p. 38.

3 Cf. Harris, *London Newspapers in the Age of Walpole*, p. 20.

4 See Rocco Lawrence Capraro, *Typographic Politics: The Impact of Printing on the Political Life of Eighteenth-Century England, 1714-1772* (doctoral dissertation, Washington University, 1984; Univ. Microfilms International, 1991), p. 90.

5 Cf. in this connection Harris, *London Newspapers in the Age of Walpole*, p. 20 and Capraro, *Typographic Politics*, pp. 80-90.

6 See Matthew Tindal, "Reasons against Restraining the Press", *The Pillars of Priestcraft and Orthodoxy Shaken*, 4 vols. (London, 1768), IV, 292-293.

7 See Daniel Defoe, *An Essay on the Regulation of the Press* (Oxford, 1948), p. 17. - Edward A. Bloom fails to give proper emphasis to the fact that Defoe, in spite of making certain verbal concessions to the supporters of censorship, was nevertheless as a matter of principle in favour of freedom of public speech: "Neoclassic 'Paper Wars' for a Free Press", *The Modern Language Review* 56 (1961), pp. 481, 484.

8 See [Joseph Addison], *The Thoughts of a Tory Author, concerning the Press: With the Opinion of the Ancients and Moderns, about Freedom of Speech and Writing. And an*

biotic relationship between a free press and party politics. Addison, too, left no doubt that curtailing the public's right to debate political issues would be at odds with the concept of a political culture of which the struggle between parties was an integral feature. Defoe, as mentioned above, also supported the idea of a free press because it gave equal chances to both parties, whose existence, however, he nevertheless regretted. The commitment of these writers to defending the right of free expression of opinion must be rated as an unmistakable sign that political parties and a free press were seen as belonging together. The arguments brought forward in support of this view showed that the concept of the printed word as a means of wooing public opinion had become an integral feature of the public political culture under Queen Anne[1].

THE CONCEPT OF PUBLIC OPINION

Finally, and in line with the scope of this study, I want to take a closer look at the concept of public opinion. This seems necessary for a number of reasons. On the one hand, it looks as if British and American scholars show only little interest in abstract definitions. Downie, for example, uses "public opinion" in the subtitle of his important monograph but does not discuss it in theoretical terms. On the other hand, Jürgen Habermas' *Strukturwandel der Öffentlichkeit*[2], which first appeared in 1962, has meanwhile been translated into English[3] and is the only German contribution to the subject with any impact abroad, is burdened with certain shortcomings which impede an adequate assessment of conditions as they prevailed in England.

For an accurate historical perspective - a glance at the past might even help to explain why major Anglo-American scholars have tended to shy away from tackling the theoretical aspects of the notion of 'public opinion'[4] - it is quite rewarding to read Matthew Prior's essay "Opinion", written in 1721. One soon notices that although nobody actually referred to it as such, public opinion did exist, despite

Historical Account of the Usage it has Met with from both Parties in England (London, 1712), pp. 3-4.

1 This is made clear even by a poem critical of the unfettered freedom of the press like *The Press Restrain'd* (1712) with its realistic view of the conditions described.

2 *Strukturwandel der Öffentlichkeit. Untersuchungen zu einer Kategorie der bürgerlichen Gesellschaft* (17th ed., Darmstadt and Neuwied, 1987).

3 Jürgen Habermas, *The Structural Transformation of the Public Sphere: An Inquiry into a Category of Bourgeois Society*, trans. T. Burger and F. Lawrence (Cambridge, Mass., 1989).

4 Note, however, the recent substantial contribution by David Zaret, who interprets the actual beginnings of public opinion emerging in the mid-seventeenth century as "a practical and not a theoretical innovation, an unintended consequence of communicative change" ("Petitions and the 'Invention' of Public Opinion in the English Revolution", *American Journal of Sociology* 101 [1996], p. 1498).

being regarded with some suspicion[1], and was also seen as closely linked to the existence of political parties[2]. In fact, as late as 1710 the clergyman Thomas Goddard had blended "Opinion and Party" in decidedly negative terms[3]. Prior's avoidance of the actual term seems to have been in some way typical of prevailing attitudes. It is true that terms like 'public interest'[4], 'public spirit' and 'vox populi' indicated that people were beginning to look beyond the confines of traditional politics, but as to 'public opinion', it was used rather late, for the first time under Robert Walpole[5]. As J.A.W. Gunn points out in a recent article[6], any theoretical assessment of political achievements does not appear to have been a concomitant feature of the historical process in England, as was the case in France, however, where the formation of public opinion was less far advanced. Furthermore, the press became known rather late as a 'fourth estate', in comparison with the equally eligible 'opposition' and 'people'[7]. This seems to indicate that the theoretical elevation of public opinion to the rank of a distinct element of political life was a rather slow process[8] lagging well behind the facts created by the actual course of events.

Contemporary Anglo-American research, too, for the most part takes an enviably pragmatic approach, given as it is to analysing historical phenomena instead of theorizing about them. Thus brilliant studies like Downie's *Robert Harley and the Press*, John Brewer's *Party Ideology and Popular Politics at the Accession of George III* (1976) and Marie Peters' *Pitt and Popularity. The Patriot Minister and London Opinion during the Seven Years' War* (1980) have analysed in great detail the historical consequences of the utilization of public opinion for political ends without, however, making any attempt to deal with the phenomenon in more theoretical terms. One of the few recent exceptions is Gunn's abovementioned contribution, in which he shows that although public opinion was increasingly regarded as an irreversible fact, actually referring to it by this name was yet to happen. In the absence of any detailed theoretical analysis of public

---

1 Cf. in this connection the derogatory remarks of Arthur Maynwaring, a prolific shaper of public opinion: Henry L. Snyder,"The Prologues and Epilogues of Arthur Maynwaring", *Philological Quarterly* 50 (1971), p. 629.

2 See "Opinion", *The Literary Works of Matthew Prior*, ed. H. Bunker Wright and Monroe K. Spears, 2 vols. (Oxford, 1959), I, 586-599.

3 See Thomas Goddard, *The Guilt, Mischief, and Aggravations of Censure, Set forth in a Sermon Preach'd in St. George's Chapel, within Her Majesty's Castle of Windsor, on Sunday the 25th of June, 1710* (London, 1710), p. 10.

4 See in this connection J.A.W. Gunn, "Public interest", *Political Innovation and Conceptual Change*, ed. Terence Ball, James Farr, Russell L. Hanson (Cambridge U.P., 1989), pp. 194-210.

5 See *The Oxford English Dictionary* (2nd ed., Oxford, 1989), X, *s.v.* "opinion".

6 See J.A.W. Gunn, "Public opinion", *Political Innovation and Conceptual Change*, ed. Ball *et al.*, pp. 247-265.

7 Cf. J.A.W. Gunn, *Beyond Liberty and Property. The Process of Self-Recognition in Eighteenth-Century Political Thought* (Kingston and Montreal, 1983), p. 88.

8 Only after the 1780s was the modern form of the expression - that is without the definite article - more frequently used; see Gunn, *Beyond Liberty and Property*, p. 281.

opinion, it is not surprising that those Anglo-American scholars who do take an interest in the theoretical aspect[1] tend to draw heavily on Habermas' book[2].

His one-sided view, however, needs to be complemented by a more function-oriented analysis, all the more so since other German contributions have failed to fill this gap. We learn very little about the exact historical situation in England in Lucian Hölscher's article written for *Geschichtliche Grundbegriffe*[3], just as Elisabeth Noelle-Neumann's otherwise useful article in *Publizistik, Massenkommunikation*[4] contributes little to our understanding of the emergence of public opinion in eighteenth-century England. Apart from the fact that Habermas' concept of 'public opinion' lacks a solid foundation of historical and empirical evidence, as Wolfgang Jäger has shown[5], it is simplistic in its application to England of ideas whose validity is restricted to the European Continent. Above all, Habermas sees the public and the state as diametrically opposed, and his central assumption is that the sole or, at least, predominant rationale of the process of cultivating public opinion instigated by the middle classes[6] was to undermine the position of the ruling aristocracy. Such a view, based as it is on class antagonisms, may provide valuable insight into the conditions of eighteenth-century Germany and even the rest of continental Europe with its absolutist regimes. But it is inadequate with regard to England, where the situation was different and where the public comprised most, if not all, social groups, especially the gentry and the nobility[7]. In no way does Habermas' approach make it easier for us to gain a better understanding of the political culture in England, where the expansion of political literature was,

---

1 See e.g Geoff Eley, "Re-Thinking the Political: Social History and Political Culture in 18th and 19th Century Britain", *Archiv für Sozialgeschichte* 21 (1981), pp. 430-431.

2 See esp. *Habermas and the Public Sphere*, ed. Craig Calhoun (Cambridge, Mass., and London, 1992).

3 See Lucian Hölscher, "'Öffentliche Meinung'", *Geschichtliche Grundbegriffe*, ed. Otto Brunner *et al.*, 4 (Stuttgart, 1978), pp. 448-450.

4 See Elisabeth Noelle-Neumann, "Öffentliche Meinung", *Das Fischer Lexikon: Publizistik, Massenkommunikation*, ed. Elisabeth Noelle-Neumann, Winfried Schulz, Jürgen Wilke (Frankfurt a.M., 1989), pp. 255-266.

5 See Wolfgang Jäger, *Öffentlichkeit und Parlamentarismus. Eine Kritik an Jürgen Habermas* (Stuttgart, 1973), e.g. p. 23.

6 In view of the heavy involvement of the aristocracy, one cannot speak of any priority of the bourgeoisie in England. Keith Michael Baker is even sceptical of this in relation to France: "But it seems difficult to characerize the new public space as a specifically bourgeois phenomenon [...]" ("Defining the Public Sphere in Eighteenth-Century France: Variations on a Theme by Habermas", *Habermas and the Public Sphere*, ed. Calhoun, p. 191).

7 For a critical discussion of Habermas' class-based concept see also Hermann Wellenreuther, "Das spanische Reich in der englischen Diskussion während des Siebenjährigen Krieges. Überlegungen zum Habermas'schen Begriff der 'Bürgerlichen Öffentlichkeit'", *Iberische Welten. Festschrift zum 65. Geburtstag von Günter Kahle*, ed. Felix Becker, Holger M. Meding, Barbara Potthast-Jutkeit, Karin Schüller (Cologne, Weimar, Vienna, 1994), pp. 723-758, esp. pp. 756-757.

significantly, not an underground phenomenon as in pre-revolutionary France[1]. Nor, for that matter, did the cultivation of public opinion simply provide a stage for exposing what was felt to be wrong with the ruling class. It was more like a free market, where political positions and views were peddled by government[2] and opposition alike. It is precisely this bipartisan element that is particularly important for any understanding of what was going on in England. Both government and opposition generously handed out political literature in order to improve their position in the eyes of the public[3], although there was a certain ambivalence in the way politicians dealt with public opinion, which, after all, was still an unfamiliar phenomenon. Thus Harley, for example, who was fascinated by the various ways of influencing public opinion[4], supported the use of propaganda[5] while at the same time he employed spies[6] as a means of surveillance and, if necessary, went so far as to suppress any undesirable activities[7]. Although in purely legal terms it was still a controversial issue whether there should be something like freedom of the press, and though governments made repeated attempts to curb free printing, there was general agreement during the reign of Queen Anne that the wooing of the public by means of the printed word had become a feature of political life which was there to stay.

The artificial dichotomy between public opinion and the state's claim to power, which also exists in Habermas' "The Public Sphere"[8] and - despite acknowledging his too monolithic notion of the public - is qualified neither in the foreword to the new edition of *Strukturwandel der Öffentlichkeit* (1990) nor in Habermas' recent contribution to a collection of essays dedicated to him[9], ought to be replaced with a less rigid, more functional concept which takes into account that both, government and opposition, were ready to acknowledge that public opinion had become an increasingly significant element of political life in its own right. The public sphere, where views and opinions vied with each other which were promulgated equally by government and opposition[10], was a kind of representative arena

---

1 See in this connection Robert Darnton, *The Literary Underground of the Old Regime* (Cambridge, Mass., 1982).

2 It was this very government that made use of propaganda; cf. e.g. Feather, "From Censorship to Copyright", pp. 181 and 184.

3 Cf. Michael Harris, "Newspaper Distribution during Queen Anne's Reign", p. 149 and Frances Harris, "Paper-Round", pp. 12-13.

4 Cf. Feather, "The Book Trade in Politics", p. 23.

5 See his early recognition of the value of propaganda in a letter to Godolphin dated 9 August 1702: BL Add. MS 28055, fols. 3-4.

6 See Snyder, "The Reports of a Press Spy for Robert Harley", pp. 326-345.

7 Cf. *ibid.*, p. 329.

8 See Jürgen Habermas, "The Public Sphere: An Encyclopedia Article (1964)", *new german critique* 1, no. 3 (Fall 1974), pp. 49-55.

9 See Jürgen Habermas, "Further Reflections on the Public Sphere", *Habermas and the Public Sphere*, ed. Calhoun, pp. 421-461.

10 Rightly emphasised by Manfred Schlenke, *England und das friderizianische Preussen 1740-1763. Ein Beitrag zum Verhältnis von Politik und öffentlicher Meinung im England des 18. Jahrhunderts* (Freiburg and Munich, 1963), p. 67.

for interaction, where the 'political nation'[1], as it was more and more often called, was able to promote its own image and express itself as effectively and freely as nowhere else. The wooing of public opinion was - despite regular complaints - an expression of an understanding of politics shared by both sides, an understanding which had left all authoritarian posturing behind. 'Interaction' in this context means two things. As regards public debate, it indicates the contest between the two (or more) opposing political camps. But - and here the term is more appropriate than the purely receptive mirror-image metaphor[2] - 'interaction' also signifies the process of influencing through public debate the decision-making authorities and Parliament, either before or after mapping out their intended course of action. The public sphere was regarded as a terrain where the political parties could measure their room for manoeuvre, where political muscles could be flexed, without the restrictions of the parliamentary arena but with clearly intended definite consequences for the latter. There were in fact instances in which the forces operating in the public sphere virtually goaded the political institutions into action. It is precisely this potential for persuasion and thereby for effecting policy changes which Capraro fails to notice when he describes the public even in George III's reign as "a readership which could participate vicariously in political life as political *voyeurs*"[3]. In fact, the mobilization of public opinion, employed by government and opposition alike as a lever against their respective opponents, had a catalytic function for the expanding indirect involvement in the political process of ever larger sections of society. As early as the beginning of the eighteenth century leading politicians began to flatter the public. They deliberately appealed to public opinion in order to justify their actions; both government and opposition saw this as an opportunity to test the popularity of their views and actions. This vying for public support thus became a kind of barometer measuring the political mood at the grass roots. Given the intensity of the political debate during the War of the Spanish Succession, it is no exaggeration to describe the culture of public contention as the lifeblood of British politics. This culture, regarded with suspicion at times, even by experienced journalists[4], exerted growing pressure on the political class to justify their decisions, although officially the political Establishment, which was still sheltered by the traditional and familiar institutions of Court and Parliament, kept its distance from this phenomenon, which was still striving for general acceptance. In the England of Queen Anne all relevant forces in society had in some way already reconciled themselves - some more readily

---

[1] Cf. Stone, "Literacy and Education in England 1640-1900", p. 85.

[2] Cf. Robert R. Rea, "Introduction: The Mirror of Politics", *The English Press in Politics, 1760-1774* (Lincoln, Neb., 1963), pp. 1-11.

[3] Capraro, *Typographic Politics*, p. 332.

[4] Cf. Snyder, "The Prologues and Epilogues of Arthur Maynwaring", p. 629. Even Maynwaring made vigorous complaints, when he felt the time was ripe, about the uncontrolled freedom of expression of the press, for example in a letter to the Duchess of Marlborough at the end of October 1709: *Private Correspondence of Sarah, Duchess of Marlborough, Illustrative of the Court and Times of Queen Anne*, 2 vols. (2nd ed., London, 1838), I, 237.

than others - to the fact that the cultivation of public opinion had become a viable instrument for increasing political participation, and we shall use the term 'public opinion' in this positive sense. It was under the spell of appealing to a public deemed competent to judge and worth any effort to influence it that the impressive amount of rhetorical ingenuity as documented in the political writings relating to war and peace was displayed.

I. THE PUBLIC CONTROVERSY ABOUT THE ENDING OF THE WAR OF THE SPANISH SUCCESSION: THE MAIN OUTLINES

1. THE WAR OF THE SPANISH SUCCESSION AS REFLECTED IN PUBLIC DISCUSSION UNTIL THE SUMMER OF 1710

This preliminary chapter briefly describes the impact of the public political culture as outlined above concerning the war which broke out in 1701. It aims to provide a backdrop for the distinctive features of the actual debate on how to end the war, which started in the latter part of 1710 and which must be regarded as the first instance of a fully developed political discourse in eighteenth-century England. Our aim is to enable both the themes and the functions of the genres participating in the debate up to 1710 to emerge in basic form. A detailed description of this debate in its successive stages lies beyond the scope of this part of the book, whose sole purpose is to prepare the way for the following chapters on the crucial phase of the discussion about war and peace. Unlike the main body of the book this section is not based on a systematic consideration of the entire corpus of relevant texts.

From the beginning the War of the Spanish Succession, which closely concerned the continuance of the political order established by the Revolution of 1688/89, had immense repercussions on the public scene in Britain. As early as December 1701, and shortly before the death of William III, the Whig-oriented dramatist and poet Nicholas Rowe brought out *Tamerlane*, in which he emphatically voiced insular expectations with regard to the fate of the French tyrant King Louis XIV and the outcome of the war[1]. When the war broke out, British domestic politics had largely returned to its former basic division between Whigs and Tories, whose growing dichotomy[2], immediately noticeable in denominational tensions, was to shape political life under Queen Anne. Whigs and Tories tended to have different views of the war, which quite often led to diametrically opposite positions in the public debate. Whereas the Whigs - because of their strong commitment to the Protestant Succession - tended to support the war on the Continent whole-heartedly, the more insular Tories, who had marked xenophobic inclinations, tended to be suspicious of, if not hostile to, the British involvement

---

1 See on this Heinz-Joachim Müllenbrock, *Whigs kontra Tories. Studien zum Einfluß der Politik auf die englische Literatur des frühen 18. Jahrhunderts* (Heidelberg, 1974), pp. 51-63.

2 Cf. Downie, *Robert Harley and the Press*, pp. 39 and 41.

in Europe[1]. Thus, almost from the outset, the War of the Spanish Sucession also assumed the role of a public catalyst for party-political rivalries.

Early in 1701, Robert Harley, the newly elected Speaker of the House of Commons, who was later to build an extensive propaganda agency to put through Parliament the Treaty of Utrecht, had tried to bring about a non-partisan stance on the approaching war. Publications such as Charles Davenant's *Essays upon Peace at Home, and War Abroad* (1704) and John Toland's *The Art of Governing by Partys* (1701) and *Anglia Libera* (1701) - all sponsored by Harley[2] - urged the need for domestic peace and a united front in face of the national challenge. With its strong Protestant and European components the last-named pamphlet already leaned towards a more strictly Whiggish point of view. In the immediately following context of closely contested parliamentary elections and mixed cabinets since late 1701 the War of the Spanish Succession was increasingly discussed in terms of party politics. The Whigs in particular, whose successful performance in the paper war of 1701[3] had proved the effectiveness of exerting pressure within doors by appealing to public opinion without doors, made skilful use of all the means of public persuasion, which included the whole gamut of genres from the noisy broadside to discursive pamphlets and sophisticated poetry.

Although the British entry into the war did not meet with the same single-minded applause from both parties, and although a growing lack of enthusiasm on the part of the Tories was noticeable by 1704, the victory at Blenheim in the summer of 1704 and the subsequent British successes secured broad acceptance of the war for a number of years. This does not mean that party-political altercations ceased altogether. Thus, for instance, Ned Ward, the Grub Street poet, even tried to give a Tory colouring to the triumph gained by the Duke of Marlborough[4], whereas High Tories did their best to play off the successes of Sir George Rooke and the Navy at Gibraltar and Malaga against Marlborough's exploits at Blenheim[5]. But the basic objectives of the war did not become a bone of public contention until much later. Discordant opinions mainly related to the effectiveness of the conduct of the war; thus, from John Dennis' *An Essay on the Navy* (1702) onwards stronger maritime efforts were regularly called for, though this hardly assumed the proportions of a major theme. Sometimes strategy in the Peninsula was subjected to critical examination. On the whole, however, Marlborough's military exploits exerted a masterful means of cohesion, as testified by the unprecedented volume of panegyric poetry of which Addison's *The Campaign* (1705) is merely the outstanding example. In the process, Marlborough, against whom High Tory

---

1 Cf. Holmes, *British Politics in the Age of Anne* (London and New York, 1967), pp. 64-65.

2 Cf. Downie, *op. cit.*, pp. 42-44, 63-64.

3 See *ibid*, ch. 2.

4 Cf. George Macaulay Trevelyan, *England under Queen Anne: Blenheim* (London, 1930), p. 419.

5 See *ibid.*, p. 420. Cf. also John B. Hattendorf, *England in the War of the Spanish Succession. A Study of the English View and Conduct of Grand Strategy, 1702-1712* (New York and London, 1987), pp. 211-212.

criticism had been perceptively voiced as early as the autumn of 1704, increasingly became the popular idol of the Whigs, although by no means Whiggish by inclination; Trevelyan puts the case correctly: "Marlborough now became the hero of the Whigs, though he was never a Whig hero"[1]. Interestingly, criticism of the Dutch share in the war developed at a comparatively early stage - notably from *The D- Deputies. A Satyr* (1705)[2] and *The D-h Politicks Examin'd: Or, the Danger of a Defensive War to the Confederates* (1705) onward - into a minor theme by no means drowned by the trumpets of patriotic jubilation.

Only after 1708 did the war begin to appear as a serious burden in the eyes of the general public[3], and Whig demands for its vigorous prosecution as expressed, for instance, in Addison's pamphlet *The Present State of the War, and the Necessity of an Augmentation, Consider'd* (1708) met with decreasing approval, especially after the summer of 1709[4]. In September 1709, apparently, complaints were already being voiced against Marlborough and the Earl of Godolphin for prolonging the war[5]. During the phase of the Junto hegemony following the summer of 1708 the discarded Harley tried to recover politically by putting before the public incriminating views of Whig rule - a deliberate appeal to the electorate in order to embarrass the Administration. More particularly, *An Account of a Dream at Harwich* (1708)[6], which has basic affinities to the approach adopted by Harley in his manuscript pamphlet *Plaine English* of the same year, was a Harleyite publication that aimed at long-term undermining effects by launching the evocative symbol of 'the family'[7] for the spoils system erected by the Marlborough-Godolphin combination. Here the conspiracy thesis that was later to be relentlessly exploited by Swift in the *Examiner* and *The Conduct of the Allies* (1711) was hatched in allegorical disguise. In spite of allusions to the attempted Jacobite invasion of Scotland there are, however, no concrete references to the war; English policy in the War of the Spanish Succession is not discussed. The same is true with regard to Mary de la Rivière Manley's *The New Atalantis* (1709), which is said to have done the most damage to the Ministry in 1709[8] through its salacious stories about Whig politicians, particularly the Duke and Duchess of Marlborough. Rumblings of discontent concerning the war still remained below the surface. Until the late summer of 1710 the liquidation of the war did not emerge as the paramount priority in domestic politics; the most controversial issues concer-

---

1 Trevelyan, *Blenheim*, p. 421.

2 Cf. on this Coombs, *The Conduct of the Dutch*, pp. 112-113.

3 Already in his *Sermon Preach'd before the Honourable House of Commons ... Feb. 1708/9* (1709) Francis Hare felt obliged to deal with the mounting criticism of Marlborough and his conduct of the war even after the victory at Oudenaarde (see esp. pp. 21-22 of the peroratio in the third and enlarged edition).

4 Cf. George Macaulay Trevelyan, *England under Queen Anne: The Peace and the Protestant Succession* (London, 1934), p. 35.

5 Cf. B.W. Hill, "The Change of Government and the 'Loss of the City', 1710-1711", *The Economic History Review* 24 (1971), p. 399.

6 See the analysis in Downie, *Robert Harley and the Press*, pp. 106-111.

7 See in more detail the chapter "Public Discourse".

8 See Trevelyan, *The Peace and the Protestant Succession*, p. 38.

ning its final outcome had not yet been put irrevocably on the public agenda, despite the foretaste of serious peace discussions after the publication of the rejected French proposals in 1709 and despite the increasingly ominous repercussions of the ill-advised Sacheverell trial early in 1710.

How does the prelude to the discussion of the ending of the war present itself in terms of genres and their share in public discourse - the more specific concern of this monograph? Some basic observations may be made. All the genres contributing to the debate on the war in its crucial phase at the end of Queen Anne's reign did so from the beginning. However, there is a marked difference in conduct between the earlier stages and the later stages of the debate starting in the late summer of 1710. First of all, the exceptionally high proportion of panegyric writings spawned by sustained military fortune is immediately noticeable[1]. The plethora of panegyric poems, in particular, gives a less professional appearance to this phase of the debate than to its concluding stage, the more so as the exultant mood of these encomia was not really matched by deflating rhetoric on a corresponding scale. Apparently the awareness of being participants in a successfully waged war put a premium on reportorial 'pamphlets' that stand out as a distinct sub-genre, with Hare among its more noteworthy practitioners[2]. As the comparatively modest output indicates, the pamphlet proper, however, does not yet seem to have played its later dominant role as undisputed *premier moyen de propagande*; in the subsequent controversy about how to end the war it assumed a pilot function in structuring the public debate and quite often relegated other genres to a subordinate position. It is revealing that, until the beginning of the peace debate proper in the summer of 1710, Arthur Maynwaring, destined to become the most important writer in the Whig camp, produced only one short pamphlet, *Advice to the Electors of Great Britain* (1708), which belongs in the context of the election campaign of the summer of 1708[3] and exploited the fears of Jacobitism, thus striking a note of opportune anti-Tory rhetoric.

As regards the 'division of labour' between the various forms of public persuasion, the discussion up to 1710 does not yet show the more sophisticated and complex pattern of the peace debate proper, but certain tentative conclusions may be drawn. For instance, in the context of the French peace-offer of 1709 pamphlets such as *Semper eadem*: *Or, Great Britain's Assurance of an Honourable Peace* (1709), which were preceded by documentary publications, took upon themselves the main burden of the argument, while supporting broadsides such as *The Character of the French King* (1709) sought to discredit Louis XIV by means of personal satire. A similar fine-tuning of genres according to their specific capacity

---

1 See, regarding the central figure, Robert D. Horn, *Marlborough: A Survey. Panegyrics, Satires, and Biographical Writings, 1688-1788* (New York and London, 1975).

2 See e.g. Hare's pamphlets *An Exact Journal of the Campaign in Germany, for the year 1704* (1704) and *The Life and Glorious History of John D. and E. of Marlborough* (1705).

3 See on the background to this publication Henry L. Snyder, "Daniel Defoe, The Duchess of Marlborough, and the 'Advice to the Electors of Great Britain'", *The Huntington Library Quarterly* 29 (1965-66), pp. 53-62.

for conveying political ideas can also be observed later, although in more concentrated form. With respect to the utilization of minor genres under party-political banners some surprisingly simple findings must be recorded. The full-scale prose romance as practised by Mrs. Manley in the form of the *chronique scandaleuse* seems to have been used almost solely as a Tory propaganda medium throughout the reign of Queen Anne[1]. In the more important genre of the drama a diametrically opposed situation prevailed. The systematic Whig patronage of the theatre, especially through the agency of the Junto-sponsored Kit-Cat Club, made the drama a virtually exclusive domain of Whig propaganda[2]. When signs of flagging enthusiasm for the war became apparent in 1704, Dennis' tragedy *Liberty Asserted* (1704), to quote but one pertinent example, forcefully voiced the Whig ideology of resolute engagement against the French tyrant in the name of liberty[3]. In prologues and epilogues alike England's efforts in the War of the Spanish Succession were emphatically and well-nigh unanimously encouraged. Right up to the Tory political backlash in 1710, when Henry St. John (later Lord Bolingbroke) applied himself to the task of supervising the theatres[4], the stage play was the favoured literary province of Whig endeavours to influence public opinion.

Although the clear-cut pattern emerging in the drama is, perhaps, exceptional, the Whigs obviously got the better of the Tories as regards the utilization of literary genres for political purposes. In travel literature, too, the Whig perspective, as illustrated by Addison's *A Letter from Italy* (1703), dominated. On the whole the Whigs were more alert to the need of cultivating public opinion and more agile in its implementation. The Whig preponderance in propaganda activity is corroborated statistically by a survey of political literature between 1701 and 1710. The professional dissemination of political propaganda by the Whigs through the theatre is proof enough that they set great store by appealing to the political nation without doors. This evaluation does not square with the appraisal of J.A. Downie for the years 1708 to 1710. Though Marlborough and Godolphin[5] - who were not

---

1 Whereas John Oldmixon's *The Secret History of Europe* (1712) was predominantly concerned with political intrigue and lacked the amorous element, the same author's *The Court of Atalantis* (1714) shared the erotic interest of Mrs. Manley's books - though in a rather inoffensive way - but did not produce the picture of all-embracing political designs.

2 See on this Müllenbrock, *Whigs kontra Tories*, ch. II ("Das Drama als whiggistisches Propagandamedium").

3 See also regarding the Whig concept of freedom Hattendorf, *England in the War of the Spanish Succession*, p. 4.

4 A piece like *The General Cashier'd* (1712), which criticised Marlborough's dismissal, was clearly not allowed to be performed under Bolingbroke's authority. Cf. John Loftis, *The Politics of Drama in Augustan England* (Oxford, 1963), pp. 61-62.

5 Godolphin was distrustful of or indifferent to the new developments in journalism. Significantly, this area remains unmentioned in William Calvin Dickinson's monograph *Sidney Godolphin, Lord Treasurer 1702-1710* (Lewiston, Queenston, Lampeter, 1990). Jeremy Black writes about the Lord Treasurer's way of dealing with propaganda: "Godolphin lacked the skills of the Junto or Harley" (*The English Press in the Eighteenth Century* [London and Sydney, 1987], p. 115).

orthodox Whigs, by the way - may have been indifferent to printed propaganda, the Junto Whigs clearly were not. That the Whigs "failed to establish further ministerial papers, or to forge stronger links with existing whig journals"[1] during that period was probably due to the fact that they felt sure of public consent at least until late in 1709 and saw no necessity to strengthen the existing propaganda apparatus. And though the Whigs may have been taken by surprise by the wave of extreme Tory sympathies aroused by the Sacheverell affair, the dexterity of their response to the journalistic moves of the reinvigorated Tories after the summer of 1710 confirmed the competence they had acquired in matters of public dispute. When the ministerial changes were made by the Queen, the man at the head of the new Government realised that, in spite of the somewhat embarrassing wave of Tory popularity produced by the Sacheverell trial, tremendous efforts would be required to beat the Whigs on their own ground and win public support for the peace policy which the new Ministers were determined to carry through. Public political culture in England was about to assume a new dimension.

2. THE TEMPORAL STRUCTURE OF THE PUBLIC DEBATE ON HOW TO END THE WAR

This chapter outlines the course of the public debate from the summer of 1710 to the conclusion of the Peace of Utrecht in the spring of 1713. Its aim is to show the macrostructure of the discussions on the ending of the War of the Spanish Succession. The following chapter entitled "Focus" investigates the context of the turning-point debate between autumn 1711 and spring 1712, a period when the Government not only succeeded in pushing its active policies through against the Opposition, but also won the public relations battle for the support of the people. This chapter looks at the microstructure of rhetorical strategies.

a) Summer 1710

It was the commotion caused by Henry Sacheverell's sermon *The Perils of False Brethren* in November 1709 and the Doctor's subsequent trial[2] that put party rivalries without doors on a new footing. The Sacheverell affair, incompetently handled by the vindictive, ill-advised Whig Government, proved the major catalyst for the change of public opinion[3], which also altered the nation's attitude towards the war. If it had not been for this stroke of luck the Tories would have ex-

[1] Downie, *Robert Harley and the Press*, p. 98.

[2] See on this A.T. Scudi, *The Sacheverell Affair* (New York, 1939) and Geoffrey Holmes, *The Trial of Doctor Sacheverell* (London, 1973).

[3] The change in the mood of the public in the wake of the Sacheverell affair was recorded by an astonished Defoe in his poem *The Age of Wonders* (1710).

perienced far greater difficulties in appealing to the country over the switch in their war-policy since late 1710. The sheer bulk of printed matter[1], among which loyal addresses to the Queen formed a major part, put on record the momentum of the volte-face in the public mood. The paper war set off by the Sacheverell trial was an unmistakable indicator that popular support was veering round towards High Church sentiments, a process whose effectiveness was spectacularly underlined in the early summer of 1710 by Sacheverell's triumphant tour of the country after his rather lenient sentence.

The beginning of the gradual challenge to the Whigs' war policy by the revitalized Tories must be placed within the context of the campaign launched on behalf of that flamboyant spokesman for extravagant High Church principles. Although the war rarely received direct treatment in the Sacheverell controversy, which hinged on religious and constitutional issues, it was at least indirectly dealt with most of the time. Thus, most frequently, the disparagement - whether overt or covert - of the principles of the Glorious Revolution and the concomitant declarations in favour of unlimited hereditary right also questioned the purpose of a war which was waged not least to secure the Protestant Succession. Although the Sacheverell controversy is not dealt with in detail in this study of the public dispute over the conduct of the war, it has to be kept in mind that it was instrumental in invigorating Tory morale and in encouraging the Tories to call their adversaries to account on all aspects of the Government's policy.

The public controversy about the ending of the War of the Spanish Succession has never been charted in its precise temporal dimensions[2]. The attempt to do so is, of course, encumbered with the knotty problem of dating[3]. In spite of many imponderables it is possible to delineate the time-structure of the debate by carefully evaluating the available evidence on a broad textual basis. Our main endeavour is directed at reconstructing the controversy by laying open the dynamics of its rhetoric. For this purpose the writings participating in the debate will be placed in a comprehensive network of interacting media; particular attention will be paid to the structuring role of certain primary texts that set the pace of the public debate.

Since the spring of 1710 there had been growing signs that Tory efforts to capitalize on the mood created by the Sacheverell trial would increasingly affect the war. From the pulpit, for example, the habitual Whig manifestations of unflagging resoluteness were increasingly matched and soon outdistanced by Tory statements of displeasure at the long continuance of the war. As early as 15 March 1710, in his fast sermon before the House of Commons, even the moderate Tory Philip Bisse[4], the future bishop of Hereford, cautiously but unmistakably voiced

---

1 See F.F. Madan, *A Critical Bibliography of Dr. Henry Sacheverell. Edited by W.A. Speck* (Lawrence, Kans., 1978).

2 This can, of course, only be maintained if one takes into account that in Harris' *A Study of the Paper War* the discussion of war and peace is embedded within the extensive and detailed, though also more specialized, treatment of Marlborough's public standing.

3 See my comments in the "Introduction", p. 14.

4 Described by Holmes as "a reconciler rather than a crusader" (*The Trial of Doctor Sacheverell*, p. 273).

misgivings about the fact that war gains were so slow to materialise[1], while at the same time emphatically warning against an ill-grounded peace[2]. By the summer of 1710[3] the grumbling voices had become so clamorous that Goddard, in his sermon preached on 25 June and dedicated to and printed on the recommendation of the Duchess of Marlborough, openly expressed his anxiety that British war aims might be endangered by growing dissension at home[4]. On the same occasion he also clearly linked increasing dissatisfaction with the Government's war policy with the general disaffection spreading in the wake of the Sacheverell affair[5]. In July 1710, during a performance of George Farquhar's *The Recruiting Officer* at the Haymarket Theatre, a ballad lashing out at Marlborough's avarice apparently led to a vehement outburst of resentment among the audience[6].

Until then displeasure at the conduct of the war, if expressed at all, was uttered by a multiplicity of individual voices and not in chorus. Up to that time there was no organized propaganda by the Opposition with regard to the war. At least no co-ordinating efforts can be discerned which indicate anything like the convergence of the media engaged in public discussion. The situation changed rather abruptly during the summer of 1710. The controversy sparked off by the publication, probably in late July or early August[7], of Simon Clement's seemingly impartial *Faults on Both Sides* (1710), his reply to Benjamin Hoadly's ironical pamphlet *The Thoughts of an Honest Tory* (1710), must be seen as the first genuine though not full-scale propaganda contest between Whigs and Tories during the last four years of Queen Anne's reign. It emerged from the journalistic maze of the Sacheverell campaign and extended beyond the caesura of the October election. Thirty-three writings, including republications and translations, have been identified as belonging to that controversy[8], but there were more. For the first time a clear-cut alignment of competing forces can be recognized, with Hoadly setting

---

1 See Philip Bisse, *A Sermon Preach'd before the Honourable House of Commons, at St. Margaret's Westminster, on Wednesday, March, 15, 1710* (London, 1710), p. 13.

2 See *ibid.*, p. 15.

3 In connection with this year James O. Richards writes: "The year 1710 marked the beginning of the most intensely partisan years of Anne's reign" (*Party Propaganda under Queen Anne. The General Elections of 1702-1713* [Athens, Ga., 1972], p. 107).

4 See Goddard, *The Guilt, Mischief, and Aggravations of Censure, Set forth in a Sermon Preach'd in St. George's Chapel, within Her Majesty's Castle of Windsor, on Sunday the 25th of June, 1710*, p. 22.

5 Soon afterwards the Whig prose sheet *The French King's Reasons against Peace* (1710) - in its concluding paragraph - explicitly ascribed the hardening of Louis XIV's attitude on war matters to his encouragement through the events centring on Sacheverell.

6 See Loftis, *The Politics of Drama in Augustan England*, pp. 54-55.

7 As regards the dating cf. *Swift vs. Mainwaring: 'The Examiner' and 'The Medley'*, ed. Frank H. Ellis (Oxford, 1985), pp. xxiv-xxv.

8 See William F.E. Morley, *Queen Anne Pamphlets. An Annotated Bibliographical Catalogue of Pamphlet Publications Spanning the Reign of Queen Anne, Held in the Eighteenth-Century British Pamphlet Collection, Douglas Library, Queen's University: 1701-1714* (Kingston, Ontario, 1987), pp. 215-228.

the Junto standard, Clement[1] disseminating Harley's[2] advances for moderation, and Joseph Trapp, in *Most Faults on One Side* (1710), voicing an uncompromisingly Tory standpoint. In *A Supplement to the Faults on Both Sides* (1710) Defoe, newly enlisted by the energetic Harley, was also coming out in favour of a coalition government and reconciliation between men of goodwill of both parties. The importance of the controversy is shown by the fact that not only pamphlets, but also other genres such as periodicals[3] and poems participated in it, albeit less extensively than in subsequent controversies. Moreover, there was a systematic tug of war between opposing points of view documented by the number of replies and counter-replies, so that the *Faults* controversy already showed the characteristics of a fairly complex, interconnecting debate.

In terms of the public debate about the ending of the war, however, the *Faults* controversy can at most be regarded as an advance-guard skirmish. Neither in its first stage nor later did the war receive full attention, being little more than a side-issue. Referred to ominously by Hoadly in his *Thoughts of an Honest Tory*[4], but dealt with only in passing by Clement in *Faults on Both Sides*[5] and even in Trapp's reply *Most Faults on One Side*, it was touched upon by other writers[6] without ever occupying centre-stage. Rather, as corroborated even by Clement's late reply to journalistic objections, *A Vindication of the Faults on Both Sides* (1710), it loomed as an impending issue upon which argumentative energies would be released after the contending parties had thrown down the gauntlet. The *Faults* controversy, in which the various political groups tried hard to come to grips with the past over party-political fundamentals, merely set the stage for the fierce debate on the burning issue of the immediate future.

---

1 As regards the identification of the author of *Faults on Both Sides* see Henry L. Snyder, "The Authorship of *Faults on Both Sides* (1710)", *Philological Quarterly* 56 (1977) pp. 266-272.

2 Regarding Clement's commissioning by Harley cf. *Swift vs. Mainwaring*, ed. Ellis, p. 11.

3 See the editions of the *Review* of 14 October 1710 (indirect reference) and of the *Medley* of 6 November 1710 and 29 January 1711, respectively.

4 See [Benjamin Hoadly], *The Thoughts of an Honest Tory, upon the Present Proceedings of that Party. In a Letter to a Friend in Town* (London, 1710), p. 9.

5 See the comments on the mismanagement of the war in Spain by [Simon Clement], *Faults on Both Sides: Or, an Essay upon the Original Cause, Progress, and Mischievous Consequences of the Factions in this Nation* (London, 1710), pp. 28-31. For the main thrust of this pamphlet see the discussion in Harris, *A Study of the Paper War*, pp. 48-52.

6 Defoe gave somewhat contradictory signals, pointing on the one hand to considerable French concessions in previous negotiations and stressing on the other hand the necessity to pursue the war in view of French insincerity; see *A Supplement to the Faults on Both Sides: Containing the Compleat History of the Proceedings of a Party ever since the Revolution: In a Familiar Dialogue between Steddy and Turn-Round, two Displac'd Officers of State* (London, 1710), pp. 47 and 75 (the latter page misnumbered in the present edition).

This debate did not really gain momentum until after the election in October 1710. Its tentative beginnings must, however, be placed in the summer of that year. At about the same time as the semi-independent *Faults* controversy, which commenced in August 1710 and was continued into the following year, the discussion about further British involvement in the war was opened. It shows none of the neat outlines of the *Faults* controversy. Whereas the latter, especially in its more important first stage, developed within a clearly recognizable cluster of closely interrelated writings, the nascent war debate spread rather irregularly though by no means haphazardly. It can, somewhat surprisingly, be said to have been started by the Whigs. Disturbed by the growing signs of Tory recovery, the first changes in the Ministry and the impending dissolution of Parliament it was they who took preventive action in the summer of 1710 in order to forestall their complete overthrow. Although, admittedly, they were far from being a match for the Tories in capitalizing on the Sacheverell trial, they were not as disconcerted as is sometimes maintained[1]. For example, the Whigs harassed the Tories with the threatened collapse of public credit so that Defoe, starting in August 1710 with *An Essay upon Publick Credit*, was commissioned to write repeatedly on this subject[2]. In the matter of war, where they might still have thought they had the better hand, they went on the offensive, outnumbering the Tories in the production of pamphlets bearing upon this subject. Thus Maynwaring's folio broadside *A Letter from Monsieur Pett(ecu)m to Monsieur B(u)ys*[3] and his longer pamphlet *Four Letters to a Friend in North Britain, upon the Publishing the Tryal of Dr. Sacheverell*, which both appeared about the beginning of August 1710, mark the starting point of a more serious dispute about the war. Both were effective pieces of propaganda and challenged the buoyant Tories over any reversal of war policy that might be envisaged, apart from trying to forestall the complete overthrow of the Ministry[4]. By trying to attach the blanket stigma of Jacobitism to the Tories in his *Four Letters* Maynwaring repeated the approach successfully tested in his *Advice to the Electors of Great Britain* and gave prominence to a standard reproach which was to re-echo in Whig rhetoric throughout the entire war controversy. Hoadly chose a similar line of attack in his provocative prose sheet *The French King's Thanks to the Tories of Great-Britain* (1710), which charged the Tories with playing the French game; only through their assistance could Marlborough's successes be thwarted. In *The Fears and Sentiments of all true Britains* (1710), published at about the same time, Hoadly also sounded the alarm-bells and - in the

1 Cf. Downie, *Robert Harley and the Press*, p. 174.

2 See Defoe's letter to Harley of 5 September 1710: *The Letters of Daniel Defoe*, ed. George Harris Healey (Oxford, 1955), pp. 276-277. For a discussion of Defoe's rhetorical strategy in the *Essay*, see John F. O'Brien, "The Character of Credit: Defoe's 'Lady Credit', The Fortunate Mistress, and the Resources of Inconsistency in Early Eighteenth-Century Britain", *ELH* 63 (1996), pp. 612-615.

3 Another possible author of this well-written piece is Robert Walpole; cf. Henry L. Snyder, "Daniel Defoe, Arthur Maynwaring, Robert Walpole, and Abel Boyer: Some Considerations of Authorship", *The Huntington Library Quarterly* 33 (1970), pp. 152-153.

4 Cf. Downie, *op. cit.*, p. 123.

midst of ministerial replacements and in anticipation of the imminent dissolution of Parliament - hurled the accusation against the Tories that they "encourage all the *Jacobites* and *Nonjurors* in the Nation; retard a good *Peace* and the Progress of the *War* both"[1]. These concerted measures clearly show that, contrary to Mary Ransome's assessment, the doctrine of Non-Resistance was not "the only stick the Whigs possessed with which to beat the Tories in 1710 [...]"[2].

The Tories' reaction indicated that they were well aware of the potential danger of the Whigs' preemptive attack. They managed to respond immediately to the Whig challenge to their rising popularity by means of a new weekly paper, *The Examiner*, which was opportunely launched at that very time. Its purpose was to call the outgoing Government to account for its past record; later, in Swift's hands, it became the leading ministerial organ. The *Examiner* replied to the *Letter from Monsieur Pett(ecu)m to Monsieur B(u)ys* in its first and third numbers[3] and to *The French King's Thanks to the Tories of Great Britain* in its second number[4]. On the whole its response can be regarded as typical of the vast majority of Tory journalism until well beyond the election of October 1710. Although it resolutely countered the charges levelled against the Tories by the Whig pamphleteers, it did so without so much as hinting that a switch of war policy aiming at a hasty peace was intended by the Tories. In its very first number the *Examiner* pronounced it absurd to assume that the Duke of Marlborough could be forced to lay down his command as a consequence of the change of the ministry[5]. Immediately afterwards the short pamphlet *Reasons why the Duke of Marlborough Cannot Lay down his Commands* (1710) slyly joined the *Examiner* in its expectations while at the same time expressing forebodings of possible recriminations. In fact, open defiance of the Duke's position by Tory writers began much later. To be sure, in religious and constitutional matters the newly established journal was quite outspoken, censured unbecoming moderation[6] and even openly spoke out in favour of Non-Resistance[7], thus diverging from Harley's line of policy. In matters relating to the war, however, the *Examiner* did not reveal any views which might be embarrassing to the Tory platform. Right up to when it was taken over by Swift it pursued a remarkably disciplined approach and did not jeopardize the reserved position initially adopted. Downie's statement, "The *Examiner*, from August to November 1710, continued to adopt an unconciliatory stance. Swift was given the responsibility of editorship to take the wind out of tory sails"[8], must be qualified

---

1 [Benjamin Hoadly], *The Fears and Sentiments of all true Britains with Respect to National Credit, Interest and Religion* (London, 1710), p. 13.

2 Mary Ransome, "The Press in the General Election of 1710", *The Cambridge Historical Journal* 6 (1939), p. 213.

3 See numbers 1 and 3 of the *Examiner*, 3 and 17 August 1710.

4 See the second number of the *Examiner*, 10 August 1710.

5 The general impression of cautious treatment of Marlborough was not even obliterated by the rather revealing reference to him as "an Ambitious *Cataline* at the head of a Mercenary Army" in the fourth number of the *Examiner*, 24 August 1710.

6 See *The Examiner*, 21 September 1710.

7 See *The Examiner*, 26 October 1710.

8 Downie, *Robert Harley and the Press*, pp. 134-135.

with regard to the war; Swift rather tightened up on the issue of war and peace. There is no essential disagreement over the peace issue between the *Examiner* and Abel Boyer's Harleyite publication *A Letter from a Foreign Minister in England, to Monsieur Pettecum* of 15 September 1710, intended in part for distribution abroad, which, while admitting that a reelected House of Commons might take up the problem of the peace, emphatically denied any dispositions on the part of the new Ministry to being less committed to the common cause. This pamphlet, which, somewhat belatedly, sought to neutralize any negative effects the Dutch Memorial might have produced, also firmly asserted that the Duke of Marlborough would be left in his command whatever ministerial changes were made[1]. Until the election in October 1710 the majority of writers in the Tory interest took up a defensive position on the war question, while the Whigs seized upon the subject as a welcome means of improving their by now precarious public standing. The most plausible explanation of the comparative neglect of the peace issue by the Tories[2] seems to be that they had misgivings about the state of opinion in the country concerning the war and did not want to put the matter to the test until firmly entrenched in power by the election. This situation might also account for the impression of a slight uneasiness sometimes discernible in Tory writings dealing with the issue of war, in contrast to the more forward handling of the topic by their Whig counterparts. Thus, while it is largely correct to say that the Whigs "fought a stalling action"[3], writing against ineluctable developments, this assessment benefiting from hindsight ought not to prevent us from appreciating that for a long time they took a bold stand on an issue which they did not think to be a foregone conclusion and which, at least rhetorically, might enable them to gain the upper hand again for a while.

The general impression of judicious restraint on the part of the Tories regarding discussion of the war between the summer and autumn of 1710 is spoiled by St. John's almost single-handed sally in his *Letter to the Examiner*, which appeared in early August 1710. Whereas the rhetoric of most Tory writers self-confidently played down the issue, St. John, whose authorship was wittily revealed by Addison in the second number of *The Whig-Examiner*[4], unabashedly took the offensive. Brashly asserting that Britain had been cheated by her double-dealing Allies into taking part as a principal in a war in which she ought to have engaged only as a confederate, he neatly laid the blame for the protraction of the war, unaccountably concentrated in Flanders, on the selfishness of the Godolphin Minis-

---

1 See [Abel Boyer], *A Letter from a Foreign Minister in England, to Monsieur Pettecum. Containing the True Reasons of the Late Changes in the Ministry, and of the Calling a New Parliament: And therefore fit to be Perus'd by all the Electors* (London, 1710), p. 12. Significantly, however, it at the same time fostered resentment against "the exorbitant Power invaded by the D. of *M*- and the late *Lord Treasurer*" (p. 6).

2 The relative scarcity of propaganda material on the war is noted, for instance, by Michael Foot, *The Pen and the Sword. A Year in the Life of Jonathan Swift* (3rd impr., London, 1966), p. 111.

3 Downie, *op. cit.*, p. 117.

4 See *The Whig-Examiner*, 21 September 1710.

try, which not only domineered over the Queen but also acted against British interests. Though not stated explicitly, the conspiracy thesis with its implications of personal enrichment at the expense of the nation was subtly hinted at in this pamphlet. Swift was to elaborate it and give it its full propaganda appeal by concentrating on the emotive symbol of 'the family' early utilized by Harley as an effective ploy of anti-Whig polemics. St. John further underscored the polarising tendency of his pamphlet by shrewdly capitalizing on the increasing unpopularity of the Dutch: "[...] may not the King of *France* reasonably Hope, tho' *Holland* should be aggrandiz'd, that *Britain* will be in proportion weaken'd?"[1] Anti-Dutch feeling[2], to which Davenant, too, pandered in *Sir Thomas Double at Court, and in High Preferments* (1710), was to be cleverly expatiated upon by Swift in *The Conduct of the Allies*. Thus the *Letter to the Examiner*, without yet setting the tone for Tory rhetoric, already exhibited the indispensable characteristics of its future direction. The existence of this seminal piece of propaganda also shows that differences of opinion in the Tory camp about the course to be adopted towards the Whigs rose to the surface from the very beginning of the serious debate on the war. It will be seen that diverse shades of opinion continued to be expressed in Tory rhetoric right to the conclusion of the war; they affected every genre and can be noticed, for instance, in the nuanced comments of the peace poems celebrating the Treaty of Utrecht[3]. In the slowly developing rivalry between Harley and St. John over determining the party's platform the *Examiner* had not yet taken sides. As late as in its election appeal in number 10[4] it did not go further than to recommend, rather diplomatically, voting for those candidates "who would push on the War with the utmost vigour, in order to end it by a safe and speedy Peace". At most its warning, in the same issue, against candidates "who wou'd avoid reducing the Power of *France*, in order to perpetuate *their own*" sounded like a discreet adumbration of harsher public oratory in store for changing conditions.

The Whigs recognized the defiant self-assuredness of the *Letter to the Examiner* and tried to retaliate. However, Lord Cowper's attempt, in *A Letter to Isaac Bickerstaff, Esq.; Occasion'd by the Letter to the Examiner* (1710), to pay St. John in his own coin by discerning "a real Conspiracy, not of the Whigs to inslave their Sovereign, but of the Tories to inslave the Nation"[5] sounded rather like a tit-for-tat response, thereby confirming the difficulties experienced by writers in a defensive position in coping with a vigorous line of attack. By fastening the

---

1 [Henry St. John], *A Letter to the Examiner* (London, 1710), p. 10.

2 Cf. also - a little later - Mrs. Manley's portentous description of the collusive dealings between Stauracious (Marlborough) and the Saracens (Dutch) in the second volume of her *Memoirs of Europe, towards the Close of the Eighth Century*: *The Novels of Mary Delariviere Manley*, Facsimile Reproductions edited with an Introduction and Index by Patricia Köster, II (Gainesville, Fla., 1971), 416-418. The reference is to the pagination added by the editor.

3 See on this the third chapter of the present book.

4 See *The Examiner*, 5 October 1710.

5 [Lord Cowper], *A Letter to Isaac Bickerstaff, Esq.; Occasion'd by the Letter to the Examiner*: [Abel Boyer], *The History of the Reign of Queen Anne, Digested into Annals. Year the Ninth* (London, 1711), The Appendix, Numb. VIII, p. 79.

standard indictment of Jacobitism on his adversary, Cowper had recourse to a well-tried polemical device to be used over and over again by the Whigs and which, dexterously employed, might always be counted upon to score a point, but which also posed the risk of losing its effect in spite of its repetitive pertinacity. That the Whigs continued to rely upon this weapon ready to be hurled at their antagonists was underlined by the publication of *A Letter from a Gentleman at the Court of St. Germains, to one of his Friends in England* (1710), in which Maynwaring seems to have had a hand[1]. In the summer of 1710, they faced at least some problems in reciprocating the brazen rhetoric of St. John, who had introduced a new note into public polemics. This becomes evident from the switch of stances in the *Whig-Examiner*, which was set up in opposition to the new party-political organ of the Tories. Addison, who had difficulties in accommodating his bland style to the rough and tumble of political strife, wrote only the first two numbers himself[2]; his rather lenient treatment of St. John's pamphlet in the second number of the *Whig-Examiner* gave way to the more trenchant criticism exhibited in the fourth number[3] of that short-lived journal. By that time the *Medley* had been launched permitting a more forceful, though by no means unproblematic, presentation of the Whig platform. Without putting its stamp on the entire debate the appearance of the *Letter to the Examiner* had a somewhat disquieting effect on the Whigs and harshly compelled them to summon adequate means of response. The stir caused by St. John's pilot publication was an important prelude to the war debate as it developed much later when the peace offensive was launched by the Tories under more propitious circumstances.

In the beginning controversy over the war, pamphlets had the lion's share both quantitatively and qualitatively. As regards the argumentative handling of current affairs they took pride of place. Weekly periodicals increased their significance and played a complementary part in the public dispute. Their complementarity is born out by the fact that the main argumentative business in the press was handled by reference to outstanding pamphlets that set the pace in the debate[4], while intra-periodical exchange was less frequent. Pamphlets and periodicals also had the main share in subsequent debates and may be regarded as the primary media of political discourse. Usually they took the lead in shaping public opinion. The secondary media such as broadsides (mainly in verse), sermons, poems and prose narratives of different kinds, however, must on no account be neglected in any analysis of the public political culture evolving in the England of Queen Anne. Often the public debate received its characteristic features through the rich instrumentation of a variety of media, each performing its own specific function not

---

1 This assumption of Oldmixon's is not invalidated by a very recent article which gives convincing reasons for Pierre des Maizeaux's playing a leading role: see P.N. Furbank and W.R. Owens, "Daniel Defoe and *A Letter from a Gentleman at the Court of St. Germains* (1710)", *Études Anglaises* 48 (1995), pp. 61-66.

2 Cf. *Swift vs. Mainwaring*, ed. Ellis, p. liii.

3 See *The Whig-Examiner*, 5 October 1710.

4 See e.g. the editions of *The Examiner* of 5 October 1710 and of *The Medley* of the same day, published during the election campaign.

easily transferable to other genres. Thus, for instance, in the intellectual climate at the end of Queen Anne's reign, especially during the turning-point debate, the sermon assumed some importance in the concert of printed propaganda as a multiplier of party-political convictions, both on the Tory and - to a slightly lesser degree - on the Whig side.

Since the function of the main genres is dealt with in the fourth chapter, it seems appropriate at this point to briefly comment on some more occasional forms. The first is the full-length prose romance. Mrs. Manley, who had made a notable contribution to the airing of discontent with the Junto through scandal-mongering in *The New Atalantis*[1], followed with another work of the same kind, *Memoirs of Europe*, the first volume of which appeared in May 1710. Though by no means suitable for an intellectually adequate approach to politics, it may nevertheless be supposed to have performed a useful function in furthering disaffection with the Whig Government. By denouncing Marlborough's avarice, for instance, it played a contributory part, preparing the ground on the level of society gossip for Swift's more incisive and damaging indictments. Expressing hopes of putting an end to the protracted war, the *Memoirs of Europe*, which reviewed the relations of the Duke and Duchess of Marlborough with the Queen during previous reigns, even anticipated a drastic change of the Ministry[2] before the dismissal of Sunderland had occurred. Books like Mrs. Manley's with their strong emphasis on corruption made it easy to commit oneself and provided Tory propaganda with an emotional undercurrent which could be counted on to have a persistently undermining effect and to do its work among readers from different walks of life. That *The New Atalantis*, which was published at a merely preparatory stage of Tory propaganda when the Whig Ministry was still in full power[3], can be ascribed such a general, subversive function can be inferred from the fact that Marlborough's description as "Count Fortunatus" was tailored to the pattern of the corrupt court-favourite and not to that of a war-mongering Whig politician. It is no mere coincidence that the second volume of *Memoirs of Europe* appeared in November 1710, when the new Government had to tackle the difficult problem of peace and further depended on sustained popular support. In this second volume Mrs. Manley, in keeping with the development of Tory propaganda, stressed the dangers to the Crown issuing from Marlborough's (Stauracius's) ruthless ambition[4], which is emotionally highlighted. At about the same time *The Secret History of Arlus and Odolphus* (1710) appeared, a notable specimen of a related genre focusing on the seamy side of Court life; for its propagandistic effect this

1 Regarding Mrs. Manley's clearly successful mixture of politics and sex see the chapter "'As long as Atalantis Shall be Read': The Scandal Chronicles of Mrs. Manley and Mrs. Haywood" in John J. Richetti, *Popular Fiction before Richardson. Narrative Patterns 1700-1739* (Oxford, 1969), pp. 119-152.

2 See *Memoirs of Europe, towards the Close of the Eighth Century: The Novels of Mary Delariviere Manley*, ed. Köster, II, 257.

3 For the pride Mrs. Manley felt in her pioneering activities, see an autobiographical remark in *The Adventures of Rivella: Novels*, ed. Köster, II, 845.

4 See *Novels*, ed. Köster, II, 413.

short narrative, which justified the ministerial changes owing to insider knowledge and further damaged Marlborough's prestige in the guise of Fortunatus, also relied on the willingness of readers to be drawn into a world of political make-believe pandering to innate curiosities.

The second remark concerns the use of occasional poetry for propaganda purposes. When, in August 1710, the Tories' campaign of addresses reached its climax with the address presented to the Queen by the Bishop of London and the clergy of London and Westminster, the Whigs arranged for the publication of a broadside poem, possibly by Maynwaring, entitled *The Humble Address of the Clergy of London and Westminster, Paraphras'd* (1710)[1] . In the guise of a high-flying London divine it mockingly prayed for scattering "those that delight in the War"[2] in order to prevent Louis XIV from being utterly ruined. Conceived as an anticlimax to High Church enthusiasm, which was threatening to drown oppositional opinion in a flood of co-ordinated statements, it was intended to take the wind out of the Tories' sails by rudely awakening them to the consequences of their about-face in foreign policy. But even when there was a lull in the public controversy, occasional poetry was also able to attract attention, thus fulfilling a useful function, albeit a modest one. Newburgh Hamilton's militant High Church poem *The Changes: Or, Faction Vanquish'd*, published in May 1711, for example, gave expression to anti-Whig feelings in order to make readers alert to the political opponent supported by the Dutch. Of course it is difficult if not impossible to judge the effect of such propaganda. However, the fact that such publications belonged to the indispensable paraphernalia of a full-blown debate shows that they were supposed to fulfil a necessary function, to open, above all, a short cut to temporary political commitment, however short-lived, whereas a prose romance by Mrs. Manley, with its malicious poisoning, relied rather on long-term impact. Their regular appearance testifies to calculated efforts to show the flag on all levels of political discourse. As a quick and pungent public relations instrument they specialized in rousing political emotions at short notice. Ephemeral poetry of this kind increased with the intensification of the public debate during the following years. Its relative importance at that time may also be gauged by the fact that the political print as a weapon of propaganda only gained genuine signficance in the later decades of the eighteenth century[3] . Of course occasional poetry of a more substantial literary character really came into its own at the conclusion of the Treaty of Utrecht, as will be illustrated in the third chapter.

---

[1] See *Poems on Affairs of State. Augustan Satirical Verse, 1660-1714*, VII: *1704-1714*, ed. Frank H. Ellis (New Haven and London, 1975), 454-457.

[2] *Ibid.*, p. 460.

[3] In contrast to the intensive reporting of the controversy between High Church and Low Church following the Sacheverell affair there were practically no political caricatures that dealt with the proper ending of the War of the Spanish Succession. Apart from copying some continental, particularly Dutch examples (cf. Dorothy George, *English Political Caricature to 1792. A Study of Opinion and Propaganda* [Oxford, 1959], pp. 64-65), the political prints basically restricted themselves to a set of playing-cards directed against France. See the reproductions in Michael Duffy, *The Englishman and the Foreigner* (Cambridge, 1986), pp. 96-121.

b) Autumn 1710 until Spring 1711

Although the elections in October 1710, which, in London, for example, also roused pacifist feelings[1], resulted in a clean sweep for the Tories, the character of the public debate over the war did not change overnight[2]. During the next six months or so, i.e. until the death of Emperor Joseph I changed the political face of Europe, the antagonists tested each other's strength, but did not really go for each other's throats. The reason why the war debate was so slow in gaining momentum must be sought in the new Government's refusal to lay open their peace plans, which were, however, pursued from the beginning. Of course the Government had to guard itself against a possible revulsion of public feeling with regard to the war. As early as December 1710[3] Harley secretly reopened peace negotiations with France[4], but preferred to pretend that there would be no slackening of Allied efforts in pursuing the war to its just and proper end. Thus the Queen, in her speech at the opening of Parliament on 25 November 1710, set forth Harley's public policy by vigorously endorsing the continuation of the war[5], thereby corroborating the expectations raised by Harleyite propaganda. It is certainly no coincidence that Thomas Swift in the sermon entitled *Noah's Dove*, which he delivered on 7 November 1710 and dedicated to Harley, concluded his appeal for unity above the level of party politics with a promise of a forceful prosecution of the war[6]. Just before Boyer had declared in an openly Harleyite publication that "our *New Ministry*, and the *New Parliament*, will insist on the Restitution of the *whole Monarchy*

1 Cf. Gary Stuart De Krey, *A Fractured Society. The Politics of London in the First Age of Party 1688-1715* (Oxford, 1985), p. 227. The Whigs tried to combat the emergent pacifism by such spirited publications as *A Letter of Advice to the Freeholders of England, concerning the Election of Members to Serve in the Ensuing Parliament* (1710) and *Serious Advice to the Good People of England: Shewing them their True Interest, and their True Friends* (1710).

2 In his article "*The Conduct of the Allies*: contexte et originalité" Guy Laprevotte writes in connection with 1711: "Peu de remous pendant les premiers mois de l'année suivante" (*Commerce(s) en Grande-Bretagne au XVIIIe Siècle*, ed. Suzy Halimi [Paris, 1990], p. 246).

3 See Brian W. Hill, *Robert Harley. Speaker, Secretary of State and Premier Minister* (New Haven and London, 1988), p. 159.

4 Cf. on the beginning of these soundings G.M. Trevelyan, "The 'Jersey' Period of the Negotiations Leading to the Peace of Utrecht", *The English Historical Review* 49 (1934), pp. 100-105.

5 See William Cobbett, *The Parliamentary History of England*, VI (London, 1810), col. 928.

6 See Thomas Swift, *Noah's Dove: An Earnest Exhortation to Peace: Set forth in a Sermon Preach'd on the 7th of November, 1710. A Thanksgiving-Day* (London, *s.a.* [1710]), pp. 23-24.

of Spain"[1] and had even held out the prospect of better conditions for the Allies. Moreover, Harley sought a modus vivendi with the disgruntled Bank of England[2], which he did not intend to antagonize for long. The debate starting after the election received its special imprint from the Whigs' obstinate but somehow vague suspicion that something was going on underhand[3] and the Tories' simultaneous endeavours to deny any reversal of the war aims while at the same time noticeably stepping up their criticism of the former Ministry[4]. Outspoken criticism of the peace policy of previous administrations, found to be gravely deficient in several respects, was vented by the author of *The Secret History of Arlus and Odolphus* published in the first half of November 1710. In *Examiner* 19 (7 December 1710) Swift, characteristically, took refuge behind the Queen's Speech, though cleverly pointing out the difficulties which would beset the new Government if it were to reverse the Whigs' war policy[5]. The overall impression resulting from the uncertainty about the further direction of foreign policy may be summed up in the metaphor that the combatants on the public scene were constantly firing at each other weapons of light or medium power while actually lying in wait for the discharge of heavy artillery.

In view of the anticipated challenge to their war policy the Whigs' main propaganda efforts consisted in creating high barriers which were not easy for the Tories to surmount in their imminent bid for public approval. The Whigs' defensive barricade consisted of an extensive presentation of circumstantial evidence establishing once again the correct conduct of the former Administration with regard to the war by pointed references to parliamentary resolutions and similar documents of seemingly unassailable conclusiveness. Hare's *Management* tracts[6], which appeared in four parts in January and February 1711, and which were probably re-

---

1 *An Essay towards the History of the Last Ministry and Parliament* (London, 1710), p. 52.

2 On the difficulties of the new Government in dealing with this institution, see Hill, *op. cit.*, pp. 134-144.

3 Significantly, suspicions of the far-reaching intentions of the new Ministry with regard to a peace to be achieved by acting in collusion with the French were at that time not yet voiced in 'responsible' journalism but only in publications of disreputable character; see esp. *The Second Part of the Impartial Secret History of Arlus, Fortunatus, and Odolphus, Ministers of State to the Empress of Grand-Insula* ([London], 1710), pp. 15 and 18. This sequel also accused the Tories of crypto-Jacobitism.

4 This task was mainly performed by Swift following his taking over of the *Examiner* (from number 14, 2 November 1710).

5 See Jonathan Swift, *The Examiner and Other Pieces Written in 1710-11*, ed. Herbert Davis (Oxford, 1941, repr. 1966), pp. 33-34. - Our numbering, however, follows that of the original editions of the *Examiner*.

6 For a detailed account of their contents see the informative Staatsexamensarbeit by Jens Metzdorf, "*The just and necessary War we are engag'd in*". *Marlboroughs Kaplan Francis Hare und die publizistische Debatte um die Beendigung des Spanischen Erbfolgekrieges in England* (University of Münster, 1993), pp. 74-82. See also the extensive treatment in Harris, *A Study of the Paper War*, pp. 83-113.

vised by Maynwaring[1], became the major instrument of the Whigs in their attempt to confront the Tories with ineluctable facts. The publication of the *Management* tracts, a substantial vindication of Marlborough, set in motion what, excepting the Galway and Guiscard episodes, turned out to be practically the only major controversy[2] of any significance for the war between the election in October 1710 and the reorientation of the public discussion in April 1711. They reminded the Tories of the premises for going to war, denied any unwillingness on the part of the former Government to work seriously for peace during previous negotiations, and emphasised - in spite of some underlying misgivings[3] - that the common ground of the Grand Alliance, the need to recover Spain[4] for Austria in order to put an end to the exorbitant power of France, was still valid. Of course the standard reproach of Jacobitism, which Maynwaring had also put forward in the summer[5], was not lacking[6]. Thus the Whigs, clearly resolved to apply pressure, of a polemic nature at least, on their opponents, continued to put up high barriers for the Tories to overcome, although their incessant war-cry of 'No peace without Spain' had lost much if not all of its persuasive power[7] since the surrender of General Stanhope's army at Brihuega, news of which reached London in December 1710[8]. In spite of their cool adherence to the solid facts of the case Maynwaring, the Whigs' *chef de propagande*[9] in the coming struggle, and Hare realised that systematic efforts were being made by their adversaries to undermine if not openly attack the very foundations of the English involvement. In the first of the pamphlets, the letter dated 23 November 1710 and reprinted in *The Management of the War; in Four Letters to a Tory-Member* (1711), the author shrewdly sur-

---

1 Cf. John Oldmixon, *Memoirs of the Press, Historical and Political, for Thirty Years Past, from 1710 to 1740* (London, 1742), p. 20.

2 Regarding this war of words cf. Henry L. Snyder, "Arthur Maynwaring and the Whig Press, 1710-1712", *Literatur als Kritik des Lebens. Festschrift zum 65. Geburtstag von Ludwig Borinski*, ed. Rudolf Haas, Heinz-Joachim Müllenbrock and Claus Uhlig (Heidelberg, 1975), pp. 126-127.

3 See *The Management of the War. In a Second Letter to a Tory-Member* (3rd ed., London, 1711), p. 37.

4 The new Government 'promised' Spain to Philip of Anjou from the outset: see Trevelyan, "The 'Jersey' Period of the Negotiations Leading to the Peace of Utrecht", p. 103. Cf. also L.G. Wickham Legg, "Torcy's Account of Matthew Prior's Negotiations at Fontainebleau in July 1711", *The English Historical Review* 29 (1914), p. 527.

5 See [Arthur Maynwaring], *Four Letters to a Friend in North Britain, upon the Publishing the Tryal of Dr. Sacheverell* (London, 1710), p. 15.

6 See *The Management of the War. In a Second Letter to a Tory-Member*, p. 38.

7 Dickinson writes on Godolphin's attitude towards the demand to recover Spain: " [...] by 1710 he had realised its senselessness and was willing to forego it" (*Sidney Godolphin*, p. 245).

8 Cf. Hill, "The Change of Government and the 'Loss of the City'", p. 407.

9 Paul Baker Patterson rightly states: "If there existed a Whig counterpart to Jonathan Swift, i.e. one who assumed the journalistic roles of literary co-ordinator, editor, censor, author, and liaison between the journalists and politicians, Arthur Mainwaring may be said to have been that counterpart" (*Robert Harley and the Organisation of Political Propaganda* [Diss., University of Virginia, 1974], p. 268).

veyed the body of printed propaganda so far produced on behalf of the new Government to call into question the fundamentals of British policy in the War of the Spanish Succession. Referring, in this order, to the *Letter to the Examiner*, *The Secret History of Arlus and Odolphus*, Davenant's *Sir Thomas Double at Court, and in High Preferments*, the *Letter from a Foreign Minister in England to Monsieur Pettecum*, *Faults on Both Sides* and Defoe's *Essay upon Publick Credit*[1], he surmised that it was the organizing skill of Harley that lay behind the variety of approaches to rally public opinion in support of the new Ministry. Besides attributing the *Letter from a Foreign Minister* to Harley himself[2], his only other mistake was to put St. John's *Letter to the Examiner* under the auspices of the new Prime Minister. The motives behind Harley's clever co-ordination of Tory propaganda were summed up thus: "But whatever various Figures these Engines of his affect to move in, and whatever different ways they take, they all make to the same End [...]; I mean in censuring the Management of the War, and endeavouring to ruin the Reputation of those, who have been hitherto the chief Directors of it"[3]. Though the *Letter from a Foreign Minister* received his highest praise and *Arlus and Odolphus* was mentioned frequently in the pamphlets, it is St. John's more daring piece of propaganda, which openly calls into question the entire rationale of the war, is mentioned first and deprecated in the supercilious manner of the author of the *Medley*, that seems to have had most portentous implications[4] for the author, for the first letter ends on an anti-Jacobite note - more typical of Maynwaring than of Hare - by evoking the danger from "our Domestick Invaders"[5], pursuing French interests in the face of Protestant Englishmen.

The Whigs' task of exposing the true aims of the new Government proved by no means easy. Through the agency of Swift, who possibly took a hand in writing replies to the first two of Hare's and Maynwaring's pamphlets in the form of an *Examination*[6] and its sequel, the *Management* controversy also got linked up with the *Examiner*, where, however, it received a rather summary treatment[7], indicating that openly taking on Marlborough's apologist did not yet appear oppor-

---

1 See *The Management of the War; in Four Letters to a Tory-Member* (London, 1711), pp. 1-2.

2 Cf. Downie, *Robert Harley and the Press*, p. 123.

3 *The Management of the War*, p. 3.

4 The following statement by George Sherburn is based on too literal a reading of the text: "Hare was contemptuous of Bolingbroke's *Letter* [...]" ("Francis Hare and the Peace of Utrecht", *The Newberry Library Bulletin* VI, no. 3 [November 1963], p. 66).

5 *The Management of the War*, p. 19.

6 Cf. Snyder, "Arthur Maynwaring and the Whig Press", p. 126. Cf., however, Harris, *A Study of the Paper War*, p. 162. *An Examination of the Management of the War* (1711), though, whose author assumes an unpretentious pose, is not, rhetorically speaking, a snide pamphlet at all.

7 See numbers 24 and 29 of the *Examiner* of 11 January and 15 February 1711. The latter issue complained about the author's "foul language" - Maynwaring's rather than Hare's doing? For Swift's abandonment of his announcement that he intended to write a detailed reply to the *Management* pamphlets, see the *Observator* of 17-21 February 1711 and the *Medley* of 5 February 1711.

tune to Swift nor - for that matter - the Ministry. For his part Maynwaring, Swift's weekly antagonist in the *Medley*, was instrumental in producing *An Answer to the Examination of the Management of the War. Written by the Medley's Footman* (1711). It was by no means accidental that the controversy about the *Management* pamphlets was, as it were, also treated as a side-issue by authors whose main business by then included weekly journalism. By quickly establishing itself as the leading opinion-journal in the Tory camp, the *Examiner* had necessitated the founding of a rival paper of comparable calibre, which was conducted by the ablest of the Whig writers. This personal constellation noticeably added to the importance of the periodical press as a medium of public debate after the installation of the new Government. The author of *Remarks upon Dr. Hare's Four Letters to a Tory Member, concerning the Management of the War* (1711), for example, frankly acknowledged the *Examiner's* superior claim to setting the pace in public dispute[1] ! Although the pamphlet, of course, did not even temporarily lose its significance as a major conveyor of political propaganda, the weekly journal gained in relative importance and to an increasing degree put its stamp on the public debate. Although it was common for the media to pay particular attention to their own kind, with regard to the weeklies this was a sign of their growing self-confidence if one considers the massive output of pamphlets, the traditional heavyweights in the journalistic fray. There were comparatively more references now in pamphlets to periodicals like the *Examiner* and the *Medley* than vice versa.

The difficulties of the Whigs in engaging their opponents can be exemplified in the *Medley's* stubborn contest with the *Examiner*[2] and corroborated by complementary observations regarding other media. The general constellation prevailing from November 1710 through the spring of 1711 was characterized by the pertinacity of Tory writers of a quite different stamp to do permanent damage to the Whig stand on the war without admitting to a change of principles. That the official attitude towards the war was changing without becoming as yet explicitly redefined was clearly reflected in Andrew Snape's fast sermon preached before the House of Commons on 28 March 1711. This seemingly balanced sermon, while admitting the justice of the struggle against France[3], sent noticeable signals of English war-weariness[4]. The final part in particular, with its unmistakable references to his private enrichment[5], made it clear that the discrediting of Marlborough was already well under way. However, the Government could not yet afford an open rupture, depending, as it did, on his services during the next campaign in

---

1 See *Remarks upon Dr. Hare's Four Letters to a Tory Member, concerning the Management of the War, etc.* (London, 1711), p. 28.

2 See the chapter "The Main Genres of the Public Debate: Profiles and Functions".

3 See Andrew Snape, *A Sermon Preach'd before the Honourable House of Commons, on Wednesday the 28th of March, 1711. Being the Day Appointed by Her Majesty's Royal Proclamation for a General Fast* (London, 1711), p. 12.

4 See esp. the remarks already pointing to the emotionalization of this debate to be brought in later by the Tories: *ibid.*, pp. 7, 13, 14, 24.

5 See *ibid.*, p. 25.

order to retain confidence in its handling of the war. Apparently the authors writing in the Tory interest were commissioned by the Harley Government to prepare for any eventuality, and to conduct a campaign of attrition instead of engaging in a battle of destruction. As early as November 1710 Mrs. Manley, in her devious way confirming Boyer's previous statement, had intimated in the second volume of her *Memoirs of Europe* that Marlborough would keep his command[1], and as late as *Examiner* 38 (19 April 1711), Swift triumphantly expostulated with his opponents that "All Care is taken to support the War"[2]. Harley's policy of camouflaging his ulterior intentions in order to maintain his freedom of action resulted in the constant harassment of Whig positions short of open revocation of official commitments.

c) Spring and Summer 1711

The real transmutation of the war debate - at first only noticeable in erratic moves on the journalistic plane - began in April 1711, when the death of Emperor Joseph I changed the setting of international affairs. In order to evaluate the process of the debate properly it is important to distinguish between its successive interconnecting phases, which permit a broad temporal placing of the printed material. This is lacking, for example, in the ninth chapter[3] of Coombs' Dutch-centered study, which therefore tends to blur the inner dynamics of the debate. Immediately after the Emperor's death the discussion of its political repercussions set in. As can be observed throughout the debate, Harley followed a double policy[4], presenting a soft approach - personified by Defoe - and a hard approach - personified by Swift - to the task of winning support for revising the aims of the war. These complementary approaches largely merged at the beginning of 1712, when Tory propaganda reached its climax of self-assertiveness. Defoe, among others, published a pamphlet, *The Succession of Spain Consider'd: Or, a View of the Several Interests of the Princes and Powers of Europe, as they Respect the Succession of Spain and the Empire*, which appeared at the end of April or the beginning of May 1711 and carefully drew attention to the need to reconsider the question of the balance of power. This pamphlet, in a kind of concerted action, appeared at about the same time as the *Review* of 28 April 1711, which saw this problem as a political issue and also realised the difficulties that would arise if the policy towards Spain were continued after the Emperor's death. Only a week after his

---

1 See *The Novels of Mary Delariviere Manley*, ed. Köster, II, 687. At the same time she undermined confidence in Marlborough's indispensability by ascribing his successes to propitious circumstances and the courage of his fellow-countrymen (pp. 418-422) as well as resorting to more fantastic explanations (p. 436).

2 *The Examiner and Other Pieces Written in 1710-11*, p. 132.

3 "The Double Game of the Oxford Ministry 1710-11".

4 Harley's "'double policy'" is described by A.D. MacLachlan, "The Road to Peace 1710-13", *Britain after the Glorious Revolution 1689-1714*, ed. Holmes, p. 204.

roguish reassurance of unflagging war efforts[1] Swift renounced the public consensus on war aims in Spain, which had not been openly challenged till then, although a Tory pamphleteer had already called "groundless" the assumption that the accession of the Duke of Anjou to the crown of Spain implied the unification of the French and Spanish monarchies[2]. In this essay (*Examiner* 39 of 26 April 1711), after expatiating on the machinations of the former Ministry and ominously mentioning their endeavours permanently to beguile the nation through addresses cunningly pressed upon it, he rather unexpectedly focuses on the point in question: "I MUST be so free to tell my Meaning in this; that among other Things, I understand it of the Address made to the QUEEN about three Years ago, to desire that her Majesty would not consent to a Peace, without the entire Restitution of *Spain*"[3]. He adds succinctly that the Whigs thereby intended "to pin down the War upon us; consequently to increase their own Power and Wealth, and multiply Difficulties on the QUEEN and Kingdom [...]"[4]. With this indictment the corrosion of the main bastion of Whig war policy had been initiated. It turned out to be an arduous process of public wrangling. Significantly, the *Post Boy* of 26 to 28 April 1711 contained a paragraph about supposed French peace intentions. Though the journal declared this to be "a meer chimera", its hint that the Allies' "Demand of the Restitution of Spain and the Indies" seemed unacceptable to the French, occurring, as it did, in close conjunction with the *Examiner's* move, must be regarded as sly assistance to Swift's *ballon d'essai*[5]. However, it is by no means clear what immediate function Swift's challenge to the 'No peace without Spain' policy fulfilled in the overall strategy of Tory propaganda. Undoubtedly its basic function, fraught with long-term consequences, was to divest of its prohibitive aura a subject which had so far not been openly dealt with by ministerial propagandists. Though it radically questioned the rationale of Whig war policy it combined aggressiveness with discretion. Maynwaring's reply in *Medley* 31 (30 April 1711) significantly accused Swift and the Tories of "pleading for the Duke of *Anjou*, and a Partition of *Spain*"[6]. Had Swift, who only doubted the feasibility of reconquering Spain for the House of Habsburg, successfully put out a bait to ensnare the Whigs? Perhaps its more immediate purpose was to spur the investigations of the Commons, whose Representation, charging the former Government with breach of public trust in the conduct of the war, was presented to the Queen at the

---

1 See above, p. 50.

2 See *An Examination of the Management of the War. In a Letter to my Lord* *** (London, 1711), p. 11.

3 *The Examiner and Other Pieces Written in 1710-11*, p. 140.

4 *Ibid.*, p. 140.

5 Cf. the Preface to *Tory Annals Faithfully Extracted out of Abel Roper's Famous Writings. Vulgarly Call'd Post-Boy and Supplement. From March 1710 to December 1711. ... Revis'd and Emprov'd by the Author of the Tale of a Tub* (London, 1712), p. v (unpaginated in original) with its satirical reference to the collaboration between Swift and Abel Roper attempting to lend support to the peace process through their publications.

6 *Swift vs. Mainwaring*, ed. Ellis, p. 295.

beginning of June[1]. The publicity which the calumnious 'pamphlet' *Oliver's Pocket Looking-Glass*, published in May 1711, received in the advertising columns of *Examiner* 42 (17 May 1711) and *Examiner* 44 (31 May 1711) indicated that the Government was not letting up in its hostility towards the war or towards its figurehead. In any case, we are confronted with the remarkable fact that Swift's kite-flying hardly produced any tangible effects, at least in the beginning. The other Tory papers did not follow suit on a corresponding note, nor did the *Medley*, though smelling a rat, pursue the argument until it ceased to appear in June 1711. Still, Swift's *Examiner* essay must at least have been seminal in removing taboos from a topic which, considering the Queen's reassuring message to the House of Commons after the Emperor's death[2], seemed to pose no immediate practical threat to the Allies' cause.

Though Defoe, in the penultimate section of his *Eleven Opinions about Mr. H-y; with Observations*, published about the beginning of June 1711[3], explicitly confirmed the validity of a tried policy and even stressed the mutual confidence between the Allies, the Whigs in that month, when rumours about an approaching peace were spreading in London, suddenly sounded the alarm bells. After hinting at secret peace moves in the last stanza of his broadside *An Excellent New Song, Called, Credit Restored* (1711), which satirized Harley's South Sea scheme, Maynwaring, who was convinced that testing the terrain with a view to a possible peace had reached a decisive stage[4], in July fully blew the Whig trumpet in *Reflections upon the Examiner's Scandalous Peace* (1711). In this densely factual pamphlet the author tries to erect a defensive barrier by cataloguing all the official resolutions backing the Austrian claim to the entire Spanish monarchy[5]. In a companion piece, *A Letter to a Member of the October-Club* (1711), which emphasised the economic drawbacks of giving up this position[6], Maynwaring[7], collaborating once again with Hare, made his point by repeatedly warning "that giving *Spain* to the Duke of *Anjou*, will be giving it to the *French* King"[8]. At about

1 Cf. Abel Boyer, *Quadriennium Annae Postremum; or the Political State of Great Britain*, 2nd ed., vol. I and II for the Year 1711 (London, 1718), 317ff.

2 See *ibid.*, pp. 284-285.

3 Cf. Coombs, *The Conduct of the Dutch*, p. 239.

4 In a letter dated 7 July 1711 Maynwaring wrote to Lord Coningsby in ironical tones: "It is generally thought that 199 [Harley] has a good Peace ready, and wants only the Dutch to like it [...]" (BL Add. MS 57861, fol. 164).

5 For the rhetorical analysis, see the chapter "The Main Genres of the Public Debate: Profiles and Functions".

6 Cf. also the eighth stanza of the broadside *An Excellent New Song, to the Memorable Tune of Lillibullero* (1711).

7 According to Snyder, this pamphlet "must at least have been seen through the press by Maynwaring" ("Arthur Maynwaring and the Whig Press", p. 128). The present author presumes that Maynwaring had a considerable hand in the authorship.

8 *A Letter to a Member of the October-Club: Shewing, that to Yield Spain to the Duke of Anjou by a Peace, wou'd be the Ruin of Great Britain* (London, 1711), p. 6.

the same time the *Review* of 16 June 1711 still marvelled that "such a Peace"[1] as giving Spain and the Indies to the Duke of Anjou could well be conceived. The *Review* remained true to this line until October 1711! As Maynwaring's bewildered request in the *Reflections* that Swift state his reasons for his sudden and portentous revelation[2] showed, the Whigs were still somehow groping in the dark as to the Government's concrete intentions. In April 1711, Swift had given the go-ahead for the final stage of calling the political enemy to account, but the public discussion went on rather erratically for the time being. Apparently the uncertainty about the progress of international politics then hindered more extensive encounters, and the Whigs, who could not but rest content with uttering Maynwaring's words of caution, wanted to give proof of being on their guard against all eventualities. The discontinuation of the *Examiner*, which was finally suspended on 26 July 1711, even led to a temporary cessation of journalistic hostility towards Marlborough, who in that month let Harley know that he was interested in coming to terms with Godolphin's successor[3], a reconciliatory move not left unreciprocated on the part of the Government, at least on the face of it. It was not until the end of August 1711, when Prior's preliminary mission leaked out, and not until the beginning of September 1711, when Marlborough's victory at Bouchain gave a new boost to Whig morale that a bitter, extensive and protracted public battle ensued that reached its densest polemical interaction in the turning-point debate between the autumn of 1711 and the spring of 1712[4].

d) Autumn 1711 until Spring 1712

The repercussions of the leaking of Prior's secret mission[5] - Swift tried straightaway to ward off the most dreadful anticipations through the "Serious Banter"[6] of *A New Journey to Paris* (1711) - were for the time being offset by Marlborough's

---

1 *Defoe's Review*, Reproduced from the Original Editions, with an Introduction and Bibliographical Notes by Arthur Wellesley Secord, 22 Facsimile Books [9 vols.] (New York, 1965), VIII, 146.

2 See [Arthur Maynwaring], *Reflections upon the Examiner's Scandalous Peace* (London, 1711), p. 21.

3 See Lord Stair's account of an interview between himself and Marlborough in July 1711: *A Selection from the Papers of the Earl of Marchmont, in the Possession of the Right Honourable Sir George Henry Rose. Illustrative of Events from 1685 to 1750*, II (London, 1831), 77-79.

4 See the separate chapter "Focus".

5 J.D. Alsop has put forward the view - by no means implausible - that it was actually St. John's purpose to launch Prior's mission into the public arena in order to further his own objectives, which were to force a political showdown at that point in time: see "The Detection of Matthew Prior's Peace Mission of 1711", *British Journal for Eighteenth-Century Studies* 7 (1984), pp. 61-67, esp. p. 64.

6 [White Kennett], *The Wisdom of Looking Backward, to Judge the better of one Side and t'other by the Speeches, Writings, Actions, and other Matters of Fact on Both Sides, for the four Years last Past* (London, 1715), p. 144.

dashing victory at Bouchain, the news of which followed hard on the diplomatic disclosure. Bouchain turned out to be a valuable incentive for the Whigs, who, even before the middle of September, appeared on the public scene with, for instance, the broadside *To the Duke of Marlborough, on the Taking of Bouchain* (1711), whose final phrase of "Lasting Peace"[1] struck a recurrent and somehow wishful note of opposition rhetoric. Roused by ominous divulgences in the *Post Boy* of 21 to 23 August and particularly in the edition of 6 to 8 September 1711 about overtures of peace[2], which at last broached the possibility of a partition of Spain[3], the Whigs really went out of their way to expose what they hoped would be seen as the Government's disgraceful retreat from essentials which were more than ever within reach of England and her Allies. Hare, in his sermon *The Charge of God to Joshua*, preached on 9 September 1711 and published on the 25th of the same month on Maynwaring's initiative[4], resolutely hoisted the Whig standard and thought fit to drive home the familiar, but highly seasonable lesson of the providential character of England's military success that unmistakably pointed towards a victorious peace that was not to be given away lightly. Although Hare also adopted a self-confident if not aggressive stance in *Bouchain: In a Dialogue between the late Medley and Examiner* (1711), this pamphlet, published a few days before the sermon, indicated that the Whigs, in spite of trying to force their adversaries to adhere to the approved principles of peace policy, did not merely return to the old agenda. Their rhetoric, which had received a considerable impetus, did not so much aim at the Government's readiness to correct itself by its own free will but rather at the eventual intervention of Parliament[5]. Their preventive oratory apparently addressed to the Tory Government, which was publicly challenged by an author supposed to be a Marlborough confidant, was increasingly directed at Parliament as the last bulwark of national interests. Thus the *Bouchain* dialogue, which, by didactically confronting the leading spokesmen for the Whig and Tory camps, forcefully demonstrates that any idea of a retreat from the 'No peace without Spain' line was untenable, put its main argumentative thrust on the conviction that it was inconceivable that Parliament would ever consent to a dishonourable peace with France[6]. Maynwaring's broadside *An Excellent New Song, Called Mat's Peace, Or, the Downfall of Trade*, which appeared about the beginning of October 1711 and painted the dire consequences of surrendering Spain to the

1 Cf. Horn, *Marlborough: A Survey*, p. 346.

2 Cf. also reports from The Hague in the *Protestant Post-Boy* of 25-27 September 1711.

3 Cf. on this Boyer, *Quadriennium Annae Postremum*, vol. I and II for the year 1711, 529-533.

4 Cf. [John Oldmixon], *The Life and Posthumous Works of Arthur Maynwaring, Esq.; Containing Several Original Pieces and Translations, in Prose and Verse, never before Printed* (London, 1715), p. 324.

5 The Duchess of Marlborough also pinned her hopes on "even this Parliament": Frances Harris, *A Passion for Government: The Life of Sarah, Duchess of Marlborough* (Oxford, 1991), p. 185. She was at that time the person with whom Maynwaring, encouraged by the Bouchain success, held a running political dialogue.

6 See [Francis Hare], *Bouchain: In a Dialogue between the Late Medley and Examiner* (3rd ed., London, 1711), p. 39.

House of Bourbon, also set its hope on Parliament's corrective power. In view of the probability of the Government's defection from the status quo the Whigs directed their efforts at Parliament as the final court of appeal without changing their basic rhetorical armoury. Of course, the publication of the Preliminaries on 13 October 1711 added highly explosive fuel to Whig ardour. Again, Maynwaring, in his ironic, well-written and effective *Vindication of the Present M-y, from the Clamours Rais'd against them upon Occasion of the New Preliminaries* (1711), published in November and probably his most influential contribution to the controversy about the Preliminaries, apparently came to the defence of the Government, which could not in fairness be suspected of such an unprecedented neglect of British interests. By harping on the shocking implications of such suppositions he at bottom appealed to the discretionary power of Parliament[1] for dispelling Whig misgivings[2]. A peace not commensurate with the sacrifices made by Britain ought to be rejected. This pamphlet also clearly states that the *Examiner's* plans never assumed the evacuation of Spain and that the Emperor's death was only the pretext for relinquishing the former position on Spain[3]. Maynwaring's complementary piece, the slightly earlier *Remarks on the Preliminary Articles Offer'd by the French King, in order to Procure a General Peace* (1711), had already highlighted the flagrant disregard of British interests by carefully pointing out the differences between the old and new Preliminaries[4].

The quick succession of the taking of Bouchain[5] and above all the premature publication of the highly controversial Mesnager Preliminaries in the *Daily Courant* of 13 October 1711 gave fresh impetus to the Whigs' publicity campaign to confront the Government on its peace plans. The Tories, though by no means taken aback by the vigour of their adversaries, did betray some embarrassment about how to match the Opposition's concerted efforts. Between September and the end of November 1711 Harley's journalistic forces were rather less efficiently arrayed than before and especially afterwards. The Whigs' propaganda battalions were comparatively strong even in the light of the fact that the Tories immediately launched a counterattack with Mrs. Manley's two rejoinders addressed to Hare[6], which showed both skill and verve[7]. Altogether the Tory policy seems to have been to counter the Whigs' polyphonic invocation of national essentials by raising the emotive pitch of their own writings. From about September 1711 Tory propa-

---

1 Cf. on this the expectations still expressed in the *Flying-Post* of 1-4 December 1711 in its controversy with Roper.

2 See [Arthur Maynwaring], *A Vindication of the Present M-y, from the Clamours Rais'd against them upon Occasion of the New Preliminaries* (London, 1711), p. 51.

3 See *ibid.*, p. 37.

4 See also Maynwaring's broadside *Seven Preliminary Articles on the Part of France, for Effecting a General Peace* (1711).

5 This event was also propagandistically exploited by the Opposition in the above-mentioned broadside poem *To the Duke of Marlborough, on the Taking of Bouchain* (1711); the latter was reprinted in the *Flying-Post* of 22-24 November 1711 to strengthen Whig stamina.

6 Regarding St. John's reaction, see *Letters and Correspondence*, I, 365-366.

7 On the journalistic significance of Mrs. Manley's replies see the chapter "Focus".

ganda distinctly appealed to the emotions - apparently intended as an antidote to the crescendo of Whig preventive oratory. Thus Mrs. Manley, in *The D. of M-h's Vindication* (1711), her reply to *Bouchain*, invoked the immense losses of human lives[1]. *A Learned Comment upon Dr. Hare's Excellent Sermon Preach'd before the D. of Marlborough, on the Surrender of Bouchain* (1711), Manley's (and Swift's) witty reply to Hare's panegyric, also struck a populist note; it concluded by calling for gratitude to "the Authors of Peace to these distressed Nations, by which we may be freed from those nearer and much more formidable Enemies, Discontent and Poverty at Home"[2]. This shift of emphasis pointed ahead, of course, to the polemical colouring of *The Conduct of the Allies.*

The growing emotionalization of Government propaganda manifested itself most clearly in Defoe's influential *Reasons why this Nation Ought to Put a Speedy End to this Expensive War*[3], published on 6 October 1711, exactly a week before the Preliminaries appeared in print. This pamphlet, which the Whigs tried to counter immediately with the somewhat laboured optimism of *A Proposal for Carrying on the War. In a Letter to a Nobleman* (1711), published on the same day, reached three editions in the month of publication and deliberately appealed to the humanitarian feelings of its readers[4]. Within this emotional framework the author, who was the initiator and most persistent proponent of this line of thought, concentrated on the supposed shift of power from France to Austria and pleaded for British equidistance from both[5]. Defoe, who had already discussed[6] the underlying principles of the balance-of-power issue[7], now became the prime advocate of this topic, which proved to be convenient for the Government. His above-mentioned pamphlet must be regarded as an important move on the part of the Tories, a sort of liberating stroke, to escape from the increasing barrage of Whig propaganda and to regain scope of action. What he envisaged early on as a volte-face on the Spanish question - there are two partition plans at the end of the pamphlet - was seconded with due delay by concomitant steps in the *Review.* Al-

1 See [Mary de la Rivière Manley], *The D. of M-h's Vindication: In Answer to a Pamphlet lately Publish'd, Call'd Bouchain, or a Dialogue between the Medley and the Examiner* (London, 1711), p. 14.

2 *A Learned Comment upon Dr. Hare's Excellent Sermon Preach'd before the D. of Marlborough, on the Surrender of Bouchain by an Enemy to Peace* (London, 1711), p. 16. Mrs. Manley followed this up with similar remarks in the second volume of *Memoirs of Europe*: *Novels*, ed. Köster, II, 414.

3 For a more detailed rhetorical analysis, see the chapter "The Main Genres of the Public Debate: Profiles and Functions".

4 See - as strategically crucial passages - the beginning and ending of this pamphlet.

5 See [Daniel Defoe], *Reasons why this Nation Ought to Put a Speedy End to this Expensive War; with a Brief Essay, at the Probable Conditions on which the Peace now Negotiating, may be Founded* (2nd ed., London, 1711), pp. 29 and 43.

6 See - as an excellent example - the *Review* of 1 June 1706.

7 On this line of thought in British politics see M. Sheehan, "The Development of British Theory and Practice of the Balance of Power before 1714", *History* 73 (1988), pp. 24-37. Cf. also Heinz Duchhardt, "Die Glorious Revolution und das internationale System", *Francia* 16, 2 (1989), pp. 29-37, esp. pp. 35-36.

though the author of *Reasons Why* pretended there was some difference of opinion in this matter between him and the author of the *Review*[1], the latter journal, while vehemently denying or at least not openly admitting any partition plans as late as its issue of 11 October 1711, chimed in from 13 October 1711 and in successive numbers emphasised the necessity of dividing the Spanish Monarchy to maintain the European balance of power now threatened by the Austrian Emperor. The *Review* of 23 October 1711, in particular, dramatically asserted in its final paragraph that the parliamentary resolutions with regard to Spain would never have been taken if the present situation had already existed. Defoe had unmistakably come round to Harley's line of policy. With its rhetoric of moderation and prudent weighing of altered circumstances *Reasons Why*, which also paid due attention to commercial aspects, addressed itself particularly to Defoe's former Whig clientele and in several respects showed well-calculated attunement to readership response with the trenchant and polarising rhetoric of Swift's more formidable *Conduct of the Allies*. In his attempt to create something like a broad-based platform Defoe also pointed to the overbearing British treatment of the French during the recent Geertruidenberg negotiations[2] and to the iniquity of Whig endeavours "to destroy the publick Credit"[3]. His insistent question with regard to military exploits, "What is this to ending the War?"[4], linked *Reasons Why* with the main body of Government propaganda, which, in this matter, was certain of being in tune with the public mood.

Although the publication of *Reasons Why* furnished further proof of the Government's stamina, the Tories were granted no respite from the pursuit of the Whigs. As Maynwaring's supercilious remark in *A Vindication of the Present M-y* indicated, "'Tis not Declamations on the Misery of the People will prove the Point, it must be done by comparing our Condition with that of the Enemies'"[5], the Whigs still relied mainly on factual enlightenment. Pamphlets such as *Anguis in Herba: Or the Fatal Consequences of a Treaty with France* (1711), opportunely reprinted, and *A Letter from an Exchange Broker to a Country Gentleman concerning the Peace and South-Sea Stock* (1711), with different emphasis, argued the identity of French and Spanish interests, while Maynwaring, in his *Letter to a High-Churchman* (1711), calmly referred the author of *Reasons Why* to his earlier *Remarks on the Preliminary Articles* for pertinent instruction[6]. In *Remarks upon the Present Negotiations of Peace Begun between Britain and France*, probably published in the second half of November 1711, Maynwaring again settled accounts with the author of *Reasons Why*, among others, and produced a kind of

---

1 See *Reasons Why*, p. 39. This rhetorical trick has also been noted by James Sutherland, *Daniel Defoe. A Critical Study* (Cambridge, Mass., 1971), p. 58.

2 See *Reasons Why*, pp. 12-13.

3 See *ibid.*, p. 22.

4 *Ibid.*, p. 9.

5 *A Vindication of the Present M-y*, p. 29.

6 See [Arthur Maynwaring], *A Letter to a High-Churchman, in Answer to a Pamphlet, Intitled, Reasons why this Nation Should Put a Speedy End to this Expensive War* (London, 1711), p. 17.

authoritative critique of the Tory manoeuvres to force the nation to come to terms with new approaches to peace. In this pamphlet he firmly substantiated the well-known Whig positions, once again pointing to Parliament as a last resort for redressing the evils of a misguided peace policy. While confidently asserting the merits of the case, Maynwaring added some indispensable emotional ingredients at the end and invoked "the Cause of Truth and Liberty"[1] on the English side. His conclusion "That the present Proposals of Peace, or any future Proposals of what kind soever, That shall leave Spain and the Indies to the House of Bourbon, ought by every true Englishman to be rejected with Scorn and Indignation"[2] somehow put the final seal on the prophylactic incantations that had become part and parcel of Whig rhetoric at this stage of the peace controversy. A broadside like *The Procession: A New Protestant Ballad*, a satirical comment on the prohibited spectacle planned for the celebration of Queen Elizabeth's birthday on 17 November 1711, capped this emotional appeal by evoking the always seasonable alternative between the Protestant Elector and the Popish Pretender. Another broadside published about this time and probably by Maynwaring, *A New Song* (1711), also exploited fears of restoring the Pretender by warning against "A Peace which our *Hanover's* Title destroys"[3].

Whig propaganda was characterized by a remarkable degree of co-ordination in which Maynwaring's guiding hand[4] can be recognized. Numerous cross-references show the close interlinking of Whig writings. Thus, to quote but one relevant example, the anonymous author of *The Ballance of Power: Or, a Comparison of the Strength of the Emperor and the French King* (1711) repeatedly referred back to Maynwaring's *A Letter to a Member of the October-Club* for support of his views[5]. Defoe, who had been instrumental in putting this topic on the public agenda, made the most of it in publications such as *The Ballance of Europe* (1711), where he again stressed to what extent the European situation had changed after the Emperor's death and once again slyly transferred the notion of

---

1 [Arthur Maynwaring], *Remarks upon the Present Negotiations of Peace Begun between Britain and France* (London, 1711), p. 34.

2 *Ibid.*, p. 35.

3 *Poems on Affairs of State*, VII, 541.

4 It is a pity that the otherwise very informative *Blenheim Papers* give us absolutely no details of Maynwaring's co-ordination of the Whigs' media strategy during the decisive phase of the public debate between autumn 1711 and spring 1712. They do, however, provide evidence of Maynwaring's faith in the principle that a government standing on shaky foundations can be toppled by the journalist's pen: see *inter alia* his letters to the Duchess of Marlborough of 12 May 1711 (BL Add. MS 61461, fols. 124-125), 15 May 1711 (BL Add. MS 61461, fol. 131) and July 1711 (BL Add. MS 61461, fol. 137). - Oldmixon's *The Life and Posthumous Works of Arthur Maynwaring* is also unforthcoming on this aspect of Maynwaring's role as public campaign co-ordinator.

5 See *The Ballance of Power: Or, a Comparison of the Strength of the Emperor and the French King. In a Letter to a Friend* (London, 1711), pp. 4, 9, 11.

"Exorbitant Greatness"[1] from France, with which it was traditionally associated, to Austria[2]. In other pamphlets like *An Essay at a Plain Exposition of that Difficult Phrase a Good Peace* (1711) he also painstakingly tried to dispel misgivings about leaving the Duke of Anjou in possession of Spain. He deserves the greatest credit for continued and unremitting Tory presence in a critical phase of the Government's public relations policy. That Defoe, who had retreated from his former Whig principles, must have experienced increasing difficulties in preserving his integrity became clear from the reactions of, among others, the penetrating author of *A Caveat to the Treaters* (1711), who took him to task on his reversal of opinion[3] and exposed the fallacy of Defoe's reasoning in the pamphlets referred to in this and the preceding paragraph. In *Armageddon*, also published at the end of October or the beginning of November 1711, Defoe actually curried favour with his former Whig clientele and emphatically denied any abandonment of the 'No peace without Spain' policy, although his consent to a possible prolongation of the war sounded rather hollow. The pressure of Whig resistance is also indicated by Boyer trying in October to recommend himself to Harley as a possible journalistic ally along moderate Whig lines in *An Account of the State and Progress of the Present Negotiation of Peace* (1711). In spite of the bold front presented especially by Defoe, one has the impression that, until the end of November 1711, the Tories, who till then had shrunk from opening the sluices of unrestrained disparagement of the Allies, did not match the Whigs in public efficacy[4]. It was more than mere coincidence that, in October 1711, the Government again had recourse to repressive measures against Opposition writers[5]. By the end of that month Swift thought the nation "half bewitched against a Peace"[6]. Although Tory writings of that particular period convey the impression of having popular feeling on their side, the massive circumstantial evidence accumulated by the Whigs in favour of existing obligations had not yet been overcome. Something was still lacking to offset the Whigs' expertise in gathering and presenting information by propagandist means of greater virulence.

This is precisely what Swift's famous pamphlet *The Conduct of the Allies, and of the Late Ministry, in Beginning and Carrying on the Present War* published on 27 November 1711 achieved. In terms of sheer numbers of replies, it was certainly

---

1 [Daniel Defoe], *The Ballance of Europe: Or, an Enquiry into the Respective Dangers of Giving the Spanish Monarchy to the Emperour, as well as to King Philip; with the Consequences that may be Expected from either* (Edinburgh, 1711), p. 39.

2 Details of this linguistic transfer can be found in the chapter "Focus".

3 See [Francis Hare], *A Caveat to the Treaters; or, the Modern Schemes of Partition Examin'd, with Relation to the Safety of Europe in general, and of Great-Britain and Ireland in particular* (London, 1711), p. 84. See also *ibid.*, p. 88.

4 The author of this study agrees with Frances Harris' judgment: "For the time being the Whigs appeared to have the best of the debate [...]" (*A Passion for Government*, p. 186). Cf. also Robert J. Allen, "William Oldisworth: 'the Author of *The Examiner*'", *Philological Quarterly* 26 (1947), p. 171.

5 Cf. Downie, *Robert Harley and the Press*, pp. 153-154.

6 Jonathan Swift, *Journal to Stella*, ed. Harold Williams, 2 vols. (Oxford, 1948, repr. 1974), II, 397.

the most effective single publication on the war during the entire debate. It exhibited the determined and ruthless effort on Swift's - and the Government's[1] - part to put public discussion on a new footing. It soon gave a new spirit and quality to Tory propaganda and forced upon the Whigs a modified debate to the latters' disadvantage. As its title implies, the pamphlet shifted attention away from problematic peace plans towards the poor war record of the Allies and the discarded British politicians acting in collusion with them. Skilfully combining a plain, vigorous and unaffected prose style with rhetorical incisiveness according to classical precepts[2], Swift caps the Whigs' factualism by relentlessly compiling a list of the sins committed by the Allies, particularly the Dutch. Their defects are virtually shouted from the housetops. However, he is not only beating his adversaries at their own game; his factualism is merely the pretext for unrestrained emotionalism. By unabashedly opening the sluices of emotion for the purpose of vituperating the Dutch[3], Swift creates a new focus of public attention. He is obviously pursuing a strategy of changing gear in the war debate. Although, in quite a number of points, he in substance summarises views already expressed by other Tory journalists[4], he fails to acknowledge such references and instead creates the illusion of starting all over again with a clean slate. Concomitantly, in spite of a few ironic reverberations, he entirely ignores the objections to a new war policy carefully built up by the Whig writers[5]. In this manner Swift tries to circumvent the enemy's lines. Even in the latter part of his pamphlet, where he wants to make the 'No peace without Spain' position appear an arbitrary addition to the original war aims[6] and also stresses the changed situation in Europe after the death of Joseph I[7], he disdains to engage in battle with Whig journalists. By high-handedly concentrating on the defects of the Allies, he can wonder at English forbearance and ask in bewilderment "by what Motives, or what Management, we are thus become the *Dupes* and *Bubbles* of *Europe*?"[8]. The ensuing conspiracy thesis then de-

---

1 From the publication of *The Conduct of the Allies* it is certainly reasonable to suppose that St. John exercised more and more influence on Swift's political writings; see *inter alia* W.A. Speck, "*The Examiner* Examined: Swift's Tory Pamphleteering", *Focus: Swift*, ed. C.J. Rawson (London, 1971), pp. 152-153.

2 See Heinz-Joachim Müllenbrock, "Cicero and Quintilian as Mentors of British Journalism: The Rhetorical Structure of Swift's *The Conduct of the Allies*", *Swift Studies* 2 (1987), pp. 57-66. A German version of this article was published in *Antike und Abendland* 32 (1986), pp. 173-185.

3 Unlike the *Observator*, the *Flying-Post* immediately realized that this anti-Dutch thrust gave politics a new quality; see esp. its issues of 29 November-1 December and 6-8 December 1711.

4 Cf. Laprevotte, "*The Conduct of the Allies*: contexte et originalité", pp. 249-250.

5 I cannot agree with the assessment of Harris, who overrates the argumentative disposition of the pamphlet (*A Study of the Paper War*, pp. 275-277) and stresses its "defensive function" (p. 277).

6 See Jonathan Swift, *Political Tracts 1711-1713*, ed. Herbert Davis (Oxford, 1951, repr. 1973), p. 48.

7 See *ibid.*, p. 51.

8 *Ibid.*, p. 40.

veloped aims, of course, at the Duke of Marlborough and 'the family'[1] who exploited England for private interests. In the rhetorical climax of the pamphlet the Duke, who was still a major obstacle to Tory peace plans, is even suspected of aspiring to royal dignity[2].

The publication of *The Conduct*[3], whose timing pointed towards the reopening of Parliament on 7 December 1711, indicated unmistakably that the Government's policy of apparent understanding with the Allies had been given up. Despite its immediate impact[4] it took some time before Swift's bombshell could give the hoped-for boost to Tory propaganda and make the latter recrystalize in new, coordinated vigour. In December 1711 the Tories still had to cope with temporary difficulties of realignment and were handicapped by the course of political events. While Defoe, in *The Felonious Treaty* (1711), tried further to drive home the new notion of equidistance from France and Austria, political events somewhat ruffled the Government's composure. On 5 December 1711 the Elector of Hanover's *Memorial* against peace without Spain was published in *The Daily Courant*[5], and two days later the House of Lords carried Lord Nottingham's motion that no peace which allotted Spain and the West Indies to any branch of the House of Bourbon would be acceptable[6]. Swift instantly tried to throw a spanner in the Whig works[7] by exposing Nottingham's time-serving practices in his trenchant ballad *An Excellent New Song, Being the Intended Speech of a Famous Orator against Peace*, which appeared on 6 December 1711.

The pressure of adverse political events on the Tories coincided with the closing of the journalistic ranks on the part of the Whigs. Significantly, the *Post Boy* of 4-6 December 1711 while welcoming the resumption of the *Examiner* drew attention to the strong Whig presence on the public scene. About the date when Parliament reconvened two major Whig pamphlets appeared in close succession,

---

1 Details of this use of political symbolism can be found in the chapter "Public Discourse".

2 See *Political Tracts 1711-1713*, pp. 44-45.

3 For further rhetorical analysis of this pamphlet, see the chapters "Focus" and "The Main Genres of the Public Debate: Profiles and Functions".

4 See e.g. the letter from a dignitary of Christ Church College in Oxford to Harley dated 4 December 1711: HMC, *Portland MSS*, VII (London, 1901), 79.

5 Cf. on this step taken by the Opposition Hill, *Robert Harley*, pp. 168 and 170 (the latter wrongly dated). The Tories tried to neutralize the impression made by this publication by casting doubts on its authenticity: see *Respectful Observations on a Late Print, Call'd a Memorial; Said to be Publish'd by the Baron de Bothmar, in the Name of his Electoral Highness of Hanover* (London, 1712). This rendered it possible for them to criticise its contents.

6 See on this and on the Lords' Address that followed, Cobbett, *Parliamentary History*, VI, cols. 1039-1042 and *Journals of the House of Lords*, XIX (London, 1774), 336.

7 On the parliamentary difficulties of the Government at that time cf. Clyve Jones, "The Division that never Was: New Evidence on the Aborted Vote in the Lords on 8 December 1711 on 'No Peace without Spain'", *Parliamentary History* 2 (1983), pp. 191-202 and G.S. Holmes, "The Commons' Division on 'No Peace without Spain', 7 December 1711", *Bulletin of the Institute of Historical Research* 33 (1960), pp. 223-234.

the Opposition's answer to Swift's challenge. Contrary to what Coombs assumes[1] they were well-concerted and fulfilled complementary functions in order to parry jointly the thrust of the *Conduct of the Allies*. The first[2] was probably Maynwaring's *Remarks on a False, Scandalous, and Seditious Libel, Intituled, The Conduct of the Allies, and of the Late Ministry, etc.* (1711)[3]. In this pamphlet the author, who at once notices Swift's strict avoidance of dealing with the serious arguments accumulated by the Whig writers, acts according to the maxim that crudeness must be met with crudeness and counters Swift's conspiracy thesis with a conspiracy thesis of his own: the Tories, who are in favour of a bad peace and want to give Spain to the Duke of Anjou, are playing into the hands of the French and the Pretender[4]. Instead of being "ineffective" because of its "appeal to reason rather than feeling" - Coombs' general assessment of the first three substantial replies to *The Conduct*[5] - it makes its appeal to the emotions and bristles with highly charged political key-terms which can be found throughout the text. Though not as carefully structured as Swift's pamphlet, Maynwaring's was a seasonable and emphatic counterblast to Swift's trumpet-call[6].

As announced at the end of the preface to Maynwaring's *Remarks*, a companion piece, Hare's massive *The Allies and the Late Ministry Defended against France, and the Present Friends of France. In Answer to a Pamphlet, Intituled, The Conduct of the Allies* (1711), the first part of which appeared immediately after Maynwaring's reply, rather performed the task of exposing the factual incompetence of the author of *The Conduct*. As its title indicates, Hare's pamphlet chimes in with the allegation that the Tories are acting as a French faction. It contains most of the political watchwords used by Maynwaring, such as "*universal Monarchy*" and "Liberty of *Europe*"[7], often in close conjunction, and continues the strategy of emotional retaliation. At the same time it has a tighter argumentative grasp and clashes with Swift's text on points of material inconsistency. Thus, to quote the most conspicuous example, towards the end of his pamphlet Hare convicts his antagonist of falsely representing the eighth article of the Grand Alliance of 1701 under the pretext of reliable documentation[8]. Factual refutation is here dexte-

---

1 See *The Conduct of the Dutch*, p. 287.

2 Cf. Snyder, "Arthur Maynwaring and the Whig Press", p. 134.

3 Whereas Snyder (p. 134) takes Maynwaring's authorship for granted and Downie (*Robert Harley and the Press*, p. 175) thinks it to be most probable, Harris (*A Study of the Paper War*, p. 300, n. 16) favours that of Oldmixon. I think that the rhetorical incisiveness of the pamphlet makes a good claim for Maynwaring's having at least been substantially involved in its composition.

4 Cf. regarding this criticism the comments made about the "French and Jacobite Faction in the Dominions of Great Britain" in the *Flying-Post* of 4-6 December 1711.

5 *The Conduct of the Dutch*, p. 288.

6 A detailed rhetorical analysis of this pamphlet can be found in the chapter "The Main Genres of the Public Debate: Profiles and Functions".

7 See [Francis Hare], *The Allies and the Late Ministry Defended against France, and the Present Friends of France. In Answer to a Pamphlet, Intituled, The Conduct of the Allies*, [part I] (London, 1711), p. 7.

8 See *ibid.*, pp. 42-43.

rously applied to the purpose of arousing moral indignation. Hare, who perceives that the author of *The Conduct* calumniates the Allies in order to justify a separate peace without Spain[1], identifies those who are in favour of overturning the Grand Alliance with enemies of the Revolution of 1688/89, thus giving an ominous ring to his warnings of the final consequences of a bad peace. Hare's rather heavy-handed pamphlet[2], which makes use of the standard repertoire of Whig polemics against a premature peace, was a weighty reinforcement of Maynwaring's more clamorous pamphlet.

In their combined endeavour to contain the pernicious influence of *The Conduct of the Allies* the two main Whig journalists received unexpected assistance from Defoe[3], who, apparently in a last valiant effort to achieve at least a modicum of independence from Harley's controlling hand, about the same time published *A Defence of the Allies and the Late Ministry: Or, Remarks on the Tories New Idol. Being a Detection of the Manifest Frauds and Falsities, in a Late Pamphlet, Entituled, The Conduct of the Allies...*(1711). This energetic pamphlet, in which Defoe, by the way, was not playing up to the Whigs at all, lays open Swift's frivolous belittlement of French aspirations to hegemony and also clearly recognizes Swift's intention to slander the Allies in order to prepare the ground for a separate peace[4]. Instead of "denying [...] that Swift [...] spoke for the ministry"[5], it voices the opinion that the author of *The Conduct* was briefed by the Government[6]; at the end this author is also stigmatized as subscribing to "Frenchified Principles"[7].

Thus, before Swift's momentous pamphlet really had its effect, it had received three substantial replies. December, with the Government crisis as a result of the obstruction of the Tory peace plans in the House of Lords[8], was a critical month for Tory propaganda. Though the Tories tried to keep up morale, the Whig journalistic presence was indeed impressive. Maynwaring's well-timed and pungent ballad *The Queen's Speech* (1711)[9] increased the emotional stir created by the pamphlets by affixing to the resolute enemy the unwonted yet revealing label of "The French, our allies". At least until mid-December the Whigs had the stronger journalistic battalions. That the Tories, whose pamphleteers hardly came to the

1 See *ibid.*, p. 31.

2 For an excellent analysis of all four parts of Hare's 'definitive' reply to *The Conduct* and its inherent drawbacks see Harris, *A Study of the Paper War*, pp. 284-290.

3 Defoe's authorship of this pamphlet is doubted by W.R. Owens and P.N. Furbank, "Defoe and the Dutch Alliance: Some Attributions Examined", *British Journal for Eighteenth-Century Studies* 9 (1986), pp. 176-177.

4 See *A Defence of the Allies and the Late Ministry: Or, Remarks on the Tories New Idol. Being a Detection of the Manifest Frauds and Falsities, in a Late Pamphlet, Entituled, The Conduct of the Allies and of the Late Ministry, in the Beginning and Carrying on the War* (London, 1712), pp. 3 and 27.

5 Coombs, *The Conduct of the Dutch*, p. 287.

6 See *A Defence of the Allies*, p. 31.

7 See *ibid.*, p. 46.

8 Cf. regarding this crisis, which had been worsening since November 1711, Keith Feiling, *A History of the Tory Party, 1640-1714* (Oxford, 1924, repr. 1965), pp. 441-443.

9 Text in *Poems on Affairs of State*, VII, 533-535.

fore, felt the need for reinvigorating measures is corroborated by the revival of the *Examiner* - under William Oldisworth's editorship - on 6 December 1711. A sort of relief attack was launched by Robert Ferguson's aggressive *Account of the Obligations the States of Holland Have to Great-Britain, and the Return they Have Made both in Europe and the Indies. With Reflections upon the Peace*. This pamphlet, which showed that the Government did not intend to eat humble pie and supplements Swift's disparagement of the Dutch on their past record, appeared on 20 December 1711, the same day as the fifth edition of *The Conduct of the Allies*, which was gradually gaining ground. The unusually dense salvo of ideologically virulent catchwords in the latter part of Ferguson's *Account* - the Whigs are fiercely reproached with pursuing the republican principles of their precursors of 1641[1] - indicated the pressure which had been brought to bear on the Tories by their robust adversaries. The Tories, who were further harassed by Harley's defeat in the House of Lords on 20 December 1711 over the Duke of Hamilton's case[2], were only relieved from this predicament through the dismissal, on 31 December 1711, of the Duke of Marlborough from all his official positions, and through the concomitant creation of twelve new Peers in order to gain control of the House of Lords. These spectacular measures restored confidence to Government propaganda, which was henceforth gradually put on the offensive.

It took the Tories until the early spring of 1712 to get the better of the Whigs in their public performance. As early as the turn of the year the broadside *The Truth's Come out at last: Or, the Downfall of a Great Favourite* (1711), one of an unusually large number of the same kind[3], exulted at the dismissal of the General and pointed expectantly towards the laying bare of the Duke and Duchess of Marlborough's fraudulent practices: "Tho' *Britain* has long time been wrong'd of its right, / Their treacherous Deeds are now coming to light". In December 1711 the House of Commons had decided to lay a report before them against the Duke of Marlborough by the Commissioners of Public Accounts[4]; during the following months anticipation and exploitation of parliamentary investigations into war finance raised the spirit of Tory propaganda and put a damper on Whig mettle. The Whigs did their best to pay the Tories back in their own coin. While the broadside *The King of France's Letter to the Cardinal de Noailles, Archbishop of Paris* (January 1712) imagined how Louis XIV rejoiced in Marlborough's disgrace, Maynwaring's *A New Protestant Litany* (1712)[5] tried to make Harley's remarkable sleight of hand, the creation of twelve new Peers, appear like French and Jacobite knavery.

---

1 See [Robert Ferguson], *An Account of the Obligations the States of Holland Have to Great-Britain, and the Return they Have Made both in Europe and the Indies. With Reflections upon the Peace* (London, 1711), pp. 40-41.

2 Cf. Jones, "The Division that never Was", p. 196.

3 See further details in the chapter "Focus".

4 Cf. William Coxe, *Memoirs of John Duke of Marlborough, with his Original Correspondence: Collected from the Family Records at Blenheim, and other Authentic Sources*, VI (London, 1820), 148-149.

5 Text in *Poems on Affairs of State*, VII, 548-551.

This rhetoric of oppugnancy could not prevent the Tory campaign from gathering momentum. From the beginning of 1712 Tory propaganda reached a particularly high degree of co-ordination, with *The Conduct of the Allies* increasingly fulfilling the function of purveyor of polemic stings against the enemy camp. Thus Swift's dominating antithesis of the Queen and the nation versus the family and the faction, which, in substance, can even be traced in a letter from Harley to the Grand Pensionary Heinsius[1], was the dominant structural feature of pamphlets such as William Wagstaffe's *The Representation of the Loyal Subjects of Albinia* and Defoe's *No Queen: Or, no General*, which in the first half of January 1712 continued Swift's approach. Within the polarising framework certain special devices became highly expedient recurrent tools of rhetoric and almost assumed the character of topoi, giving coherence to the Government's resurgent, never-ending appeal to public opinion. Thus, to quote but a few relevant examples, both the broadside *The Queen's and the Duke of Ormond's New Toast* (1712) - the latter in the parenthetical line "(For a Town in a Year will not make the War cease)" - and Wagstaffe's *Representation* reiterated Swift's argument that the idea of finishing the war by just one more campaign was an illusion. Several broadsides took up Swift's reproach that Marlborough had aspired to royal dignity[2]. A related instance of the efficient co-ordination of Government propaganda can be seen in the steady dissemination, from the beginning, of the assertion that Marlborough had merely been fortunate, by means of which the Tories wanted to detract from the General's prestige. Highly idiosyncratic pamphlets such as Wagstaffe's *The Representation*[3] and Defoe's *No Queen: Or, no General*[4] - the one written by a Non-Juror, the other by a dissenting journalist with Whig inclinations - made use of this agreed formula. Such verbal streamlining gave a remarkably modern ring to the public battle fought by the Tories[5] against the Whigs.

On 11 January 1712 the Dutch resident L'Hermitage reported home that English opinion was not yet ripe for a separate peace[6]. The air of suspense which, in spite of rapidly increasing Tory confidence, still hung over British politics with regard to the war was reflected in the chequered appearance of the fast sermons of 16 January 1712. Roger Altham's sermon preached before the House of Commons and cautiously expressing official views diplomatically confirmed the justness of the struggle with France while at the same time stressing the calamitous conse-

---

1 Cf. Ottocar Weber, *Der Friede von Utrecht. Verhandlungen zwischen England, Frankreich, dem Kaiser und den Generalstaaten 1710-1713* (Gotha, 1891), pp. 416-417.

2 For instructive examples see the chapter "Focus".

3 See [William Wagstaffe], *The Representation of the Loyal Subjects of Albinia* ([London], 1712), p. 8.

4 See [Daniel Defoe], *No Queen: Or, no General. An Argument Proving the Necessity Her Majesty Was in, as well for the Safety of Her Person, as of Her Authority, to Displace the D- of M-borough* (London, 1712), p. 6.

5 A detailed account of the unanimity of journalistic policy in the Government camp can be found in the chapter "Focus".

6 Cf. Coombs, *The Conduct of the Dutch*, p. 294.

quences of an unnecessarily protracted war[1]. Other shades of opinion were also well represented. Trapp's highly emotional sermon expressed more radical Tory sentiment and reproduced the antithetical pattern which was quickly becoming part and parcel of Tory propaganda through the proliferation of Swift's primary text of *The Conduct of the Allies*. Thus, in Trapp's sermon, Queen Anne as the nation's protector is put into sharp contrast with Marlborough, who, though unnamed, is unmistakably made responsible for dragging out the war in order to plunder his country. Trapp's belligerent sermon[2] voiced growing Tory determination to carry through the campaign promisingly launched by *The Conduct of the Allies*.

The Whigs, too, used the pulpit to stake their claims. While Samuel Wright's moderate discourse cautioned against the proven perfidy and cruelty of Louis XIV[3], William Fleetwood's sermon, though avoiding a strident tone, tenaciously and pointedly reaffirmed the Opposition's fundamental objections to a precarious peace[4]. In contrast to these temperate sermons the overtly propagandist sermon of the Dissenter Daniel Mayo utilized the whole register of polemical warfare and, raising the spectre of "Popery and Slavery"[5], vehemently remonstrated against a peace which might put the liberties of Protestant England at the risk of being threatened by the aspirant to universal monarchy. Though differing in tone, both Fleetwood's and Mayo's ideologically well-attuned sermons put the emphasis on a "lasting" peace - in addition to the generally accepted criteria of being "just and honourable" as recently sanctioned in the carefully phrased[6] Queen's Speech to Parliament on 7 December 1711[7]. Thus Whigs and Tories also pitted their relative strengths against each other in the pulpit.

In the following weeks the public destruction of the Duke of Marlborough was completed with renewed vigour by the Tories, who used the entire gamut of genres[8] from broadsides such as the pseudo-financial prose report *The D-e and D-s of M-h's Loss* (1712) to accounts using the thin veil of ancient history such as *Rufinus* (1712), an historical essay ascribed to William King. Though the Whigs

---

1 See Roger Altham, *A Sermon Preach'd before the Honourable House of Commons at the Church of St. Margaret Westminster, on Wednesday, Jan. 16. 1711/12. Being the Fast-Day for a General Peace* (London, 1712), p. 19.

2 For further remarks on this sermon see the chapter "The Main Genres of the Public Debate: Profiles and Functions".

3 See S. Wright, *A Sermon Preach'd at Black-Fryars, on Occasion of the Publick Fast, January, 1712* (London, 1712), p. 18.

4 See esp. the closing passage of this cleverly constructed sermon, which receives detailed commentary in the chapter "The Main Genres of the Public Debate: Profiles and Functions".

5 See Daniel Mayo, *Pray for the Peace of Jerusalem. Being a Sermon Preach'd at Kingston upon Thames on the Publick Fast, January 16. 1711/12* (London, 1712), p. 17.

6 See J.A. Downie and David Woolley, "Swift, Oxford, and the Composition of Queen's Speeches, 1710-1714", *The British Library Journal* 8 (1982), pp. 122-123.

7 Cf. Cobbett, *Parliamentary History*, VI, columns 1035-1036.

8 The interplay between the various genres is explained in the chapter "Focus".

tried to counter with such lengthy productions as *The Conduct of the Duke of Marlborough during the Present War, with Original Papers* (1712), Hare's definitive, yet uncontentious apology for the General published on 17 January 1712, the day appointed for the parliamentary debate on Marlborough's record, the Tories were gradually getting the upper hand - which they achieved by the middle of March. For the time being they still had a lot of work on their hands to pacify, for example, the malcontents of the vindictive October Club, a difficult task Swift took upon himself in *Some Advice Humbly Offer'd to the Members of the October Club* published in the second half of January 1712. All the while Defoe assiduously plodded on with pamphlets, published towards the end of January 1712, like *The Conduct of Parties in England, more especially of those Whigs who now Appear against the New Ministry, and a Treaty of Peace*, which stressed the Junto origin of current reproaches against Marlborough, and *Peace, Or Poverty*, which, with its pithy title, confirmed Defoe's recent attempts at dramatic gesture and once again emphatically denied any designs of a separate peace[1]. Altogether Tory confidence must have been growing in anticipation of the results of parliamentary inquiries. As early as 19 January 1712 Swift's successful broadside poem *A Fable of the Widow and her Cat*[2] had, in its last line, pointedly delivered Marlborough up to the avenging power of Parliament: "Here, *Towzer*! - Do Him Justice"! With the controversial Barrier Treaty brought before the House of Commons on 29 January 1712 such expectations were raised even further. This new bone of contention proved particularly conducive to propagandist exploitation by the Tories, who, from about the time - 5 February 1712 - the Commons passed their Resolutions against the insufficiency of the Dutch contribution to the War[3], steadily gained the advantage over their adversaries.

The - from the Tory point of view - welcome event in Parliament was immediately highlighted by a prose broadside whose suggestive title reflected the interaction between political debates in Parliament and outside as well as the need to show the legitimacy of parliamentary decisions to the increasingly wider audience of the political nation at large. Synchronized with the proceedings in Parliament, the *Resolutions without doors, upon the Resolutions within doors, in the Votes of the H- of C- Martis 5 Die Febr. 1711* (1712) transformed the sober language of the Lower House into the vindictive war cry "That no Nation, no, not a petty Conquer'd Province, was ever treated with more Contempt, or more infamously Bubbl'd and Abus'd, than *Great-Britain* has been by its *Al-s*, especially the *D-h*". Swift's pointedly disrespectful language in *The Conduct of the Allies* seems to reverberate here - evidence of a linguistic orchestration that will be illustrated in the next chapter, which focuses on the turning-point debate. The rallying call was

1 See [Daniel Defoe], *Peace, Or Poverty. Being a Serious Vindication of Her Majesty and Her Ministers Consenting to a Treaty for a General Peace. Shewing the Reasonableness, and even Necessity, there was for such a Procedure* (London, 1712), p. 15. See also the editions of the *Review* of 1, 5 and 17 January 1712.

2 For the function of this broadside see also the chapter "The Main Genres of the Public Debate: Profiles and Functions".

3 Cf. Cobbett, *Parliamentary History*, VI, cols. 1090-1091.

readily echoed in all kinds of Tory propaganda. Following his own personal journalistic line, Defoe in the *Review* of 9 and 12 February 1712 stressed the Emperor's failure to fulfil his treaty obligations. Although the Whigs, as indefatigable as ever, tried to hit back to the best of their ability, their public performance was rather less impressive than in preceding stages of the grand controversy, and with the publication of the Representation of the House of Commons concerning the state of the war and the Barrier Treaty[1] at the beginning of March 1712 - a parliamentary incentive with even wider repercussions - the Tories were finally precipitated on to the path of victory.

In this parliamentary context the Whigs betrayed some uneasiness in coping with the growing tide of Tory militancy. Thomas Burnet's pamphlet *Our Ancestors as Wise as We: Or, Ancient Precedents for Modern Facts* (1712), which reflected prevailing Whig attitudes, obviously lacked punch[2]. Interestingly, this pamphlet, which dealt with notable Government publications of the immediately preceding period, in concluding singled out Swift as the mastermind of Tory propaganda who especially aimed at influencing opinion among the landed gentry[3]. In its subtitle it was also indicative of renewed Whig recourse to factual evidence based on historical precedents. Even Hare's[4] subsequent pamphlet *The Treaty between Her Majesty and the States-General* (1712), which put the threat to the Protestant Succession as the ultimate issue before its readers[5], relied heavily on factual information and ended with an historical appendix illustrating the importance of the Dutch barrier for England. This was quite typical of Whig practice in or around February 1712. The documentary publications *The Sense of the Nation, concerning the Duke of Marlborough* (1712) and *The Information against the Duke of Marlborough* (1712) may also be named here. The fact that the Whigs were in the process of being pushed on to the defensive and felt the need to ward off mischief also became apparent in the "apotropaic refrain"[6] of Maynwaring's *A New Protestant Litany*. Meanwhile the Tory demolition of Marlborough was going on at full blast with such popular pieces as Wagstaffe's *The Story of the St. Alb-ns Ghost* (1712).

As things at Utrecht - the congress had been opened at the end of January 1712 - were not yet developing satisfactorily[7], the Tories themselves were not wholly free from misgivings in spite of increasing support at home. The sermon preached by William Ayerst before the British plenipotentiaries at Utrecht on 7 February 1712 left no doubt, however, that Dutch intransigence would not be tolerated. The

---

1 See *ibid.*, columns 1095-1105.

2 For the rhetorical 'embarrassment profile' of this and other Whig pamphlets during this period, see the chapter "Focus".

3 See [Thomas Burnet], *Our Ancestors as Wise as We: Or, Ancient Precedents for Modern Facts, in Answer to a Letter from a Noble Lord* (London, 1712), p. 34.

4 Hare's authorship is not really certain.

5 See [Francis Hare], *The Treaty between Her Majesty and the States-General, for Securing the Succession to the Crown of Great-Britain, and for Settling the Barrier for the States-General against France, Consider'd* (2nd ed., London, 1712), pp. 4 and 21.

6 Ellis' formulation in *Poems on Affairs of State*, VII, 547.

7 Cf. Coombs, *The Conduct of the Dutch*, pp. 295-297.

divine's conclusion that, in default of Dutch acquiescence, it would be justified for Britain "to change Sides"[1] was echoed by *The Fable of the Cods-Heads: Or, a Reply to the Dutch-Men's Answer to the Resolutions of the House of Commons* (1712): "Or *B-ain* thou art not to blame,/ If thou the Dance of War disclaim,/ By paying *Europe's* Piper". This broadside confirmed the careful orchestration of Tory propaganda at all levels of public discourse. Still, some additional efforts were apparently deemed necessary by the Government in order to prevail completely against their adversaries. It was with this view that Swift's *Some Remarks on the Barrier Treaty*, which did not come out in time for the Commons debate on 14 February 1712[2], was published on 22 February 1712. With their malicious exposure of the preposterous terms of this treaty and their well-timed publication of the text itself, which was then being submitted to close parliamentary scrutiny[3], the *Remarks* were intended to put the final seal on the Government's anti-Dutch campaign and adroitly did so in concert with the authoritative moves of the House of Commons. In spite of some casual attacks on the author of *The Allies and the Late Ministry Defended*[4] - three parts of which had by then appeared - Swift's *Remarks* was not so much a response to Hare's *The Treaty between Her Majesty and the States-General*[5] as a final release of vituperative energy which, irrespective of individual antagonists, completed the work begun by the *The Conduct of the Allies*. That the latter pamphlet was still useful in crystalizing Tory propaganda around which a wide variety of other writings could cluster was corroborated by Defoe's later *A Farther Search into the Conduct of the Allies* (1712), which also chimed with the recent Resolutions of Parliament.

The publication of the *Representation of the Commons to the Queen on the War in Spain, the Barrier-Treaty, and the State of the Nation* coincided, significantly, exactly with the publication of John Arbuthnot's *Law Is a Bottomless-Pit*, the first part of his history of John Bull: both appeared on 4 March 1712[6]. This date may well be regarded as the symbolic turning-point of the Tories' peace-campaign; from now on the Government was finally heading for victory in the public acceptance of its peace-policy. Thus the boost given to the Tory cause by the Commons' massive criticism of Allied deficiencies was immediately exploited with polemical brilliancy by Tory propaganda. Arbuthnot could all the more easily highlight those parliamentary findings as the extensive Representation itself[7], com-

1 William Ayerst, *The Duty and Motives of Praying for Peace. A Sermon Preach'd before their Excellencies the Lord Privy Seal, and the Right Honourable Thomas, Earl of Strafford, Her Majesty's Plenipotentiaries at the Congress of Utrecht. In St. John's Church. January 27. February 7. 1711/12* (London, 1712), p. 18.

2 Cf. Hill, *Robert Harley*, p. 180.

3 Cf. Swift, *Political Tracts 1711-1713*, ed. Davis, p. xv.

4 See *ibid.*, pp. 95-96.

5 Yet cf. Snyder, "Arthur Maynwaring and the Whig Press", p. 134.

6 Cf. Coombs, *The Conduct of the Dutch*, p. 308.

7 See the wording in Cobbett, *Parliamentary History*, VI, columns 1095-1105. The document is also reprinted in Jonathan Swift, *The History of the Four Last Years of the Queen*, ed. Herbert Davis, with an Introduction by Harold Williams (Oxford, 1951, repr. 1973), pp. 80-94.

pared with the more prosaic and official tone of the earlier Resolution, was dressed up in combative language and did not stop short of using, for example at the end, emotionally charged words such as "private counsels of ill-designing men" with regard to the intentions of the former Ministry. In its detailed gloating over Allied shortcomings the Representation, which sometimes verges on pamphlet form proper, seems to re-echo Swift's *The Conduct of the Allies*[1].

With *Law Is a Bottomless-Pit* and the further parts of the series Arbuthnot exactly hit the public mood prepared by the long-term undermining campaign against the Dutch. His vigorous political allegory of the irascible but honest Englishman John Bull shamelessley cheated by the cunning Dutchman Nicholas Frog in a protracted lawsuit graphically underpinned the Tories' insistence on the necessity of British withdrawal from a wasteful war. Marlborough was denigrated as the avaricious and cunning attorney Hocus, who is acting in collusion with Frog at the expense of his fellow-countryman. *The History of John Bull* (1712) proved a most effective relay station for transmitting messages whose contents had already been approved; in his down-to-earth allegory Arbuthnot utilized an ideal medium for propagating political views largely based on popular resentment. That Arbuthnot was about to win the day and successfully complete the work begun by Swift becomes apparent from the volume of Whig criticism[2]. Significantly, the main salvos against *Law Is a Bottomles-Pit* and its sequels were launched in the periodical press, with the *Medley* and the *Protestant Post-Boy* taking pride of place in April 1712[3]. Rather surprisingly, no front-rank pamphlet seems to have appeared on the Whig side.

That the pamphlet weapon as used by the Whigs had become a rather blunt weapon by the spring of 1712 is corroborated by other specimens of the same genre. Some of these, like the fourth part of Hare's *The Allies and the Late Ministry Defended* (1712), belong in the original context of the long drawn-out controversy initiated by Swift's *Conduct*. The weakening drive behind Whig propaganda is also illustrated by the fact that the last two parts of Hare's series of pamphlets published in February and March 1712 never saw a second edition[4]. A belated and lengthy reply to Swift's pamphlet, *A Full Answer to the Conduct of the Allies* (1712), somewhat ineffectively interpolated the text of the Letter of the States General to the Queen about the Barrier Treaty of February 1712[5]. *The Treaty be-*

---

1 While Swift's boast that "the Resolutions [...] are almost quotations from it [*The Conduct of the Allies*]" (*Journal to Stella*, ed. Williams, II, 482) is not borne out by the text, the Representation shows signs of his hand. The remarkable similarities between *The Conduct* and the Representation are, incidentally, noted by the author of *Law not a Bottomless Pit: Or, Arguments against Peace: And some Queries pro and con* (London, 1712), p. 4. Coombs (*The Conduct of the Dutch*, p. 291) supports the wrong view of L'Hermitage with regard to the Resolutions.

2 Cf. on this John Arbuthnot, *The History of John Bull*, ed. Alan W. Bower and Robert A. Erickson (Oxford, 1976), pp. xvii-xviii.

3 Cf. *ibid.*, p. xviii and Coombs, *The Conduct of the Dutch*, p. 316, note 1.

4 Details taken from the *Eighteenth Century Short Title Cataloge* (*ESTC*).

5 See *A Full Answer to The Conduct of the Allies: To which is Added, Some Observations on the Remarks on the Barrier Treaty. By the same Author* (London, 1712), pp. 80-82.

tween Her Majesty and the States-General, while dealing out the tried anti-Jacobite formulae, obviously lacked punch. The same can be said with even more justification of *Remarks on Some Extracts, Published in a Paper, Called The Supplement, of Friday, March 28, 1712* (1712). The latter pamphlet took up the seasonable topic of treacherous Dutch conduct at Nijmegen broached by the *Examiner* in March 1712[1] and rather tamely reproached the Government with intentions of going "into a *Separate-Treaty*"[2] itself. The *Reflections upon the Present Posture of Affairs: With Relation to the Treaty of Peace, now on Foot* (1712), too, lacked bite and meekly appealed for a consensus between parties on matters of national interest. In other media as well, the Whigs lacked mettle at that time. Thus, for instance, in *Aesop at Utrecht* (1712) published a few weeks earlier, the second fable conveys the time-honoured message of the French King's treacherous dispositions with innocuous blandness[3]. These publications may be regarded as representative of Whig propaganda, which, in the spring of 1712, was to all intents and purposes losing bite. By then Tory propaganda had arrived at an unprecedented high and had clearly outdistanced its Whig counterpart.

e) Spring 1712 until Spring 1713

The Tories, meanwhile, asserted their newly won self-confidence with increasing vigour. As early as 8/19 March 1712, in his letter to the Grand Pensionary Heinsius, Harley had expressed the buoyant mood of the Government with regard to its opponents. Interestingly, the wording of this letter, which warns foreigners against mistaking "a faction for the people" and maintains that "there are not ten in a hundred against the peace"[4], shows close affinity with Swift, who time and again hammered away at this point in almost identical phrases[5]. While negotiations at Utrecht were not at all developing smoothly - as intimated by Thomas Dibben in his sermon preached there on 9/20 March 1712[6] -, the Tories expanded their journalistic platform with a good deal of self-assurance. Their growing assertiveness without doors indicated the determination of the Government to carry through its peace policy irrespective of temporary setbacks. An outward sign of the shifting of weights in party-political presentation is in the fact that within a month - from March to April 1712 - the number of pamphlets published in the Tory interest outstripped the number of those supporting the Whig cause. In the

---

1 Cf. Coombs, *The Conduct of the Dutch*, p. 309.

2 *Remarks on Some Extracts, Published in a Paper, Called The Supplement, of Friday, March 28, 1712* (London, 1712), p. 10.

3 See *Aesop at Utrecht* (London, 1712), p. 6.

4 Weber, *Der Friede von Utrecht*, p. 417.

5 See e.g. the *Examiner* of 1 February 1711: *The Examiner and Other Pieces*, ed. Davis, p. 78.

6 See Thomas Dibben, *A Sermon Preach'd in St. John's Church in Utrecht on Sunday March 9/20 1711. Being the Day after the Anniversary of Her Majesty's Happy Accession to the Throne* (Utrecht, 1712), p. 17.

ongoing Tory publicity campaign the publication of the various parts of Arbuthnot's *The History of John Bull* provided focal points around which political sentiment could crystalize. The third part of the series, *John Bull still in his Senses*, appeared on 16 April 1712, and thus followed closely on the publication, in *The Daily Courant* of 7 and 8 April 1712, of the Dutch Memorial in reply to the Resolution and Representation of the House of Commons - an emergency measure of the Whigs which nettled the Tories, who took retaliatory measures[1]. *John Bull still in his Senses* ridicules the Dutch objections in the guise of "Nic. Frog's *Letter* to John Bull", in which the latter is confronted with the following question by his Dutch partner, who still laments Marlborough's dismissal: "*Why hast thou chang'd thy Attorney? Can any Man manage thy Cause better for thee?*"[2]. In a similar, though more ferocious vein Charles Leslie, who had earlier reflected on Dutch insidiousness in *Natural Reflections upon the Present Debates about Peace and War* (1712), in the following month vilified the discarded Duke and the former Ministers for having plotted poor John Bull's ruin in *Salt for the Leach. In Reflections upon Reflections* (1712). The latter pamphlet, a reply to the Whig *Reflections upon the Present Posture of Affairs* mentioned above[3], high-handedly defended the Tory peace moves against Whig intransigence. In its almost exultant vituperation *Salt for the Leach* asserts: "Their [the Whigs'] Wickedness is Detected, and they are Abhorred of all True *English* Men, who see how they have been Peeled, Squeezed, and Loaded with immense Debts for Ages to come [...]"[4]. As Arbuthnot had already made the necessity of a peace unmistakably clear in the first two parts of his political allegory, the publication of the further parts apparently served as a welcome catalyst for perpetuating political resentment. *A Letter from the Famous Sir Humphrey Polesworth*, sometimes attributed to Arbuthnot and printed in the *Examiner* of 8-15 May 1712, served exactly this purpose by drawing further attention to the collusive dealings between the Whigs and the Dutch. In a way *The History of John Bull* took over and completed the function adopted by *The Conduct of the Allies* - that of a major crystalizing agent with the aid of which the Tories were able to close their ranks and fasten their grip on public opinion. The continuity of function in Swift's and Arbuthnot's writings, which will be more explicitly pointed out below, is epitomized linguistically in the pointed use of the taunting word "bubble", which - reprehensively, as the Whigs rightly saw it - is echoed in other Tory publications[5].

The new relative strength of Whig and Tory performances in public, which became noticeable in spring, was maintained throughout the summer of 1712. The turning of the tables in journalistic efficiency may at least partly be ascribed to the fact that Maynwaring's co-ordinating hand was loosening its grip on Whig propa-

---

1 Cf. Abel Boyer, *Quadriennium Annae Postremum or The Political State of Great Britain*, 2nd ed., vol. III and IV for the Year 1712 (London, 1718), III, 233-234.

2 *The History of John Bull*, p. 70.

3 See p. 71.

4 [Charles Leslie], *Salt for the Leach. In Reflections upon Reflections* (London, 1712), p. 8.

5 See details in "Focus".

ganda at that time[1]. In any case, to judge by their printed output, the Whigs had lost much of their former resilience. Thus, in May 1712, Fleetwood's Preface[2] to his *Four Sermons* (1712), reprinted by Richard Steele in *The Spectator* of 21 May 1712 together with a revealing passage from the *Post Boy*, was the most remarkable feat on the Whig side and caused quite a stir[3] without seriously endangering the standing of the Government in the eyes of the public. To be sure, *Some Observations upon Bishop Fleetwood's Four Sermons: Wherein his Preface is Fully Consider'd* (1712) showed some mettle, but more characteristic was another supporting pamphlet, *A few Orthodox Remarks upon a late Preface, Publish'd before some Occasional Sermons, Preach'd by the L- B- of St. Asaph* (1712), which turned out to be less forceful. Even when the notorious 'Restraining Orders' to the Duke of Ormonde became known in London at the end of May 1712[4], this news, though embarrassing to the Government, did not result in any recovery of Opposition propaganda. Coombs' statement "the Whigs were in full cry"[5] may be true with regard to some of their parliamentary activities[6] but is not corroborated by their journalistic production. Although their periodicals tried to disconcert the Government, Coombs has to admit the half-heartedness of their attacks[7]. In the other genres they were remarkably ineffective; the pamphlet was not utilized with any forcefulness - Maynwaring's *The French King's Promise to the Pretender* published in June 1712 merely reiterated fears about the Protestant Succession in a routine-like manner. Another pamphlet published in the same month and addressed to the ideologically most sensitive section of the Tories' clientele, *All at Stake, Hannover or Perkin: In a Letter to a Country Clergy-Man* (1712), stated Whig grievances correctly enough but, in spite of its dramatic title, did so in a resigned rather than in a combative spirit. The deterioration of the pamphlet as a genre utilized by the Whigs is highlighted by the fact that - between April and June 1712 - Tory pamphlets gained a remarkable numerical superiority over their Whig counterparts - a dramatic statistical volte-face. It is quite revealing that the protest of a group of Lords against the orders for not fighting published shortly after proceedings in the Upper House[8] virtually proved the most impressive public relations measure of the Whigs at that juncture. Altogether their propagandistic endeavours were colourless and lukewarm and made it easy for their opponents to gain further ground on the public scene. While the Whigs relied heavily on documentary evidence and historical analogies (of the half dozen or so Whig pamph-

[1] Due to his poor state of health, Maynwaring's journalism came practically to a standstill in 1712. Cf. Oldmixon, *The Life and Posthumous Works of Arthur Maynwaring*.

[2] For the rhetorical side of this foreword see the chapter "The Main Genres of the Public Debate: Profiles and Functions".

[3] For the controversy provoked by this publication see John C. Stephens, Jr., "Steele and the Bishop of St. Asaph's Preface", *PMLA* 67 (1952), pp. 1011-1023.

[4] See the *Postscript* to the *Flying-Post* of 24-27 May 1712.

[5] *The Conduct of the Dutch*, p. 322.

[6] The broadside *A Plot or no Plot* (1712) celebrated the ministerial victory over Whig machinations.

[7] See *The Conduct of the Dutch*, p. 324.

[8] Cf. Boyer, *Quadriennium Annae Postremum*, III, 329-331.

lets in June 1712, three were of that kind), the Tories made further progress by exploiting the by no means exhausted anti-Dutch vogue.

Defoe again fulfilled the function of making a broad appeal in favour of the Government platform. While he stated the fallacy of Dutch remonstrances recently put forward through their Letters and Memorials in sedate and moderate terms in *A Farther Search into the Conduct of the Allies*, he also hung on to the bitter resentment built up against Holland. In *Reasons against Fighting* (1712) he briskly defended the 'Restraining Orders' as a legitimate and seasonable measure of the Government to neutralize the collusive dealings between the Whigs and the Dutch[1]. Publications like this, which capitalized on the emotional topic of Dutch tutelage over England, had a sting which the vast majority of Whig writings at that time certainly lacked. Significantly Defoe, whose particular task was to present the Government's new policy towards the House of Habsburg, did not exempt the Emperor from criticism, and referred back to an earlier pamphlet of his, *Imperial Gratitude* (1712)[2].

In midsummer 1712 the Whigs were losing further ground to the Tories in public estimation. Boyer's assertion that the English public was surprised at the conditions of peace communicated in the Queen's Speech to both Houses of Parliament on 6 June 1712[3] cannot be verified by pointing to a corresponding situation in printed propaganda, although the Opposition again managed to issue a vigorous remonstrance, *The Protest of the L-s upon A- Her M- for Her S-, with the Names of the L-s* (1712), which was countered by Wagstaffe's *The Second Representation of the Loyal Subjects of Albinia* (1712). The new confidence felt in Government circles found expression, for example, in the *Review* of 10 June 1712[4], in which Defoe, while stating that he was not qualified to comment on whether King Philip's renunciation of the French Crown could be trusted, was optimistic that Holland and England would agree on a common policy. On the whole, moreover, the public debate at this time was clearly less lively than at earlier stages; in particular, the network of statements and counterstatements and similar references was less tight in pamphlet literature than it had been before. The observer's impression that, in the summer of 1712, the Whigs were unable to shake the position of the Government is confirmed by the emphatic approval of the peace moves in Parliament in June 1712. Even in the House of Lords, the former bastion of the Whigs, whom Swift addressed moderately but with self-assurance in *Some Reasons in a Letter to a Whig-Lord*, opportunely published on 31 May 1712, the Government, in spite of one opposition group making a last stand, carried a handsome victory[5] and saw the last obstacle to its peace policy

---

1 See [Daniel Defoe], *Reasons against Fighting. Being an Enquiry into this Great Debate, whether it is Safe for Her Majesty, or Her Ministry, to Venture an Engagement with the French, considering the Present Behaviour of the Allies* ([London], 1712), pp. 35-36.

2 See *ibid.*, p. 31.

3 Cf. *Quadriennium Annae Postremum*, III, 336.

4 On the use of political imagery in this edition, see the chapter "Public Discourse".

5 Cf. Boyer, *Quadriennium Annae Postremum*, III, 341.

being removed. The judgment of a foreign observer that the Whigs had never been as insignificant as they were in the summer of 1712[1] is fully born out by the inconsequentiality of their propaganda performance. The slackening of Whig efforts here is all the more surprising as in the months following the Commons' Representation in March Parliament had played a minor role in the wrangling about peace policy, which had been mainly passed over to the media. At a time when forceful propaganda might have rendered final victory in Parliament somewhat more difficult for the Government, the Whigs, who as a last resort fell back upon publishing the Letter of 5 June 1712 from the States General to the Queen[2], failed to put their former weapon to effective use. Their temporary period of weakness in the field of propaganda is almost as hard to explain as their simultaneous weakness in the parliamentary arena.

The situation on the public scene as reflected in the relative strength of Whigs and Tories remained very much the same throughout the mid and late summer of 1712. The Whig propaganda profile as it stood out in relief at that time can be confirmed by taking a look at such a publication as *The Secret History of the Geertruydenbergh Negotiation*, which was a reprint of an earlier pamphlet of the same title and appeared early in July 1712. Heavily documented and thus relying on factual information rather than on persuasion, this pamphlet took a derivative approach by recommending Hare's *Management* tracts for their earnestness and showed its well-meaning attitude by meekly acquitting the new Ministers of any suspicions of "consenting to a Peace that may endanger the Liberty of *Europe*, and the Protestant Religion"[3] - this was Maynwaring's effective rhetoric with a difference! The republication of this uncontentious pamphlet squared with the diffidence of the Whigs' public performance at this juncture. While the Whigs showed no signs of recovering from their comparative weakness, the Tories continued their offensive. The reaction provoked by the occupation of Dunkirk in July 1712 was quite typical of the propagandistic set-up as it had by then developed. Whereas the Tories gleefully took advantage of this occasion in order to show off the Government's achievement - with Swift firing an unusually dense barrage of writings in prose and verse[4] - the Whigs, who, for instance, published the ineffective pamphlet *Concordia Discors* (1712), completely overburdened by the subject of standing armies, and exerted much more effective public pressure on the Dunkirk issue in 1713[5], almost completely disappeared from sight. In July and the succeeding months the Tory propagandists relentlessly pursued their anti-Dutch campaign. Pamphlets such as *A Search after Dutch Honesty*, *The History*

1 Cf. Weber, *Der Friede von Utrecht*, p. 280.

2 Cf. Boyer, *Quadriennium Annae Postremum*, III, 351, 359-360.

3 *The Secret History of the Geertruydenbergh Negotiation. With Several Original Papers. To which are Prefix'd two Letters* (London, 1712), p. 14.

4 In July 1712 Swift published *It's Out at last: Or, French Correspondence Clear as the Sun; A Dialogue upon Dunkirk; Peace and Dunkirk; Dunkirk still in the Hands of the French; A Hue and Cry after Dismal.*

5 See also John Robert Moore, "Defoe, Steele, and the Demolition of Dunkirk", *The Huntington Library Quarterly* 27 (1963-64), pp. 279-302, esp. p. 288.

of the Dutch Usurpations, *Dutch Alliances* and Defoe's[1] *The Justice and Necessity of a War with Holland* all published in midsummer 1712 hammered away at Dutch intransigence, fully exploiting the topic of Holland's ingratitude towards England[2], with which the Tories - even through moderate statements such as *The Speech of a Noble Peer* (1712) - were keeping the public debate alive. With *Lewis Baboon Turned Honest, and John Bull Politician*, the last part of his extensive political allegory published on 31 July 1712, Arbuthnot once more seasonably expressed popular political feeling by making John Bull indignantly refer to the "Ingratitude"[3] of his Dutch partner. Although the Whigs tried to counter, for example, with the rather innocuous pamphlet *Dutch Generosity and English Gratitude* (1712)[4], their altogether meagre efforts were submerged by the Tory flood of exultant vituperation. Coombs expresses his surprise at the unremitting dissemination of anti-Dutch propaganda after the Government's successful parliamentary handling of its peace policy: "There was no longer any obvious reason for the ministry to inflame public feeling to the degree to which its hacks evidently aspired"[5]. However, as the Dutch reaction to the peace plans disclosed in the Queen's Speech of 6 June 1712 was still uncertain, the Government prudently used a proven strategy to maintain its propaganda advantage, less "as a safeguard against a popular reaction in favour of the Allies"[6] than in order to keep control of the public debate, underpinning the process of diplomacy and - here one can agree with Coombs - "as a means of maintaining pressure on the wavering Dutch leaders"[7]. This campaign of preventive denigration did not subside until the end of September 1712, when it became obvious that the Dutch would comply with the British peace plans. In that month the Whigs issued another 'relief publication', *Belga-Britannus: Or, the Hollander always in the English Interest* (1712), which - somewhat plaintively - testified to the impact of previous Tory indictments[8]. During this period the Tories consolidated their supremacy in propaganda won in the spring in the wake of the parliamentary inquiries into Allied deficiencies. The advantage gained by the Tories can be measured by the fact that practically the only Whig pamphlet of real weight to appear in the summer of 1712 was *A Dialogue between a New Courtier and a Country Gentleman*, probably published at the end of June. This pamphlet skilfully turned the pretended loyalism of the Tories to good party-political account by making the relinquishment of the Queen's

1 As always, Defoe acted as a second in the *Review*: see *inter alia* the editions of 8, 10 and 15 July 1712.

2 This indignant note is also struck at the end of the *Occasional Poems on the Late Dutch War, and the Sale of Dunkirk* (1712) in "A Satyr against the Dutch".

3 *The History of John Bull*, p. 101.

4 Cf. Coombs, *The Conduct of the Dutch*, p. 348. For further details of this controversy see *ibid.*, pp. 348-349.

5 *Ibid.*, pp. 345-346.

6 *Ibid.*, p. 346.

7 *Ibid.*, p. 346.

8 See *Belga-Britannus: Or, the Hollander always in the English Interest. With Remarks on the late Ill Treatment the Dutch have Met with from a certain Kingdom that is in Alliance with them* (London, 1712), pp. v-vi.

many and carefully listed claims to the recovery of the whole of Spain for the House of Habsburg appear as a defection from received country doctrine. A similar argumentative strategy was pursued in the longer and even more heavily documented, but rhetorically less impressive pamphlet *A Letter from a Tory Freeholder to his Representative in Parliament* (1712)[1], published at about the same time. The pretended acceptance of the Tory stance of loyalism in these two pamphlets indicated, of course, the defensive position into which Whiggism had been forced. While, with regard to the Dutch, the *Dialogue* merely deplored the fact "that nothing is too bad to be said or done to them"[2], its more provocative appeal lay in its pointed references to the dangers lurking behind the Government's withdrawal from long accepted positions: "[...] from the hour the *House of Bourbon* is left in quiet Possession of *Spain*, and the *West Indies*, we may date that *Universal Monarchy* which the *French* King has so long been aspiring at"[3]. Such rhetoric was aimed at the weak point of the partition policy and adumbrated a resurgence of at least part of former Whig pugnacity.

The political summer doldrums of 1712 dragged on longer than usual, which may to a certain extent be due to the prorogation of Parliament until the following year. That - with some exaggeration - they lasted virtually until December 1712 may in some measure be accounted for by the fact that the Government had made decisive headway with its peace policy in June 1712, which left things quiet for a while, as well as by the scarcity of news from Utrecht. From August 1712 there was a sharp fall in the overall production of political propaganda which even affected the usually prolific pamphlet. During the second half of 1712 the public debate about war and peace reached its most unproductive phase. This state of public discussion was also reflected by the periodical press, as is shown by a glance at the *Review*, which gave distinctly less space to peace themes. The public debate was obviously going through a period of fatigue and showed signs of revitalization only towards the end of the year. The prevailing impression of stagnation throughout the late summer of 1712 and beyond is hardly modified by some erratic publications which, amidst the scarcity of printed propaganda, even managed to attract a modicum of attention. Thus, for instance, Edmund Chishull's sermon at the assizes at Hertford, preached shortly after Lord Bolingbroke's departure to France on 2 August 1712, was an ex cathedra pronouncement of the Queen's and the Government's unremitting resolution to go through with their peace plans; in confident tones it asked: "Is not, in one word, the End of the War obtain'd?"[4] In

---

1 The 'protective' technique of slipping into Tory shoes was at that time apparently a favourite device of Whig pamphleteers; see also Burnet's ironic pamphlet *Truth if you can Find it* (1712), published in May, which was cast in the form of a letter from a Tory backbencher who uncritically reiterates standard reproaches against Marlborough and the Whig leaders.

2 *A Dialogue between a New Courtier and a Country Gentleman* (*s.l.*, 1712), p. 15.

3 *Ibid.*, p. 17.

4 Edmund Chishull, *The Duty of Good Subjects, in Relation to Publick Peace. Being a Sermon Preach'd at the Assizes at Hertford, on August the 11th, 1712* (London, 1712), p. 17.

the following month Joseph Browne tried to curry favour with the Ministry by celebrating Bolingbroke's return from his peace mission to France in *Britain's Palladium* (1712). His reference to "BRITAIN's Wealth,/Imbezzel'd lately, or purloin'd by Stealth"[1] relied on the undiminished effectiveness of the 'argument from purse', which the Tories were to serve up right to the end of the peace debate and which lent popular fervour to their vindictiveness against the Dutch. In spite of the homage paid to Bolingbroke in this poem there is no inkling of the rising differences of opinion about peace policy between Harley and Bolingbroke, which became manifest in the Cabinet in September and October 1712[2]. Even later poems dealing with the advent of peace do not overtly reflect the growing division between the two Ministers so that Tory propaganda, at least, does not seem to have been seriously impaired on account of internal dissensions. In September 1712 Charles Hornby, in *The Fourth and Last Part of a Caveat against the Whiggs*, once again heaped opprobrium on the Whigs, who "by a Juggle and Combination between some crafty, selfish Neighbours, and an Intestine Faction" were said to have "been made the Cat's Paw, to pull the *Dutch* Chesnuts out of the Fire [...]"[3]. The publication of Ward's collection *The Poetical Entertainer* (1712) in October also showed that the Tory propaganda machinery was to be kept going; in particular the poem *The English Foreigners: Or, the Whigs Turn'd Dutchmen*, designed to prick the anti-Holland nerve, employed all the well-tried devices of journalistic warfare.

After several months of delaying action on the part of the States General, it became known in London at the beginning of October 1712 that the Dutch were about to give in to the British peace plans. In the wake of these events attention was turned towards the effectiveness of the proposed renunciation of the French throne by Philip V. At the beginning of November 1712 the English translation of Jean Dumont's *Les Soupirs de l'Europe* sought to expose the inadequacy of such an arrangement to effectively separate the kingdoms of France and Spain. But this opportune publication did not have a lasting impact in favour of the Whigs and was, after causing a preliminary stir[4], quickly neutralized by the appearance of *The Queen, the Present Ministry, Lewis XIV and Philip V Unanswerably Vindicated* (1712), with its aggressive preface once again brandishing the big stick of abuse at the war-mongering Whigs. While, on the one hand, this pamphlet relied on the readers' discernment by stating with composure "That *France* is powerful

---

1 [Joseph Browne], *Britain's Palladium: Or, my Lord Bolingbroke's Welcome from France* (London, 1712), p. 7.

2 Cf. Hill, *Robert Harley*, pp. 187-188.

3 [Charles Hornby], *The Fourth and Last Part of a Caveat against the Whiggs, etc. In a Short Account of their Behaviour in the Reign of Her Majesty Queen Anne* (London, 1712), p. 101. The same image is used in *The Queen, the Present Ministry, Lewis XIV. and Philip V. Unanswerably Vindicated, with Respect to his Catholick Majesty's Possession of Spain and the Indies Confirm'd to him in the Treaty of Peace now on foot. In a Letter to a Noble Lord, concerning a Scandalous Libel, Entitled, The Groans of Europe, etc.* (London, 1712), p. 22.

4 Cf. Abel Boyer, *Quadriennium Annae Postremum or, the Political State of Great Britain*, 2nd ed., vol. V and VI for the Year 1713 (London, 1719), V, 50-72.

enough to withstand the greatest Efforts of her Enemies, and yet is not strong enough to attack the Liberties of *Europe*"[1], on the other hand it skilfully kindled the readers' emotions by pointing out in its conclusion that a successful continuation of the war would lead to nothing "but to double the Territories of the *Dutch*, and to quadruple those of the Emperor"[2]. In spite of the republication - a little later - of *The Barrier-Treaty Vindicated*, which set out the case for a strong barrier for the Dutch with great skill and couched in unpolemical language, the Whigs did not succeed in taking the lead again on the public scene, but remained curiously on the defensive. On the whole their journalistic performance towards the end of 1712 was, with the exception of the *Flying-Post*, which sometimes stung the Government almost single-handedly, characterized rather by low-spiritedness than vigorous remonstration. They still gave the impression of having somehow conceded defeat. A poem with Whig leanings published at the end of October, Thomas Tickell's complimentary *To his Excellency the Lord Privy-Seal, on the Prospect of Peace* (1712)[3], took for granted the Government's ability to shape events at Utrecht according to schedule. When it became known that Marlborough would be leaving England at the end of the year, Tory malice[4] as epitomized in the irreverent poem *A Trip to Germany, or the D. of M-h's Farewel to England* (1712) was rather more pronounced than the gallant defence expressed in its Whig counterpart *To his Grace the Duke of Marlborough on his Going into Germany* (1712)[5]. Was it a sign of the Government's self-confidence that no attempts were made by Tory propaganda to charge Marlborough personally with the design of rousing European resistance to the peace plans of the Ministry? In December the news that the Dutch would positively submit to the British demands including the abandonment of the Barrier Treaty put the seal of final success on the Government's staying power. As the year 1712 was drawing to its close, the first stanza of *A New Ballad* emphatically expressed Whig forebodings of the new year:

> Now, now comes on the Tories Year,
> *Frenchmen* have Hopes, and *Britons* Fear;
> Perkin intends to govern here,
> And be our Faith's Defender.
> For *France* is become our good Ally,
> Th' Emperor too and the *Dutch* must fly,

---

1 *The Queen, the Present Ministry, Lewis XIV. and Philip V. Unanswerably Vindicated*, p. 24.

2 *Ibid.*, p. 24.

3 For details on this poem see the chapter "The Treaty of Utrecht (1713) as Reflected in Peace Poems".

4 See also *The Examiner*, 6-13 November and 22-26 December 1712.

5 Reprinted in Boyer, *Quadriennium Annae Postremum*, IV, 332. See also Ridpath's vindication of Marlborough in the *Flying-Post* of 18-20 and 27-29 November 1712.

Unless they will bow to our M-y,
And *Flanders* and *Spain* surrender[1].

In its dismal mood this ballad also reflected the inability of the Whigs during the previous months to imprint their views of war and peace on the public's mind. In the course of 1712 their former combativeness had given way to rather erratic and feeble manifestations of political resistance. Whig propaganda had to a large extent lost its former punch and resilience in the previous stage of the great debate, depending rather on isolated shots than dense barrage. However, with their vivid and plucky allusion to weaknesses in the Government's position the lines quoted above also recalled earlier Whig stamina and pointed towards at least a partial recovery of Whig efficiency in propaganda. Revitalization[2], though at something not quite like the former level of public assertiveness by the Whigs, took place at the beginning of 1713.

Although the Whigs were then still falling short of their usual effectiveness, the revived *Examiner* of 22 December 1712 noticed that the Whigs were "once more rally'd and got together" - probably in order to summon up vigilance in anticipation of a final counteraction by the Opposition. With the coming of the new year the controversy about war and peace to a certain degree regained its former vigour, the Government finding itself once again confronted with concerted Whig objections of some weight. Quantitatively a marked increase in printed propaganda gave evidence of the revitalization of the public debate. The latter was reinvigorated by the publication, in the *Flying-Post* of 13-15 January 1713, of parts of the Letter of the States General to the Queen, in which they put forth their reservations concerning the new Barrier Treaty demanded by Britain since December 1712[3]. That the Whigs had not entirely lost their former mettle could be seen from the uproar raised against the French ambassador, the Duc d'Aumont, in January 1713. A satirical ballad, *The Merchant a-la-Mode* (1713), cast scurrilous aspersions on the latter as well as on the Ministry, which was accused of Jacobite sympathies. The Tories immediately retaliated by publishing a ballad of the same title which, significantly, called attention to the burdens of the war iniquitously loaded upon Britain - still the safest argument in the continual bid for popular support.

Although the Whigs understandably did not disdain to fire such inflammatory broadsides of populist militancy, they made their last stand in the first months of 1713 on a predominantly somewhat different note. Apparently convinced that complete polarisation would be of little or no avail against a Government which had repeatedly demonstrated its hold on the public at large, they mainly resorted

[1] *A Pill to Purge State-Melancholy: Or, a Collection of Excellent New Ballads* (London, 1715), p. 143.

[2] See also the outspoken criticism of Tory policy in Burnet's pamphlet *A Certain Information of a Certain Discourse that Happen'd in a Certain Gentleman's House in a Certain Country* (1712), which went into three editions between December 1712 and February 1713.

[3] Cf. Coombs, *The Conduct of the Dutch*, p. 367.

to a rhetoric of what may be called 'restrained oppugnancy'. Mindful of the efficacy of Tory reproaches of Whig disloyalty towards the monarch, they adopted a more deferential attitude towards the Queen and did not flatly deny any well-intentioned efforts on the part of her Ministers. This newly chosen approach of 'respectful dissidence' became most noticeable in pamphlet literature, which the Whigs again put to effective use; after a long period of neglect or at least restricted activity this weapon was once more dexterously wielded by the Whigs - in the first quarter of 1713 the Whigs published more pamphlets than the Tories. Whig objections to the impending peace were voiced on two interrelated planes. The revived discussion of the Dutch barrier became the Whigs' first foothold in their attempt to regain the favourable attention of the public. The appearance of the second edition of Hare's[1] reserved but substantial *The Barrier-Treaty Vindicated* in December 1712, and the publication of the Letter of the States General to the Queen at the turn of the new year, set the stage for this debate. In its numbers of 11 and 18 December 1712 the *Examiner* had made slashing attacks on the views upheld in that pamphlet, testifying to the latter's impact through its angry retort. The intrepid *Flying-Post* tried to cash in on the stir caused by the publication of the Letter of the States General[2]. At the very same time the Tory 'pamphlet' *The Testimonies of Several Citizens of Fickleborough, in the Kingdom of Fairy-Land, concerning the Life and Character of Robert Hush, commonly Called, Bob*, published - according to Coombs[3] - on 20 January 1713, took pains not to release the emotional grip on the English public by again applying Swift's ready-made conspiracy thesis - as outlined by himself[4] and quickly exploited for propaganda purposes[5] - to the dealings of the Whigs with the Dutch. The Tories obviously felt this sort of emotional 'mugging' to be fully adequate; significantly the author of *The Testimonies* did not engage in factual argumentation with the author of the rhetorically effective *The Present State of Fairy-Land. In Several Letters from Esquire Hush, an Eminent Citizen of Fickle-Borough, to the King of Slave-Onia* (1713), a further indication of Whig recovery on the public scene. The appearance of a new edition of *The Barrier-Treaty Vindicated* about that date was promptly countered by the publication of *Remarks on the Barrier-Treaty Vindicated* (1713) and *A Letter to the Examiner, concerning the Barrier Treaty Vindicated* (1713). The first of these two pamphlets, in particular, conveys the impression that Tory propaganda was in general more adept at hunting down the enemy

---

1 The authorship is unclear. According to Walpole, Stephen Poyntz was the author: see William Coxe, *Memoirs of Horatio, Lord Walpole. Selected from his Correspondence and Papers, and Connected with the History of the Times, from 1678 to 1757* (London, 1802), p. 436.

2 Cf. Coombs, *The Conduct of the Dutch*, pp. 368-369.

3 See *ibid.*, p. 368.

4 In the last verse of *Peace and Dunkirk* we find the words "the Dutch-hearted Whigs".

5 See, most notably, Ward's *The English Foreigners: Or, the Whigs Turn'd Dutchmen* (1712). Cf. also the succinct formulation "our *English Dutch*" in *A Search after Dutch Honesty: Or, the Old Use and Custom of that Nation to their Friends and Allies ever since they have been a Common-wealth; faithfully Taken from their own Histories and Authentick Records* (*s.l.*, 1712), p. iii.

on the emotional plane than at bringing him to bay by demolishing his arguments through superior expertise. The most important contribution on the Whig side was *An Answer to the Examiner's Cavils against the Barrier Treaty of 1709* (1713), which made ample use of material previously published in the *Flying-Post* and probably appeared about the beginning of February 1713. This pamphlet restored Whig propaganda to something of its former quality and must be regarded as one of the highlights of the newly revived debate; together with *The Barrier-Treaty Vindicated* and the *Observations* characterized in the next paragraph it posed a serious if transitory threat to Tory dominance on the public scene, where the Whigs had been on the retreat since the summer of 1712. Full of spirit and with a dogged factualism, this brisk piece of political writing summed up the Opposition standpoint in a rhetorically trenchant manner exceptional in Whig pamphleteering at that moment and raised the banner of Whig contradiction for the last time.

Correlated efforts to show the Whig colours centred on the *Observations upon the State of the Nation, in January 1712/13* (1713). Perhaps because of its posture of reluctant disapprobation and its concomitant moderateness in tone, this pamphlet with its statesmanlike approach as testified by its very title drew the most replies. The gist of the argument expanded in the *Observations* was that the European balance of power was going to be jeopardized by the imminent convergence of French and Spanish interests. As the Tories had made the changed situation after the death of Joseph I in the spring of 1711 the pivot of their volte-face on the Spanish question, the political discussion had come full circle. Although the *Observations* did not present new arguments, they were impressive because of their scrupulous insistence on a point of national magnitude which could not be relinquished in spite of the respect due to the Queen and her Government. Through his attitude of humble remonstration and by even admitting to unwarrantable behaviour of the Whigs towards the Church when they were in office[1], the author of the *Observations* seems to be appealing to the sense of responsibility of the moderate section of the Tory party. In spite of its conciliatory tone, however, the pamphlet is by no means lacking in rhetorical pithiness. Thus the Tories' overstatement of Dutch economic rivalry is mocked through the repartee "we strain at Gnats, and swallow Camels, when we bellow at the *Dutch*, and overlook the *French* in this Article of Trade"[2]. And the main point, indeed the ultimate objective of all Whig writings at that time - the danger to the Protestant Succession - is driven home in words which ironically stress the sudden confidence in the King of France's[3] word: "[...] and the next Thing which we are to look for, is, that he will join in a *Guarantee* to secure the *Barrier* for the Dutch, and the *Hannover Succession* against himself"[4].

---

1 See *Observations upon the State of the Nation, in January 1712/13* (London, 1713), pp. 24-26.

2 *Ibid.*, p. 13.

3 Of course the latter's perfidy continued to be exposed, for instance by the author of *John Bull's last Will and Testament, as it was Drawn by a Welch Attorney. With a Preface to the Ar-p of C-ry* (London, 1713), p. 8.

4 *Observations upon the State of the Nation*, p. 24.

As can be seen from a quick glance at a number of replies, the polemics with a difference deployed in the *Observations* discomfited the Tories, although they did not seriously disconcert them. Even the most spirited of them showed, however, that the Tories had some difficulty in coping with the constructive antagonism of the *Observations*. *An Answer to the Observations upon the State of the Nation, in January 1712/13. By the Author of the Examiner* (1713) identified the Earl of Nottingham as the author of the Opposition pamphlet and tried to ridicule him by harping ironically on his pretended apprehensions as well as on his ostentatious modesty. George Sewell's *Remarks upon a Pamphlet Intitul'd, Observations upon the State of the Nation, in January, 1712/13*, published after the signing of the second Barrier Treaty on 30 January 1713, roguishly pointed to the concord that now prevailed between England and the States General[1]. Interestingly, another reply to the *Observations* also published about mid-February 1713 and ascribed to Defoe, *Not-am Politicks Examin'd*, observed that Whig propaganda had again achieved a considerable degree of coherence[2]. However, this Whig recuperation did not prove more than a last-ditch attack on the Tories; it could not effectually stem the tide of public opinion, which was set for the coming of peace. Notably Defoe, who clearly did not find it necessary to deal with the balance-of-power question yet again in his journal, had said on the question of peace in the *Review* of 24 January 1713: "[...] it is not so much the Subject of our present Debate as it used to be, the Matter is as good as over [...]"[3]. It is very much in keeping with this statement that Defoe in three subsequent issues of the *Review*, all dealing with the *Observations*[4], only marginally concerned himself with aspects of peace policy in the last number, concentrating instead on the alleged author of the *Observations* and anxieties with regard to the Pretender.

At Utrecht things were on the verge of being brought to a conclusion, and at home - as signalled by the appearance of Defoe's pamphlets *Reasons against the Succession of the House of Hanover* (1713) and *And what if the Pretender Should Come?* (1713) - political discussion turned increasingly towards the problem of the Succession after March 1713. This new emphasis was confirmed by George Ridpath's pamphlet *Some Thoughts concerning the Peace* (1713), written after the conclusion of the treaty, in which, despite warnings to be vigilant in the matter of the Succession[5], there was nonetheless a certain resignation to the fact that the Whigs had lost not only a political, but also a public relations battle. Altogether the Government, which had successfully taken the lead in the battle for public

---

1 See [George Sewell], *Remarks upon a Pamphlet Intitul'd, Observations upon the State of the Nation, in January, 1712/13* (London, 1713), p. 24.

2 See *Not-am Politicks Examin'd. Being an Answer to a Pamphlet lately Publish'd, Intituled Observations upon the State of the Nation* (London, 1713), p. 7.

3 *Defoe's Review*, VIII, 99.

4 See the *Review* of 21, 24 and 26 February 1713.

5 See [George Ridpath], *Some Thoughts concerning the Peace, and the Thanksgiving Appointed by Authority to be Observed for it. In a Letter from an Elder to a Minister of the Church of Scotland* ([London], 1713), p. 15.

support in the course of 1712, managed to go through with its campaign. This, however, did not prevent the Whigs from again voicing their unease at the advent of peace and later stiffening on the trade issue.

II. Focus: The Dynamics of the Polemical Interaction In the Turning-Point Debate

The aim of this chapter is to throw more light on the turning-point debate - the decisive period of public controversy between the autumn of 1711 and the spring of 1712, at the end of which the Government had gained the upper hand in the media - by bringing out representative features more sharply than was the case in the general outline. There now follows a sharpening of the focus on events of the polemical interaction, taking special account of the rhetorical realisation of political creativity. The rhetorical realisation is examined in many revealing details of the verbalisation of political concepts in order to bring the process of public political communication to light precisely as it is reflected linguistically. How is the turning-point debate represented from the perspective of the theme complexes that determine the large structures, how is it revealed in the linguistic realisation of political intentions?

1. End of August until mid-October 1711

The turning-point debate falls chronologically into two distinct periods. The caesura lies around the end of the year 1711 after the volte-face initiated by the publication of *The Conduct of the Allies* on 27 November 1711 had given first indications of a consolidation of Government propaganda. During the first phase the Whigs had the more powerful journalistic battalions, and were endeavouring to perpetuate the long undisputed national consensus on the question of war; in the second phase it was the Tories who dominated the propaganda scene through a qualitative leap. The inner dynamics of this increasingly intense journalistic trial of strength can be made transparent by localising the respective theme complexes, which party-politically were differently accented, and identifying their potential for development. The obvious point to begin with is the fact that, following the leak of Prior's peace mission at the end of August 1711, the struggle for public opinion was bound to flare up more openly and in a more direct manner and that before long the Government would be obliged to come clean in the press, too, a situation that was further aggravated by the publication of the Preliminaries in mid-October 1711, all of which so clearly defined the political constellation that the Duke of Marlborough, who had hitherto been exposed to anticipatory critical assessment, was bound to move right into the crossfire of public debate.

Marlborough's military success at Bouchain allowed the Whigs to enter the turning-point debate under full sail when it began in the autumn of 1711. With ostentatious optimism they discharged the task of taking further steps to maintain England's readiness for war, a task which political developments had rendered necessary. Even in September 1711 Hare, in his pamphlet *Bouchain*: *In a Dialogue between the Late Medley and Examiner*, which opened the Bouchain controversy, announced with a self-confidence which challenged the Government "*That no Man in* England *dare sign a Peace, which shall give up* Spain *to* France"[1] ! After the publication of the Preliminaries in the middle of the following month pamphlets such as Maynwaring's *A Vindication of the Present M-y, from the Clamours Rais'd against them upon Occasion of the New Preliminaries* and the anonymous *Letter from an Exchange Broker to a Country Gentleman, concerning Peace and South-Sea Stock* took an identical line and endeavoured to more or less exorcise the Government by uttering the unutterable. In his sermon *The Charge of God to Joshua* in September 1711, the same Hare attempted to surround the Duke of Marlborough, who had already been subjected to an unpleasantly realistic examination in Swift's *Examiner* - frequent references to which over quite a long time during the turning-point debate bear witness to its enduring effect -, with a religious aura again by means of a providential interpretation of his victories[2]. With their pointed references to England's by no means exhausted material resources pamphlets published in the first half of October such as *A Proposal for Carrying on the War. In a Letter to a Nobleman* and *The Taxes not Grievous* complete the picture of the consolidation of the Whig campaign in early autumn 1711.

The more remarkable political signals were at this time already being transmitted by the Tories, however, who, particularly provoked by the appearance of *Bouchain*[3], resumed their war of attrition against Marlborough. It has hitherto remained unnoticed that Mrs. Manley's prompt replies to Hare's pamphlet and sermon, *The D. of M-h's Vindication* and *A Learned Comment upon Dr. Hare's Excellent Sermon Preach'd before the D. of Marlborough on the Surrender of Bouchain*, anticipate in a nutshell the strategy of Tory propaganda in the coming months[4] ! These two complementary publications, written under the particular auspices of St. John, revealed, even at a time of comparative reserve on the part of the Tories, that the Government would in the end be unable to avoid stepping up

1 Hare, *Bouchain*: *In a Dialogue between the Late Medley and Examiner*, p. 41. - As Harris supposes, the 'official' aura of the pamphlet suggested "a determination to involve Marlborough publicly in the Whig opposition to the peace, with or without his active consent" (*A Study of the Paper War*, p. 231).

2 See Francis Hare, *The Charge of God to Joshua*: *In a Sermon Preach'd before his Grace the Duke of Marlborough, at Avenes le Sec, September 9 1711, Being the Day of Thanksgiving for Passing the Lines, and Taking Bouchain* (London, 1711), p. 17.

3 Cf. Harris, *A Passion for Government*, pp. 185-186.

4 This also applies to Gwendolyn B. Needham's instructive article, which does not reveal rhetorical strategies: "Mary de la Rivière Manley, Tory Defender", *The Huntington Library Quarterly* 12 (1948-49), pp. 253-288. The immediate importance of the pamphlet *The D. of M-h's Vindication* as a warning to Marlborough of the consequences of allowing himself to get further involved in Opposition measures is, however, fully realized by Harris, *A Study of the Paper War*, pp. 236, 242.

the pace in its use of propaganda. Thus there is a unity of theme stretching over this half-year which, despite all continuity with previous discussions, gives the turning-point debate its own character. Evidently as an antidote to Whig persistence in the matter and the glorification of Marlborough, both of Manley's writings introduced the emotionalization of the war into the public debate as a new direction in Government propaganda. Thus *The D. of M-h's Vindication* lamented "the Blood of these poor Wretches that are yearly sacrific'd in vast Numbers [...]"[1]. In the face of the sacrifice of men and material values, the humanitarian appeal to the public's feelings was set as a counterpoint against the alleged hardheartedness of the Whigs and was in the ensuing months to be an essential asset of Tory propaganda in all political groupings and all genres. This emotionalization of the war debate paved the way towards the goal - aimed at by Tory propaganda strategy and certainly achieved through the publication of *The Conduct of the Allies* - of making short shrift of complex issues by delivering them up to rejection purely on the grounds of resentment. In addition to the pointed reference to the use of the affective potential for the purpose of peace propaganda, both *The D. of M-h's Vindication* and *A Learned Comment* viciously attacked the Duke of Marlborough, whom ministerial journalists had for some time treated with considerable leniency but who had been restored as the figurehead of those opposing the peace, and, even at the time of the early skirmishes, showed unmistakably that the only way to get the better of the Whigs was by thoroughly dismantling their figurehead[2]. *The D. of M-h's Vindication*, which on its last page preferred a separate peace as the lesser of two evils to the continuation of the war, was then the first text on the Government side - after the terminological precedent in Mrs. Manley's own *The New Atalantis* (1709) and *The Secret History of Arlus and Odolphus* (1710), in which Marlborough was named Fortunatus -, which again deliberately introduced the element of luck[3] into the debate[4], namely the argument that the Duke of Marlborough owed his successes more to favourable circumstances than to his skill[5]. This was the first of a series of incriminating charges which subsequently were eagerly assembled by all genres to produce a powerful arsenal of propaganda with which to destroy Marlborough's reputation. At the beginning of 1711 Defoe, in *A Short Narrative of the Life and Actions of His Grace John, D. of Marlborough*, had already noted the new tendency to chop away at Marlborough's mili-

---

1 *The D. of M-h's Vindication*, p. 14.

2 As early as in July 1711, in a letter to the Duchess of Marlborough, Maynwaring had predicted that "their [the Tories'] whole business from henceforward will be to blast 39's [Marlborough's] character, and to set him down" (*Private Correspondence of Sarah, Duchess of Marlborough, Illustrative of the Court and Times of Queen Anne*, II, 73).

3 That this was propitious to him is not even denied by those historians who are well disposed towards Marlborough: "There is no question but, in addition to skill and judgment, he had luck on his side" (Henry L. Snyder, "Marlborough and the Reign of Queen Anne: The Status of Current Studies", *The British Studies Monitor* 8, 3 [1978], p. 5).

4 See *The D. of M-h's Vindication*, p. 8.

5 Journalists of the Opposition camp immediately made efforts to counter this argument, which was used with increasing frequency; cf. the alleged letter from an officer of the Confederate Army in *The Protestant Post-Boy*, 4-6 October 1711.

tary prestige by attributing his successes to sheer luck[1]. Alongside the emotionalization of the war and the incrimination of Marlborough, Mrs. Manley's two pamphlets, which follow the argument adumbrated in *A Letter to the Examiner* (1710), also set the other main aspects of the ensuing months of Tory propaganda, some of which were intertwined with the above: the alleged jeopardising of the balance of power in Europe on account of the growth of Austrian power[2], the cheating of England by the Dutch[3] and the neglect of the Allies to supply the agreed quotas[4]. The presence of all the important aspects of subsequent Tory propaganda in these writings of Mrs. Manley suggests long-term planning, the acceptance of a possibly lengthy incubation period for the full rhetorical implementation of certain aspects and careful timing. In Mrs. Manley's two pamphlets, which betray insider knowledge[5], Government journalism stubbornly and ominously announced the potential it had for influencing public opinion without, however, making full use of it, at least for the time being[6].

The fact that the emotionalization of the peace debate[7] represented a long-term propagandistic move on the part of the Government is confirmed by the publication of Defoe's widely debated pamphlet *Reasons why this Nation Ought to Put a Speedy End to this Expensive War* on 6 October 1711, which made known in its own way the Government's intention to take up and fight the journalistic battle against the increasing strength of the Opposition even before the publication of the Preliminaries. As the emotional appeals at the beginning and the end show, Defoe subordinates his whole argument in this pamphlet to influencing the reader emotionally. While the very first sentence appeals to "A Mind possest with any Tenderness for the Miseries, Sufferings and Distresses of its Native Land"[8], the last words condemn "this Bloody and Expensive War"[9]. The emotional address to the reader, which became a common point of departure for the entire Tory propaganda campaign, as confirmed, for instance, immediately afterwards by the *Post Boy* of 13-16 October 1711 and later by *Law not a Bottomless Pit: Or, Arguments against Peace* (1712), published at the end of the turning-point debate, was im-

1 See [Daniel Defoe], *A Short Narrative of the Life and Actions of His Grace John, D. of Marlborough* (1711), ed. Paula R. Backscheider, The Augustan Reprint Society, Publication Number 168 (Los Angeles, 1974), p. 26.

2 See *The D. of M-h's Vindication*, p. 13.

3 See *A Learned Comment*, pp. 5 and 9.

4 See *ibid.*, p. 11.

5 On the 'briefing' of Mrs. Manley at an earlier date cf. Needham, "Mary de la Rivière Manley", pp. 265-268.

6 There is no evidence in the journalism at this or later stages of the dramatic confusion in the Tory camp as maintained by Coxe; cf. *Memoirs of John Duke of Marlborough, with his Original Correspondence: Collected from the Family Records at Blenheim, and other Authentic Sources*, ed. Coxe, VI, 147.

7 This phenomenon was also given due attention in *The Case of a British General. Collected from Several Late Celebrated Papers: And Laid down in two Plain Propositions* ([London], 1711), p. 2.

8 *Reasons Why*, p. 3.

9 *Ibid.*, p. 47.

mediately and consistently continued by Defoe in such pamphlets as *Reasons why a Party among us, and also among the Confederates, are obstinately Bent against a Treaty of Peace with the French at this Time* (1711), *The Ballance of Europe* (1711) and *An Essay at a Plain Exposition of that Difficult Phrase a Good Peace* (1711). The second cornerstone of *Reasons Why* was the updating of the balance-of-power theme, which accompanied the entire public discussion of the War of the Spanish Succession, by shifting the perspective from France to Austria. A possible increase of Austrian power in the event of the Emperor ascending the Spanish throne became the central argument in Defoe's foreign-policy platform, which made Defoe the leading exponent of a new balance-of-power casuistry - already set out in *The Succession of Spain Consider'd* (1711) -, which, with its pseudo-rational demand for equidistance from France and Austria, lent itself to damaging the Opposition, which was insisting on the maintenance of the status quo, but also to exerting at least argumentative pressure on the Whigs to reveal where they stood. Defoe's specific option to give propaganda support to the Government, which essentially was only pursued by himself[1], found its distinctive linguistic expression in the reclassification of the terms "exorbitant" and "exorbitance", which focused the hegemony problem as in a burning mirror. By transferring these key-words, hitherto employed to signalise Louis XIV's striving for supremacy[2], to Austria, Defoe summarised his change of perspective on foreign policy, which was dictated by Government strategy, in a manner that effectively caught public attention.

The words "exorbitant/ exorbitance" had previously been only associated with France, so their transfer to Austria by Defoe in *Reasons Why* was spectacular. Their application to Austria was maintained consistently in pamphlets such as *The Ballance of Europe* and *An Essay at a Plain Exposition of that Difficult Phrase a Good Peace*. The linguistic transfer, signalling the domination of a political theme, was executed by the *Review*[3], too, which from mid-October 1711

1 Sutherland's assertion that Defoe did no more than jump on to a bandwagon already in full swing - he writes: "The argument he was now using in his anti-war pamphlet had already become common property among the Tory writers [...]" (*Daniel Defoe. A Critical Study*, p. 59) - is not born out by a perusal of the published material.

2 The *Examiner* of 24 August 1710, for instance, had still - in a completely matter-of-fact manner - referred to "the *exorbitant* Power of France [...]". Under Swift's responsibility the key-word - recoined in such phrases as "*exorbitant Interests and Annuities*" or "monstrous Encroachments of exorbitant Avarice and Ambition" - was soon systematically turned into a term of abuse against the domestic enemy; see the following issues of the *Examiner*: 2 November 1710; 14 December 1710; 22 February 1711; 19 April 1711; 26 April 1711; 24 May 1711; 31 May 1711. In its original application to France it was only used again one other time - in a quotation, significantly (see the *Examiner* of 25 January 1711)!

3 See esp. the editions of the *Review* of 13, 16, 18 and 25 October, also those of 10, 15, 17, 20, 22 and 24 November 1711.

performed in a kind of functional symbiosis with Defoe's pamphlets[1] in order to bring more forcefully to public notice a topic which was welcome to the Government[2]. The pointed reference to the dangers posed by an increase in Habsburg power gave Defoe repeated opportunities to demand equidistance from both France and Austria in the interest of maintaining the balance of power - so the pair "exorbitant/ exorbitance" was often applied in symmetrical reference to both nations - and to present this attitude as mere common sense. The fact that by adopting this procedure Defoe touched the Whigs' argumentative nerve and put them under pressure to justify themselves is seen in the violent reaction of some of them. In October and November 1711, for instance, the *Observator* published its reply in a series of issues in which the word "exorbitant" already appeared in the table of contents, a reply which expressed indignation at Defoe's balance-of-power rhetoric, which the Opposition apparently found troublesome[3]. Even the *Protestant Post-Boy* of 6-8 March 1712 still added its voice to those opposing the volte-face in foreign policy manifested in the reapplication of the word "exorbitant". But pamphlets such as *The Ballance of Power* and especially the more substantial *A Caveat to the Treaters* (1711)[4], too, rejected Defoe's attempts at repolarisation. In November 1711, when Whig pressure on public opinion was particularly strong, it became clear that the word "exorbitant" was predominantly used with reference to Austria in the *Review*[5], which indicated that Defoe had been assigned the task of regularly leaping to the Government's defence. How purposefully Defoe pursued a given political line is shown, for example, in the 'individual' defence of *A Defence of the Allies*[6], published in December 1711, where he returned just for once to the old use of "exorbitance" with reference to France[7]. Interestingly, the use of the 'Austria argument' in Tory propaganda was almost entirely restricted to Defoe, although the latter found a rare supporter from another genre in, for instance, the writer of the poem *The Peace-Haters* (1711), who uses it towards the end. In addition the prominent use of this argument was largely confined to the first phase of the turning-point debate, although it appeared sporadically in the second phase, too, as for example in *A Fair View of our Present Case* (1712)[8]. This indicates that with his specific line Defoe was only taking advantage of a temporary option

---

1 On the fine-tuning between the author of the *Review* and the pamphleteer Defoe cf. also Lawrence Poston III, "Defoe and the Peace Campaign, 1710-1713: A Reconsideration", *The Huntington Library Quarterly* 27 (1963), p. 11.

2 Cf. Bolingbroke's use of language: *Letters and Correspondence*, IV, 21.

3 See the editions of the *Observator* of 20-24, 24-27 and 27-31 October, also those of 3-7, 7-10 and 24-28 November 1711.

4 The second sentence of this well-written pamphlet (probably by Hare) reads as follows: "Europe *has smarted too much already by the Exorbitant Power of* France *alone, to add any more to it*" (*A Caveat to the Treaters*, Preface).

5 See esp. the editions of the *Review* of 10, 15, 17, 20, 22 and 24 November 1711.

6 Defoe's authorship of this pamphlet is, however, doubted by Owens and Furbank; see above, p. 63, note 3.

7 See Defoe, *A Defence of the Allies and the Late Ministry: Or, Remarks on the Tories New Idol*, p. 19.

8 Cf. *A Fair View of our Present Case* (London, 1712), p. 18.

in Government propaganda and - as is suggested particularly by the public appeal of the *Review* - was given the task of addressing possible Whig sympathisers in order at least to give rise to a measure of uncertainty in the Opposition camp. The 'Austria rhetoric' was primarily a manoeuvre to give temporary relief to the Government, which is clearly shown by the fact that, although Defoe did not fundamentally change his balance-of-power argument until the peace settlement, this approach was all but abandoned in the second phase of the turning-point debate, when the Government camp was presented with topics which had a more powerful appeal. Significantly, in this second phase Swift applied the key-word "exorbitant" to the arch-enemy Holland[1] in *Some Remarks on the Barrier Treaty* (1712)[2] ! The balance-of-power argument, as tailored to Austria, was obviously part of an intermediate stage in the Government's long-term media strategy, in which presumably they initially sounded out how Marlborough would act at the decisive moment[3] .

It is interesting that the Whigs realized early on that the public debate was approaching a turning-point and that the Government was employing fresh options to guarantee the necessary journalistic support for their political plans. In *A Vindication of the Present M-y*, for instance, Maynwaring stated, firstly, that since the publication of Mrs. Manley's *The D. of M-h's Vindication* the Government had been staking everything on the tactic of emotionalizing the peace debate: "[...] the Author sets forth with all his Eloquence the Misery of the People, and infers from thence the Necessity of a Peace [...]"[4] . Secondly, he perceived the apparently rational touch in Defoe's approach to the breaking up of the Opposition's status quo front: "But there is one Point indeed relating to a Peace, upon which the Writers of this Side advance something that has the colour of an Argument; and that is, that the Face of Affairs is chang'd by the Death of the Emperor [...]"[5] . In *An Account of the State and Progress of the Present Negotiation of Peace* (1711), Boyer, too, pointed to the restructuring of the balance-of-power argument to apply to Austria as an important constituent of the most recent change in public perception[6] . In this pamphlet, in which the author reviews the Government's preparatory steps in the public arena from St. John's *A Letter to the Examiner* to Swift's number 39 of the *Examiner* (26 April 1711), thereby demonstrating that he knows the new Ministry's long-term propaganda strategy only too well, he subjected Swift to violent polemic and thereby offered Harley his services in the obvious expectation

---

1 The reference has been stated by Irvin Ehrenpreis in *Swift: The Man, his Works, and the Age*, II: *Dr Swift* (London, 1967), 498, who does not, however, take note of Swift's switch in terminology.

2 See Swift, *Political Tracts 1711-1713*, ed. Davis, p. 88.

3 In Winston Churchill's estimation in *Marlborough: His Life and Times*, VI (New York, 1938), 486 Harley had known of Marlborough's final opposition since the beginning of November 1711. Regarding advances made to Marlborough after that, cf. Coxe, *Memoirs of John Duke of Marlborough*, VI, 137.

4 Maynwaring, *A Vindication of the Present M-y*, p. 31.

5 *Ibid.*, p. 32.

6 See [Abel Boyer], *An Account of the State and Progress of the Present Negotiation of Peace. With the Reasons for and against a Partition of Spain, etc. In a Letter to a Noble Lord in Worcestershire* (London, 1711), pp. 34-35.

that the latter would not be able to avoid taking account of Whig ideas when peace was made[1]. Both publications betray sensitivity to changes occurring on the journalistic plane, in which the Government was exploring new directions of its propaganda in order to prevail in the dispute with the Opposition.

2. FROM THE PUBLICATION OF THE PRELIMINARIES TO THE APPEARANCE OF *THE CONDUCT OF THE ALLIES*

After the publication of the Peace Preliminaries in mid-October 1711 the 'No peace without Spain' problem occupied the centre of the public debate. And though "War naturally generates journalism"[2], the problem of how to end it proved even more gratifying in this respect. The Opposition, suspecting the abandonment of the declared aim of the war, reacted by setting off the alarm bells in the press. With the full weight of the previous resolutions touching Spain in nearly all the pamphlets behind them, the Whigs tried to put the Government under pressure by sharply drawing attention to the contradiction between the favourable war situation and giving in to France, which now seemed to be on the cards. Maynwaring, for instance, fully trusting in the corrective influence of public opinion[3], poked fun at the Government's new attitude to the old enemy when, in *A Letter to a High-Churchman* (1711), he wrote: "[...] two Victories more obtain'd by the Duke of *Marlborough*, would be an undeniable Reason for leaving the *Spanish* Monarchy entire with the Duke of *Anjou*"[4]. With reference to long-standing French intentions regarding Spain the same author sarcastically asked a short time later in *Remarks upon the Present Negotiations of Peace Begun between Britain and France* (1711): "[...] and shall they gain it now by being beaten nine Campaigns?"[5]. By means of this rhetoric of 'manifest inconsistency'[6] the Whigs tried to proclaim from the roof-tops the Government's departure from

1 See *ibid.*, p. 39.

2 Leslie Stephen, *English Literature and Society in the Eighteenth Century* (London, 1910), p. 68.

3 In a letter to the Duchess of Marlborough that probably dates from July 1711 Maynwaring had announced his confident conviction that "it is possible to scribble these men [the new Ministers] down [...]". In the same letter he says "that the more they are expos'd the more impossible it will be for them to cover their Abuses" (BL Add. MS 61461, fol. 137).

4 Maynwaring, *A Letter to a High-Churchman*, p. 35.

5 Maynwaring, *Remarks upon the Present Negotiations of Peace Begun between Britain and France*, p. 11.

6 Defoe attempted to counter this in a linguistically pointed way as well as factually; see e.g. - ascribed to Prince Eugene and ironically emphasising the hopelessness of the Spanish situation - the following comment from the *Review* of 18 October 1711 that the Allies would not even leave Philip in Spain "[...] *Land enough to bury him in*".

the essentials of the war policy thus far pursued and to build up a corresponding sense of public outrage.

At the same time the Whigs confidently[1] expressed their conviction that Parliament would prevent the worst from happening. Thus, pointed references to Parliament's ability to intervene are to be found in rhetorically prominent places in Whig writings, for example at the end of Maynwaring's two pamphlets *A Vindication of the Present M-y* and *Remarks upon the Present Negotiations of Peace*. Towards the end of the former Maynwaring makes the confident assertion: "[...] yet we have a sure Refuge in the P——t, which may put us out of our Pain"[2]. Even at the end of December 1711 a similar chord was struck at the end of the prose broadside *Prince Eugene's Welcome to England: Or, a Dialogue between Two Great Generals, relating to the Peace*. The clear references to the possibilities Parliament had to intervene, mainly to be found in pamphlets, provided as it were the cue that mobilised Whig supporters for an all-embracing rallying cry which pinned its hopes on the Whig majority in the Lords.

The Whig 'rhetoric of objection' was carried by impressive semantic unity and temporal co-ordination in the different genres. Under Maynwaring's aegis a clear complementarity of function can be seen particularly between pamphlet and broadside. For example, at the beginning of *An Excellent New Song, Called Mat's Peace* (1711) there are the ironical lines "For why have we spent so much Treasure in vain, /If now at the last we must give up *Spain*,/If now we must give up *Spain*" and "Why so many Battles did *Marlborough* win?/ So many strong Towns why did he take in?"[3]. The line "If now we must give up *Spain*" is a refrain which runs through the entire text. Towards the end of this broadside there is a pointed reference to the possibility that Parliament could call Bolingbroke and Harley, the Government politicians responsible, to account[4]; the prose broadside *Queries upon the Prorogation* (1711) begins with the provocative question whether it is not mysterious "that the best Ministry the Nation was ever bless'd with, shou'd be afraid to meet the best Parliament that was ever chosen, when they have nothing to offer to them, but what is for the Good of their Country?" The skilful orchestration of the media - the broadsides as it were announced to the world the essence of what was discursively worked out in the pamphlets - showed that the Opposition, which in November and December 1711 clearly put its mark on the public scene[5], was determined to offer resistance. The co-ordination achieved by Maynwaring was also reflected in the way the Whigs used their rhetoric for mutual support; to

---

1 On the strength of the Whig press campaign cf. briefly Holmes, "The Commons' Division on 'No Peace without Spain', 7 December 1711", p. 224.

2 *A Vindication of the Present M-y*, p. 51.

3 *Poems on Affairs of State. Augustan Satirical Verse, 1660-1714*, VII, ed. Ellis, 508. For an ironical exposure of the abandonment of the original war aims cf. also the last stanza but two of the broadside *The Truth at last* (1711).

4 Cf. - with appropriately threatening tone, though without explicit reference to Parliament - Hare, *Bouchain*, pp. 42-43.

5 On the efforts made by the Whigs cf. also *Memoirs of John Duke of Marlborough*, ed. Coxe, VI, 132-133.

confirm his own position in *A Letter to a High-Churchman*, for example, he referred to his earlier writings *A Letter to a Member of the October-Club* (1711)[1] and *Remarks on the Preliminary Articles Offer'd by the French King* (1711)[2]. However, despite this self-referentiality, which marked the consistent attitude of the Opposition, the Whig press campaign, even during this period of impressive public presence, did not have at its disposal a basic text which laid down the rhetorical course for all genres, as did *The Conduct of the Allies* a short time later for the Government camp.

The Government's press campaign between the publication of the Preliminaries and the appearance of *The Conduct of the Allies* was mainly in the hands of Defoe, whose indefatigable defence endeavours were responsible for the continued presence of the 'No peace without Spain' problem on the political agenda being drawn to a not inconsiderable extent into the wake of his questioning of the agreed balance-of-power maxim. The obstinacy with which Defoe pursued his own version of the theme, which compelled the *Observator* to respond[3], was met with a corresponding concentration of the Opposition's attention; it is no coincidence that, with *A Letter to a High-Churchman*, Maynwaring devoted a whole pamphlet to the refutation of *Reasons Why*. Defoe's persistent desire for argument absorbed the Opposition's attention and was reflected in his preoccupation with the position of Austria, an issue whose potential for controversy was temporarily fully exploited but which was nevertheless obviously only chosen as a 'reserve' topic, since after the onset of the phase of fierce confrontation it was surprisingly quickly and completely dropped again. In a difficult period for Government publicity Defoe's function was apparently that of a kind of buffer, and in his endeavours to make topics his own he set temporary directions for a debate which in retrospect can be seen in many respects as artificial and cleverly staged by the Government. The prominence of Defoe's approach also makes it clear that until the appearance of *The Conduct of the Allies* the line taken by the Tory pamphlet campaign was almost exclusively aimed at 'convincing' rather than polarising. Occasional militant replies such as *Cursory but Curious Observations of Mr. Ab-l R—er upon a Late Famous Pamphlet, Intituled, Remarks on the Preliminary Articles Offer'd by the F.K. in Hopes to Procure a General Peace* (1711), which are impaired by streaks of involuntary self-irony, do not blur this general impression. The reserve of the Government's publicity campaign reflected in Defoe's writings as regards vicious attacks on Marlborough[4] and the Dutch[5] at any rate indicates

1 See *A Letter to a High-Churchman*, p. 32.

2 *Ibid.*, p. 17.

3 See p. 90, note 3. On Defoe's argument with the *Observator* see also *The Letters of Daniel Defoe*, ed. Healey, p. 362.

4 See the references - which merely express criticism, but never descend to invective or even irreverence - in *Reasons why this Nation Ought to put a Speedy End to this Expensive War*, pp. 8-9, 11-13 and *Reasons why a Party among us, and also among the Confederates, are obstinately Bent against a Treaty of Peace with the French at this Time* (London, 1711), pp. 9-10, 44-47.

5 In his restrained rhetorical stance towards the Dutch Defoe may be assumed to have been the mouthpiece of Harley, of whom it is said with regard to the period preceding

that in late autumn Harley still showed particular consideration for the Whig elements in his Ministry and had perhaps not entirely given up hope, either, of maybe still being able to come to some arrangement with the Duke of Marlborough[1], or had at least kept up the appearance of such hope.

Defoe's pamphlet of the end of October or the beginning of November 1711 entitled *Armageddon: Or, the Necessity of Carrying on the War, if such a Peace Cannot be Obtained as May Render Europe Safe, and Trade Secure* shows both the flexibility which the Government then still felt obliged to maintain in the way it presented itself in public, as well as the fierce pressure created by Whig attacks. The Government's difficult position, incidentally, was also confirmed by the simultaneous persecution of unaccommodating Opposition journalists[2]. In this pamphlet, which was published by John Baker[3], and in which Defoe even avoids invoking the Austrian threat to the balance of power in Europe, the author everywhere makes clearly recognisable verbal concessions to the Whigs[4] and, going far beyond previous attempts at reaching a consensus, he does not even rule out the possibility of a continuation of the war, although this alternative is very half-heartedly presented. The attempt to deflect Opposition criticism on to extremists in the Government - Roper is branded as an instrument of the High-Fliers - and the emphatic denial of any intention to give up Spain[5] also identify this pamphlet as a document which exemplifies a domestic balance-of-power rhetoric that is still characterized by an apparent attempt to reach an understanding with the Whigs instead of provoking them. *Armageddon*, especially, is evidence of the Government's dilatoriness in finally coming clean in public; the Government's deliberate hesitation is also seen in the fact that no journalistic relief troops were sent to the aid of Defoe, who - as late as early December 1711 - brought out a further pamphlet, *The Felonious Treaty* (also published by Baker and advertised as written by the author of the *Review*), aimed at accommodating the Whigs. While maintaining the rhetoric of equidistance towards France and Austria[6], it earnestly presses

---

the crisis in December 1711: "Oxford had previously pursued a more moderate policy towards the Dutch" (Roderick Geikie and Isabel A. Montgomery, *The Dutch Barrier 1705-1719* [Cambridge, 1930], pp. 237-238).

1 Harley was, in any case, apparently more obliging to him than St. John; cf. Sheila Biddle, *Bolingbroke and Harley* (New York, 1974), p. 226.

2 See Boyer, *Quadriennium Annae Postremum or the Political State of Great Britain*, 2nd ed., vol. I and II for the Year 1711, 645-646.

3 Defoe's pamphlets published by John Baker tend to show a moderate, conciliatory rhetoric of consensus in contrast to the sharper, more aggressive tone found in the pamphlets published by John Morphew. No absolute contrasts can of course be established between the pamphlets published by these two gentlemen. Cf. on this point the instructive remarks of Backscheider, *Daniel Defoe: His Life*, pp. 292, 315-318.

4 See e.g. [Daniel Defoe], *Armageddon: Or, the Necessity of Carrying on the War, if such a Peace Cannot be Obtained as May Render Europe Safe, and Trade Secure* (London, [1711]), p. 12.

5 *Ibid.*, pp. 30-33.

6 See [Daniel Defoe], *The Felonious Treaty: Or, an Enquiry into the Reasons which Moved His Late Majesty King William of Glorious Memory, to Enter into a Treaty at two*

for the partition of Spain and gives the impression of being a last-minute attempt at some sort of agreement with the Opposition.

Leaving aside the orchestrated balance-of-power rhetoric in Defoe's journal and his pamphlets, it is at this point almost impossible to detect any co-ordination of propaganda efforts in the form of a concerted action in the rhetoric of the various genres used in the Tory campaign. In this respect Tory journalism clearly lagged behind the Whig approach at this time, which betrayed a stronger tendency to pursue a common cause; in the second phase of the turning-point debate the contrast with the Government's public image is considerable.

On account of the concealed presence of the Government's determination to carry through its peace policy, a determination revealed more between the lines by Defoe, the debate did not until the end of November 1711 concentrate on Marlborough, nor were the Dutch, despite the increased attention paid to the role of the Allies, yet the focus of the debate on foreign and war policy. Clearly, despite the earlier criticism in, for example, Davenant's *New Dialogues upon the Present Posture of Affairs* (1710)[1] and poems like Hamilton 's *The Changes*: *Or*, *Faction Vanquish'd* (1711) and the later, perceptibly more aggressive *The Peace-Haters*[2], the Government had not yet announced the end of the close season for the Dutch[3]. On the contrary, a survey of the countries figuring in the polemical interaction still shows a remarkably slight presence of the Dutch in Tory writings[4], which shortly afterwards subjected them to vehement attack, while the prominence of Austria in the writings of both parties at this time reflects how far Defoe had succeeded in forcing the opposing camp to bring before the public the balance-of-power debate which he, Defoe, had turned against the House of Habsburg. So, despite early indications of their intended journalistic course at the time of the Bouchain controversy, the Government had still not let the cat out of the bag at the end of November 1711. Despite the continuity of theme there was a different polemical focus in each of the two phases of the turning-point debate with specific points of view in each case.

---

several Times with the King of France for the Partition of the Spanish Monarchy (London, 1711), pp. 23, 41.

1 See e.g. [Charles Davenant], *New Dialogues upon the Present Posture of Affairs, the Species of Mony, National, Public Revenues, Bank and East India Company, and the Trade now Carried on between France and Holland* (London, 1710), p. 245. Cf., however, Davenant's lengthy account of the commercial disadvantages suffered by England because of Dutch machinations, especially in the *Second Report to the Honourable the Commissioners for ... Stating the Publick Accounts of the Kingdom*, published in 1712.

2 Advertised as "this day" published in *The Post Boy* of 1-3 November 1711.

3 Defoe's forbearing attitude towards the Dutch is also noticed by Laprevotte, "*The Conduct of the Allies*: contexte et originalité", p. 255.

4 Nevertheless, the Whigs could not fail to take notice of the increasing signs of a changing attitude towards the Dutch. See, for instance, the first paragraph of the preface to *The History of the Peace with France and War with Holland in the Year 1672...* (London, 1712). Although the imprint bears the date 1712, it seems probable from the context that the preface was written late in 1711. This documentary pamphlet was advertised in the *Evening Post* of 15-17 November 1711 as "This Day is published [...]".

3. THE PUBLIC DISPUTE BETWEEN DECEMBER 1711 AND APRIL 1712

With the publication of Swift's *The Conduct of the Allies* on 27 November 1711 the Government unequivocally indicated its determination to prevail in its diplomatically already advanced peace efforts, even if it meant a tough confrontation with the Opposition. On account of the extraordinary cohesive power of *The Conduct of the Allies* for the immediate development of Tory propaganda the publication date of this pamphlet, which was at once enthusiastically praised by the *Post Boy* of 29 November-1 December 1711 and, as early as its issue of 29 November-1 December 1711, strongly denounced by the *Flying-Post* as "a perfect Declaration of War against the Confederates, by the French Faction in Great Britain", can be regarded as the starting-point[1] of the journalistic volte-face in the turning-point debate. So the second phase of the debate began with Swift's thunderbolt, although of course a certain amount of time was to elapse before *The Conduct of the Allies* became the gravitational centre of the public debate. Thus the Whigs were able to launch a spirited counterattack, for, with Maynwaring's *Remarks on a False, Scandalous, and Seditious Libel, Intituled, The Conduct of the Allies*, the first part of Hare's *The Allies and the Late Ministry Defended against France* and - surprisingly - Defoe's *A Defence of the Allies and the Late Ministry: Or, Remarks on the Tories New Idol*, Swift's pamphlet had three substantial replies to consider in the first ten days of December 1711, even before it was able to succeed in easing journalistic pressure on the Government camp. At the same time it is indicative of the provocative effect of *The Conduct of the Allies* that with the first reply from the opposing camp, Maynwaring's *Remarks on a False, Scandalous, and Seditious Libel*, a work entered the fray that, in its overheated polemics - which find expression in the continual use of emotionally charged, polarising vocabulary such as "religion", "liberty", "slavery", "universal monarchy", "the Revolution", "the Protestant Succession" and "High Church" -, clearly sought to outdo Swift's pamphlet. At any rate, until the middle of December, the Whigs maintained their strong position in the leading journalistic genre, whose breadth of approach was underlined by the 'Harleyite' publication *The Whigs Appeal to the Tories* (1711).

In the second half of the month, towards the beginning of the new year, however, powerful fanfares issued from the Tory camp in the form of two pamphlets which broadcast militant polemics and proclaimed the Government's determination to go on the offensive. Both pamphlets evidently shared the work of further hotting up the Tory campaign, which came into full swing in January 1712 and was intended to take over leadership in the formation of public opinion. Functional complementarity was maintained by the one pamphlet having a primarily

---

[1] This pamphlet did not, as J.A. Downie, "*The Conduct of the Allies*: The Question of Influence", *The Art of Jonathan Swift*, ed. Clive T. Probyn (London, 1978), p. 111 states, represent the climax of a campaign that had already been started, but marked the spectacular overture to the decisive phase of the Government's propaganda.

foreign-policy bias, while the other concentrated on domestic affairs. Whilst public resentment against the Dutch was stirred up by the gross exaggeration of Ferguson's *An Account of the Obligations the States of Holland Have to Great-Britain, and the Return they Have Made both in Europe and the Indies. With Reflections upon the Peace* (1711), which unambiguously shows that the Government had now thrown the Dutch to the wolves, the anonymous - and almost twice as long - popular 'pamphlet' *Oliver's Pocket Looking-Glass, New Fram'd and Clean'd, to Give a Clear View of the Great Modern Colossus* (1711), which received even wider publicity through a further edition and reproduced Swift's conspiracy thesis from *The Conduct of the Allies*, presented an extensive treatment of the sins attributed to the Duke of Marlborough by the Tories and, immediately before the beginning of the heated phase of the debate, put at the disposal of the Tory propaganda machine the surely welcome aid of a rich treasure-house for the final dismantling of the Commander-in-Chief. The greater length of *Oliver's Pocket Looking-Glass*, with its emphasis on domestic policy, was a clear indication of what the Government was going to make its main priority in the weeks to follow. This intention was also unmistakably indicated by the publication, on 22 December 1711, of the Votes of the House of Commons reviewing government expenditure and implicating Marlborough; within a week *The Report of the Commissioners for Taking, Examining, and Stating the Publick Accounts of the Kingdom* (1711) was also printed. By openly placing the present Whigs on the same level as the republicans and regicides of 1649, which only reflected the dramatic intimidation of the Queen by her leading Ministers[1], incidentally, both Ferguson's *Account* and *Oliver's Pocket Looking-Glass* manifested the Tories' resolve to seek confrontation.

Resolute party-political confrontation was also signalised early in December 1711 and towards the turn of the year by two broadsides, Swift's *An Excellent New Song, Being the Intended Speech of a Famous Orator against Peace* (1711) and William Shippen's *The Character of a Certain Whigg* (1712), which exposed two prominent Opposition politicians, the Earl of Nottingham and the Earl of Wharton[2], to public denigration. Also right at the end of 1711 *The Story of Typhon* bore unmistakable signs of the Government's intention to deal severely with Marlborough. In contrast, even the Whig prose broadside *Prince Eugene's Welcome to England: Or, a Dialogue between two Great Generals, relating to the Peace*, a spirited reply to the "delight in war" reproach, showed first signs of the Whigs defensively giving way, in spite of persistently pointing to the "*Chymaera of Universal Conquest*". In this genre, too, which visibly and audibly testified to polemical presence, there was quantitative proof of a fresh consolidation of the Government's publicity campaign during the transition month of December. If in November 1711 the Whigs still had a numerical advantage over the Tories in terms of broadsides, the Tories up to then making practically no use of the genre, the Government campaign at least caught up with the Whigs in the next month, and at

1 Cf. Churchill, *Marlborough*, VI, 503.

2 This politician was also subject to a satirical attack in the prose broadside *The Earl of Wh-on's Speech to the House of Lords* (1711).

the turn of the year already showed unmistakable signs of taking the offensive, an initiative strikingly manifested by the broadside during January 1712.

In January 1712 there was a quantum leap in the public controversy surrounding the termination of the War of the Spanish Succession. This leap can be traced back to the thorough intensification of the Government campaign and was most clearly reflected in the lively participation of the most varied forms of political propaganda in the Tories' attempts to shape public opinion. This new level of participation can be especially well illustrated from the angle of the media which generally did not stand in the centre of the public debate. At the beginning of 1712 both the sermon and the broadside articulated with impressive unanimity the Government's determination to carry through its peace programme; with a hitherto unknown intensity both genres were called upon by the Government to conduct its broad-based publicity campaign. After the first phase of the turning-point debate, in which the Tories made no use at all of the sermon, mid-January 1712 saw no fewer than three fast sermons lending resonance to the Government position by continuing the emotionalization of the peace debate already begun in Tory propaganda and pleading for an end to the war for humanitarian reasons. While Trapp's sermon does this in the style of rigorous ideological confrontation, the sermons of Altham and George Smalridge express the same desire in a more reserved manner[1].

The impressive level of participation on the Tory side, which gave Government propaganda unprecedented cohesion, is confirmed by the broadside, which - even if in a different way from the sermon - constitutes a particularly event-oriented genre. After it had for months played a very limited role in the Tory campaign and had, as it were, to be rediscovered in December 1711, the broadside - stimulated no doubt by Marlborough's dismissal and the creation of twelve new Peers - took on the distinctive function of building up the novel opinion-forming pressure of Government propaganda. In the short term the broadside, which also hung on to the emotionalization[2] of propaganda well orchestrated by the Government, even became the focus of Tory dominance in the shaping of opinion, reflecting the way the Tories' public image outstripped that of the Whigs at the beginning of the year. In January 1712 the Tories not only succeeded in gaining a numerical advantage over the Whigs in the medium of the broadside, they also drove them on to the defensive by their political spiritedness. The broadside became the spearhead[3] of Government propaganda in so far as it tailored the discussion to the role of the Duke of Marlborough more rigorously than all the other genres, though

---

1 See on this the section on the sermon in the chapter "The Main Genres of the Public Debate: Profiles and Functions".

2 In *A New-Years Gift for the Plunderers of the World: With an Ancient Prophecy* (1712) Francis Hoffman reproaches those who want to prolong the war: "*Great Britain* feels them to her cost, / And *Infants* who have Fathers lost".

3 The dramatic increase in broadside production on the Tory side is documented by the activity of Hoffman, whose numerous broadsides lampooning Marlborough in Harley's service almost all appeared in quick succession in the first months of 1712 and reflected, as in a burning-mirror, the Government's propagandistic punch.

quite in line with them. The determination of the Government to settle their account with their party-political opponent was nowhere so clearly expressed as in the massive bombardment with which the Whig hero was to be finally knocked off his pedestal at the beginning of 1712. In order to increase its impact there was an almost modern synchronisation of Tory propaganda, which can be seen in the way several genres, the *Examiner* among them, united to shower Marlborough with a barrage of regularly repeated accusations designed to completely destroy his public reputation. After Mrs. Manley, at the beginning of the first phase of the turning-point debate, had still argued with accusations of rapacity, ambition and luck[1] in *The D. of M-h's Vindication*, and after Swift, at the beginning of the second phase, had explicitly formulated the conspiracy thesis in *The Conduct of the Allies* and added the incriminating point of Marlborough's reaching out for the throne - an accusation most likely suggested by Harley[2] or others around him[3] and immediately reproduced in *Oliver's Pocket Looking-Glass* -, the broadsides were in a position to aim their polemical arrows at Marlborough with more accuracy on the basis of 'evidence' made available in pamphlets. Marlborough found himself as it were subjected to a political X-ray examination and, in the spectrum of interrelated accusations, he was completely taken apart in public.

The specific function of the broadside as the vanguard of the campaign of destruction to which the Tories took off in January 1712 is illuminated by the fact that for the moment this medium dropped all other propagandistically exploitable aspects and on only few occasions played the card of stirring up anti-Dutch resentment[4], which had quickly been introduced by the pamphlets; thus the absolute concentration of the broadside on Marlborough shows that at the decisive point Tory propaganda put all its faith in the effect of the anti-Marlborough campaign. The arsenal of incriminating evidence mustered in the broadsides at this time preempted - sometimes quite plainly - the findings that would hopefully be presented by the investigating committee set up against Marlborough, as is shown by the broadsides *The Truth's Come Out at last: Or, the Downfall of a Great Favourite*, *The Grand Enquiry, Or, What's to be Done with Him* and Swift's *A Fable of the Widow and her Cat.*

"Avarice[5] and Ambition"[6] formed as it were the first links in the chain of accusations; it was easy to associate with them the charge of conspiring against

---

1 That the reproach of having been merely fortunate could be easily disproved in logical terms (see, for instance, *The Secret History of the Geertruydenbergh Negotation*, pp. 10-11 and the *Medley* of 21-24 March 1712) did not prevent its being voiced regularly.

2 Harley (named Epiboulius) and his associates had already been accused of such wiles by the author of *The Impartial Secret History of Arlus, Fortunatus, and Odolphus, Ministers of State to the Empress of Grand-Insula. ...* ([London], 1710), pp. 18-19.

3 Cf. Churchill, *Marlborough*, VI, 492.

4 See, for example, Hoffman's broadside *Vulpoon in the Snare; or, a Hue and Cry after Eight and Twenty Millions Sunk by the Hawkubite Crew* (1712).

5 In the foreword "To the Reader" of *Mars Stript of his Armour: Or, the Army Displayed in all its True Colours*, first published in 1707, Ward had used the ominous terms "*Avarice*" and "*private Advantage*", in this way levelling his guns at Marlborough, though in

Queen and country to Marlborough's own advantage and that of his family. The accusations of personal ambition directed at him, as reflected also in his desire for supreme command for life, culminated in the charge that he coveted the crown, an accusation that clothed his hybrid claims to power in memorable symbolism and formed the climax of the Tory incrimination rhetoric. Virulent articulations of the latter charge are to be found in *The Story of Typhon* and in Elijah Fenton's *M. Manlius Capitolinus* as well as Richard Newcomb's *The Queen's and the Duke of Ormond's New Toast* at the beginning of 1712. This sensational accusation[1], incidentally, merely made public the internal whisperings of Government politicians[2]. The name "King John" applied to Marlborough, which is also used in Newcomb's broadside, can be found as early as in Mrs. Manley's *The Secret History of Queen Zarah* (1705) and is supposed to have been used in the meantime with particular spitefulness by Abigail Masham[3]. The charge, which was supported, for example, by the *Examiner* in its issues of 21 and 28 February 1712 and later particularly by the poem *Peace, Or, no Peace* (1712)[4], was among the few 'argumentative' items not immediately connected with the investigation against Marlborough that remained topical well into March because they did not merely serve as 'documentary evidence' in the campaign to achieve a condemnation but rather contributed further to Marlborough's political and moral disqualification.

But the intense journalistic bombardment of Marlborough in the broadsides[5] must not be seen in isolation; it is only in conjunction with the other genres that the streamlined concentration of Tory propaganda on Marlborough's 'destruction' really becomes apparent. Although it is correct to point to "the convenient oversimplification of a complex issue"[6] by the use of verse fables, the importance in propagandistic terms of such broadsides lay in their being able to engage in concerted action together with other media. Indeed, the Tory propaganda network had

---

the chapter "Of a Captain-General" (1709 ed., pp. 10-12), in spite of a slightly critical tone, these were not yet directly fired off.

6 This dual formula was used on the last page of [William Wagstaffe], *The Story of the St. Alb-ns Ghost, or the Apparition of Mother Haggy. Collected from the Best Manuscripts* (London, 1712).

1 Late in 1710 a Whig publication had explicitly referred to this strategy of the new Ministers to intimidate the Queen: *The Second Part of the Impartial Secret History of Arlus, Fortunatus, and Odolphus*, p. 14. It could only be capped by the more lurid but also more transient allegation of an attempt on her life (see *The Story of the St. Alb-ns Ghost*, pp. 14-15).

2 See a remark in this connection made by Earl Poulett in a letter to the Earl of Oxford dated November 1711: HMC, *Portland MSS*, V (Norwich, 1899), 119.

3 Cf. David Green, *Sarah Duchess of Marlborough* (London, 1967), p. 146.

4 See *Grandsire Hambden's Ghost. And Peace, Or, no Peace. Two Poems. Together with a Prefatory Answer to Some Late Whiggish Scurrility, especially, a certain Dedication* (London, 1712), p. 37.

5 In the broadside *No Queen or no General, or a Story Told to Prince Eugene upon his Arrival in England* (1712) the Duke figures as Belisarius and is subject to the sinister influence of his wife.

6 Harris, *A Study of the Paper War*, p. 310.

reached a degree of coherence at the beginning of 1712 such as had hitherto not been seen in the public controversy over the termination of the War of the Spanish Succession. As early as in its issue of 12-15 January 1712 the *Protestant Post-Boy* testified to the impact of the campaign. The various genres achieved such perfect co-ordination that they succeeded as it were in spinning a web of political incrimination so dense that Marlborough was left with no means of escape. His rapacity, which did not stop short of embezzlement, made him unfit for royal service, according to the pamphlet *The Birth, Parentage, and Rise of J——D. of M——, together with the Reasons of his Present Disgrace* (1712)[1]. The 'royal' charge, the culminating myth of Tory propaganda which Swift had opportunely revived in *The Conduct of the Allies*, was echoed in pamphlets, for instance in King's *Rufinus*[2] in January, and indirectly in Wagstaffe's popular allegory *The Story of the St. Alb-ns Ghost, or the Apparition of Mother Haggy* in February. It was also presented in *No Punishment, no Government: And no Danger even in the Worst Designs* (1712)[3]. How skilfully Tory public relations work was orchestrated at the crucial moment of the turning-point debate was underlined in the already mentioned issues of the *Examiner* of 21 and 28 February 1712, in which the graphic 'Man of Gold' vision[4] is used to present Marlborough as a man driven by unscrupulous ambition and rapacity[5] making a grab for the crown, whilst Harley, the Queen's selfless adviser, pursues the welfare of the deceived sovereign. The application to Marlborough of the code-word "arbitrary" in the second issue, a word much used by the Whigs to denounce absolutist conditions[6], also demonstrated the self-assurance of Tory propaganda, the sheer quantity of which was impressive. The new image of Marlborough about to be forced on the public consciousness by the relentless Tory propaganda machine could soon be written large on the very title-page of the satirical oriental narrative *The Perquisite-Monger; or the Rise and Fall of Ingratitude* (1712). The *Examiner* of 24 January 1712 had condemned Marlborough for converting "BREAD, defrauded from poor half-famished Soldiers, into a new Name of PERQUISITE". The joint thrust of all genres participating in the shaping of public opinion was a manifestation of the Tory claim to leadership in the propaganda war at the beginning of 1712. The unscrupulous concentration of the polemics on Marlborough, and the unprecedented personalisation of the public debate, show how forceful Tory propaganda had become and to what extent the rhetorical profile of Government publicity had been

---

1 See *The Birth, Parentage, and Rise of J——D. of M-, together with the Reasons of his Present Disgrace* (London, 1712), p. 7.

2 See [William King], *Rufinus: Or an Historical Essay on the Favourite-Ministry under Theodosius the Great and his Son Arcadius* (Edinburgh, 1712), p. 6.

3 (London, 1712), pp. 8 and 16.

4 In Hoffman's broadside *The D- of M- Turn'd Conjurer: Or, the History of the Golden Apple* (1712) Marlborough is said to have "Turn'd *Bread* to *Gold*, which is his God".

5 With regard to Marlborough's mercenariness cf. also Hoffman's broadside *The White-Hall Prophecy, lately Found under the Ruins of that Royal Chapel* (1712).

6 Thus in *The Observator* in its edition of 20-23 February 1712, whose detailed reply directed against "*our* French *Faction*" did not of course succeed in tackling the harmful image of greediness.

switched from the factual argumentation of the first phase to polarisation through personalisation in the second, where no important Tory pamphlet appeared which genuinely engaged in factual discussion.

The Government's new political line was also supported by Defoe, who, in January 1712, once again became the most prolific pamphleteer on the Tory side, this time, however, largely adopting the more intense polemical course of Government propaganda. This adaptation of Defoe the pamphleteer[1] completes the Government's amazingly homogeneous public image at the beginning of 1712. Defoe's first pamphlet of January 1712, a work bearing the meaningful alternative title *No Queen: Or, no General*, to which - certainly not accidentally - Leslie approvingly alluded a short time later in *Salt for the Leach* (1712)[2], largely took up the charges made against Marlborough, for instance in the symbolic accusation of favouring his family at the expense of national interest[3]. Without vilifying Marlborough it insinuated under the cover of historical analogy that the latter's involvement in Whig politics posed a threat to the Queen herself. *The Conduct of Parties in England, more especially of those Whigs who now Appear against the New Ministry, and a Treaty of Peace* (1712), as the title already shows, demonstrated the pressure of the incriminations generated by Swift's pilot publication; conceived as a purely domestic dig at the Junto, this pamphlet made concentrated use of the word "Spoils" to attack the political opponent at home[4] and once again took up the suggestive charge of Marlborough's power-hungry feathering of his family's nest[5], to which the meaningful words "Exorbitant Gain"[6] are applied. Precisely this pamphlet, in which the author presents the thesis that all the charges made against Marlborough by the Tories ultimately went back to the Whigs or, to be more precise, the Junto, underlines the fact that Defoe was fully incorporated as a 'Whig' writer in the hardening of propaganda in Government journalism. Finally, the emotional pamphlet *Peace, Or Poverty* (1712), published by John Morphew, evoked the contrast between the Dutch amassing of wealth and English impoverishment and thus completed the impression that at the beginning of 1712 the pamphleteer Defoe was at last toeing the line of Tory propaganda.

The reaction of Whig propaganda to the Tory offensive launched in early 1712 can be very well illustrated by the more supporting genres, the sermon and espe-

---

1 Significantly, the author of the *Review* - doubtless owing to the difficulties caused by his previous open and vigorous support of Marlborough - did not join in the intensified polemics against him, which was an easier task for the pamphleteer with his greater anonymity. Cf. a pertinent observation by Sutherland, *Daniel Defoe*, p. 55.

2 See Leslie, *Salt for the Leach*, p. 6.

3 See Defoe, *No Queen: Or, no General*, pp. 11 and 17. - Cf. also the reference in another pamphlet which appeared about that time and could well have been written by Defoe: *Plunder and Bribery further Discover'd, in a Memorial Humbly Offer'd to the British Parliament* (London, 1712), p. 5.

4 See [Daniel Defoe], *The Conduct of Parties in England, more especially of those Whigs who now Appear against the New Ministry, and a Treaty of Peace* (London, 1712), pp. 29, 30 and 33.

5 *Ibid.*, pp. 15-16.

6 *Ibid.*, p. 29.

cially the broadside. Both in the fast sermons of 16 January 1712 and in the broadsides of this period the Whigs, who had reacted at once to Marlborough's dismissal through Steele's intrepid but excessively eulogistic public letter *The Englishman's Thanks to the Duke of Marlborough* (1712), were still developing quite a powerful rhetoric of resistance[1] aimed at shocking the public by references to the dangers of a bad peace. But it soon became clear that the Whig broadsides were a poor match for the intense concentration on Marlborough in the corresponding Tory media, which, as it were, amounted to virtually coercing the Whigs with this theme. While Tory broadsides, which temporarily ignored even the Dutch as a potentially worthwhile topic, unanimously turned on Marlborough and made him the only target of their attacks, while leaving the repeated objections of Whig journalism without a reply, the Whigs lacked a comparable target and felt compelled to pay more attention to Tory topics such as Marlborough[2] and the Dutch, against which genuine Whig concerns like, for instance, the danger of French hegemony were pushed into the background or not mentioned at all. From the fact that, for example, in *The Protestant Post-Boy* the 'No peace without Spain' topic was touched on only in the issue of 1-3 January 1712, whereas Marlborough was always present, it may be concluded that in January 1712 the Whig periodicals, too, went on the defensive. At the same time it became apparent that the broadside was a genre with inherent rhetorical limitations, which made it basically unsuited for concrete argument and difficult to operate from the defensive position to which the Whigs now fled. So the broadsides - although some like the not very powerful *Where's Your Impeachment Now? Or the D- ['s] Safe Delivery* (1712)[3] tried to exploit the circumstance that the Commons' proceedings of 24 January 1712 did not result in impeachment - had to leave comments on the wide-ranging accusations against Marlborough to discursive genres like the pamphlet, which, however, seemed to lose its sharpness in the second half of January. Especially effective propaganda, like for example the charges in the *Examiner* that Marlborough had conspired against Queen and country and coveted the crown, could not be dealt with in broadsides at all and had to be taken up by other media[4]. But in the final analysis there was no appropriate defence against such tactics.

In the dismantling of Marlborough at the beginning of 1712, in which broadsides played an essential part, the Tories relied on the fact that it was difficult to counter well-timed and emotional polarisation with sound argument. In view of the violent escalation of Tory invective against Marlborough, which approached

---

1 In fact, this kind of rhetoric became increasingly less frequent towards the end of the turning-point debate, occurring almost exclusively in periodicals and newspapers; see, e.g., the *Medley* of 21-25 April 1712.

2 See, for instance, the *Flying-Post* of 26-29 January and 31 January-2 February 1712.

3 Although this beast-fable is by no means unambiguous, its topical thrust squares ill with Horn's assignation as "anti-Marlborough " (*Marlborough: A Survey*, p. 419).

4 For the difficulties experienced by Whig journalists to respond adequately to the reckless Tory detraction of Marlborough see, for instance, *The Protestant Post-Boy* of 7-9 February 1712. See also *The Medley*, 17-21 March, 21-24 March and 4-7 April 1712.

its climax in January, the statement from *The King of France's Letter to the Cardinal de Noailles, Archbishop of Paris* (1712), a Whig prose broadside in the form of a fictitious letter[1] from an exultant Louis XIV, can certainly be applied to the public scene: "[...] we have receiv'd the agreeable News of the surrender and demolishing of the strong important Fortress of *Marl——gh*, hitherto thought impregnable [...]". In the light of the political adversities it is not surprising that as early as the beginning of 1712 texts appeared whose very titles contain an element of melancholy, for instance *The Soldiers' Lamentation for the Loss of their General* and even the energetic broadside *A New Protestant Litany*, attributed to Maynwaring. A truly elegiac aura surrounds Charles Dive's *On the Duke of Marlborough. A Poem*, a broadside which appeared in the first half of February 1712. *The Fable of the Shepherd and his Dog, in Answer to the Fable of the Widow and her Cat* (1712), a meek reply to Swift's aggressive piece, fitted in with the picture of Whig discouragement. The Whig broadside was now only rhetorically effective when it ignored the Marlborough issue and focused on the disappointment about the aims of the war. The fifth stanza of the broadside *The French Preliminaries. A New Ballad to the Old Tune of Packington's Pound*, which appeared in mid-February 1712, for instance, ironically conveyed the following message: "*The King consents likewise, that instead of* Spain/ *A Barrier shall for the Empire remain*". Characteristic of the relative strengths which became clearly visible in February 1712 was the aggressive self-confidence of the Tory broadsides *Resolutions without doors*, *The Fable of the Cods-Heads* and Swift's *The Fable of Midas*, to which the discomfited Whigs had no answer. This self-confidence also manifested itself in the retrospective description contained in *Grandsire Hambden's Ghost* (1712), in which, as in Hoffman's broadside *The Portraiture of Oliverus Secundus* (1712), Prince Eugene's visit presents an opportunity for further reviling of the General. In the public battle surrounding Marlborough the Whigs were visibly throwing in the towel.

The mood conveyed at least partially by the Whig broadside is confirmed by a glance at the propaganda giant, the pamphlet. The pamphlet, still employed by the Whigs with great energy in the first phase of the turning-point debate, had lost its cutting edge - it seems to be symptomatic of the Whig pamphlet's loss of thrust from 1712 on that there were no more front-rank pamphlets by Maynwaring in this period. Characteristic of the state of Whig pamphleteering at the climax of the agitation surrounding Marlborough was the resignation with which the author of *Our Ancestors as Wise as We: Or, Ancient Precedents for Modern Facts* (1712) addressed his supposed reader at the beginning and challenged him to look for any precedents in the writings of the past: "*See whether in them you can find any Generals that, after such great and eminent Services, after so many Victories and such Successes, were first turned out by their Prince, and then affronted by every paultry Sribler*"[2]. With its high proportion of purely factual instruction and its

---

1 Regarding this genre cf. also the broadside *The French King's Letter to Pope Clement XI, Anno 1712* (1712).

2 Burnet, *Our Ancestors as Wise as We: Or, Ancient Precedents for Modern Facts. In Answer to a Letter from a Noble Lord*, p. 4. - The epithet "outspoken" (Harris, *A Study*

forced recourse to historical analogies, the quoted pamphlet by Burnet, *Our Ancestors as Wise as We*, was at the same time characteristic of current Whig pamphlets, which, in order to change political opinion, seemed to rely solely on factual information[1], particularly the imparting of historical data. In its pronounced emphasis on historical argumentation Whig journalism showed that it was no longer a match for Tory polemics and was seeking refuge in a second-choice expedient. It is true that Whig pamphleteers, as illustrated by many of Maynwaring's writings, had relied quite conspicuously on factualism, but this massing of facts had always led to a corresponding polemical militancy, as can be seen in the deliberate use of highly-charged, polarising language. Of course, some of this well-tried repertoire of set phrases was still present, but now it often seemed more like an addition born of resignation rather than an expression of a fighting spirit, as is documented by the pamphlet *The Duke of M-h's Vindication. In Answer to a Pamphlet Falsely so Called* (1712). It seems to square with this prevailing fatalistic mood that Maynwaring's *The History of Hannibal and Hanno* (1712), which severely criticised Harley, was "dispers'd chiefly among his own Friends"[2].

The rhetorical 'makeshift profile' just described of Burnet's *Our Ancestors as Wise as We* can also be seen in such pamphlets as Hare's *The Barrier-Treaty Vindicated* (1712), the same author's *The Treaty Between Her Majesty and the States-General* (1712), the *Remarks on Some Extracts, Published in a Paper, Called The Supplement of Friday, March 28, 1712*, which appeared at the end of March 1712, and even Maynwaring's pamphlet *A Short Account and Defence of the Barrier-Treaty*[3], which was not published at the time. Even Hare's factually solid pamphlet *The Barrier-Treaty Vindicated*, which is impressive for its wealth of instruction, seemed by its almost spectacular refusal to adopt a polemical course to betray that in this respect the Whigs could no longer keep pace with the Tories and were deliberately employing secondary options. With the virtual elimination of polemics these pamphlets, which obviously also pursued the long-term aim of preventing historical events from being distorted by the Tories[4], sometimes approach the objective style of justification employed in documentary accounts such as *The Sense of the Nation, concerning the Duke of Marlborough* (1712) or *The Information against the Duke of Marlborough. And his Answer* (1712)[5]. Practically the only exception - alongside the plucky *The Dutch Barrier Our's* (1712)[6],

---

of the Paper War, p. 335) does not fit the rhetorical approach of the pamphlet as a whole.

1 On this see also the *Flying-Post* of 5-8 April 1712 with its extensive cataloguing of English and Dutch computations of quotas of ships.

2 Oldmixon, *The Life and Posthumous Works of Arthur Maynwaring*, p. 144.

3 See *ibid.*, pp. 227-247.

4 See a remark in this connection made by Hare in *The Allies and the Late Ministry Defended against France and the Present Friends of France* [part IV] (London, 1712), p. 84.

5 Regarding the latter, cf. *The Marlborough-Godolphin Correspondence*, ed. Henry L. Snyder, 3 vols. (Oxford, 1975), III, 1685, note 2.

6 Geikie and Montgomery (*The Dutch Barrier 1705-1719*, p. 253) do not differentiate between the Whig Barrier pamphlets in terms of rhetorical profile.

which was probably written by the same author - was the pamphlet most often attributed to Oldmixon, *Remarks upon Remarks: Or the Barrier-Treaty and the Protestant Succession Vindicated* (1712), which could still have come out of Maynwaring's workshop - at least it displays much of his polemical brilliance. For instance, the author defuses Swift's antithesis between advantages for the Dutch and disadvantages for the English with reference to the Dutch barrier by asking the following question: "Do we not in effect conquer for our Selves, when we conquer for Them?"[1] In Hare's *The Barrier-Treaty Vindicated* and Oldmixon's *Remarks upon Remarks* there seemed once again to be something like the division of functions that was adopted by Maynwaring and Hare in their immediate responses to *The Conduct of the Allies* in December 1711. Despite the polemical resistance of *Remarks upon Remarks*, however, it is impossible to overlook the declining vitality of Whig pamphlets, which had lost the capability of decisive remonstrance that had long characterized them and broadly speaking no longer had any rhetorical equivalent to pit against the political aggression of Government propaganda. In the new year genuine polemical commitment[2] on the Whig side could mainly be found in the press, the *Flying-Post*[3] and the *Observator* especially having retained much of their former vigour and subjecting the opposing camp to stinging attacks even under adverse circumstances.

The ever widening gulf between Whigs and Tories with respect to polemical 'bite' can be further illustrated by comparing Tory pamphlets of the same period. In January and February 1712 Wagstaffe's popular publications *The Representation of the Loyal Subjects of Albinia* and *The Story of the St. Alb-ns Ghost* as well as Swift's *Some Remarks on the Barrier Treaty, between Her Majesty and the States-General* exhibited a polemical aggressiveness to which the Whigs had no comparable answer. *A Vindication of Oliver Cromwell, and the Whiggs of Forty One, to our Modern Low Churchmen. With some Reflections upon the Bar-r Treaty* (1712), which openly accused Marlborough of treachery, though not by name, even went beyond the by now customary imputations by advancing the thesis that the present Whigs were much worse than their evil predecessors who had not betrayed England to Holland. In his detraction of Marlborough and the Whigs the author of the last-named pamphlet expanded on his slightly earlier publication

1 *Remarks upon Remarks: Or the Barrier-Treaty and the Protestant Succession Vindicated. In Answer to the False and Treasonable Reflections of the Author of The Conduct of the Allies* (London, 1711 [1712?]), p. 17.

2 Whig polemical diffidence even affected a genre normally devoted to noisy expression of political sentiment see the 'dialogue broadside' *You-Trick, or I-Trick: Or, we Trick you all* (1712), where the French king turns out to be the beneficiary of Anglo-Dutch dissensions. The Whig objection in the supplement *To be Given gratis to the Buyers of the Half Sheet, Entituled, A View of the Taxes, Funds, and Publick Revenues of England* (1712) was also remarkably mild.

3 The *Flying-Post* of 31 January-2 February 1712, for example, contains the following reproach: "Therefore this Libeller [the *Examiner*] is for preferring the worst Peace that France can allow us, to a successful War and 'tis none of his Fault if Lewis XIV don't take the Hint, and insist on Terms still lower than those which he has offer'd us by his new Preliminaries".

No Punishment, no Government: And no Danger even in the Worst Designs. The relentless pursuit of Marlborough as a war-profiteer and would-be usurper showed that the final humiliation spared him through Parliament stopping short of impeachment was offset by his public execution through Tory propaganda. The concern about the Tories' unrestrained use of language in *Reflections upon the Present Posture of Affairs* (1712)[1] was a clear expression of the Whigs' embarrassment in the face of the Tories' polemical vigour. The tendency of Government propaganda to indulge in emotionally-charged, polarising polemics was further pursued by Defoe who, in his pamphlet *Imperial Gratitude, Drawn from a Modest View of the Conduct of the Emperor Charles VI and the King of Spain Charles III*, published at the end of February 1712, simultaneously continued his own particular line by applying to Austria the rhetoric incriminating the Dutch Ally and tried to find a polemical link with the topic imposed by *The Conduct of the Allies*. At the same time, however, Defoe presumably did not wish to lose sight of Whig addressees and put his work on a firm factual basis in order to present them with a broad persuasive approach[2]. With Defoe's application to Austria of the 'inadequacy rhetoric' used by Swift to pillory Dutch shortcomings the last piece of an energetic Tory publicity campaign fell into place in *Imperial Gratitude*.

4. THE POLEMICAL IMPACT OF *THE CONDUCT OF THE ALLIES*

The repeated mention of *The Conduct of the Allies* is an indication of the outstanding significance of Swift's pamphlet for the progress of the public debate. Indeed, *The Conduct of the Allies*, which was reprinted no fewer than seven times by the end of March 1712, may be seen as the key-text of the turning-point debate, and it had both short- and long-term effects on the course of the public discussion. This can also be seen in the regular references to it during the second phase of the turning-point debate. In frequency of reference in other texts *The Conduct of the Allies* far surpasses all other pamphlets and is quoted almost as many times as all other pamphlets together! The fact that Whig writings explicitly refer to *The Conduct of the Allies* about four times as often as Tory writings shows how great a challenge this aggressive pamphlet presented to the other side. The high frequency with which it is mentioned in Whig writings underlines the fact that the Whigs simply could not help taking up Swift's arguments and how he weighed them. The catalytic effect of *The Conduct of the Allies* is not only revealed by the ubiquity of references to it in the writings of the other camp, however. It is also

1 See *Reflections upon the Present Posture of Affairs: With Relation to the Treaty of Peace, now on Foot. In a Letter to a Friend* (London, 1712), pp. 41-44. Cf. also *The Medley* of 12-16 May 1712.

2 Sober rhetoric is a distinguishing mark of the pamphlet *A Prospect for Establishing the General Peace, by a more Equal Partition than has hitherto been Proposed* (1712), which followed Defoe's anti-Austrian approach but was also critical of the Dutch.

shown - and at least as powerfully and impressively - in the cohesive power that *The Conduct of the Allies* exercised over the direction taken by the whole Tory propaganda campaign. Tory writings of all genres visibly followed Swift's firm thematic and linguistic guidelines, so that the comparative paucity of explicit intertextual references in Government journalism is not a reliable gauge of the thrust emanating from *The Conduct of the Allies* for the Tories. The smaller number of references to *The Conduct of the Allies* in Tory writings can also be explained by the paramount position of o n e text which almost as a matter of course provided the basis for the more subordinate endeavours of Tory propaganda. Thus, with reference to anti-Dutch polemics, the caustic Whig pamphlet *The Dutch Barrier Our's: Or, the Interest of England and Holland Inseparable* was quite right to emphasise the preeminent influence of *The Conduct*, "under whose Auspices, the little Curs that have since fall'n upon their High Mightinesses have their Being and Merit"[1].

In conclusion I want to take a closer look at the thematic and linguistic aspects of *The Conduct of the Allies* in order to show the polemical impetus that was its essential contribution to the superior profile of Tory propaganda at the end of the turning-point debate. For it was not least owing to *The Conduct of the Allies*' expansive polemical power that the Tories were able to gain decisive political ground in the debate while at the same time the Whigs had to abandon their topics or have them restricted. With his conspiracy thesis, prepared in *The Examiner*[2], which expressly put the Duke of Marlborough in direct opposition to Queen and country, Swift set a topic for which on the one hand Tory propaganda provided a richly-orchestrated sounding-board, while on the other it was almost impossible to reply to on account of its assertive character. An instructive example of the way Swift gave an enduring topic polemical bite is provided by his treatment of the Succession question, which in *The Conduct of the Allies* he coupled with his expounding of the Dutch Succession guarantee in the Barrier Treaty[3]. While previously this combination of topics was to be found neither in Whig nor in Tory pamphlets, after the publication of *The Conduct of the Allies* it determined the argumentation to such an extent that the majority of Whig pamphlets followed Swift's lead, and only few retained the traditional approach of the first phase of the turning-point debate, which only brought in Jacobitism. The significance of Swift's shift in emphasis can be seen in the fact that in its wake both the four most important explicit rejoinders to Swift's pamphlet, that is Maynwaring's *Remarks on a False, Scandalous, and Seditious Libel*, Hare's *The Allies and the Late Ministry Defended against France*, Defoe's *A Defence of the Allies and the Late Ministry* and *A Full Answer to The Conduct of the Allies* (1712), and the central Whig

---

1 *The Dutch Barrier Our's: Or the Interest of England and Holland Inseparable. With Reflections on the Insolent Treatment the Emperor and States-General Have Met with from the Author of the Conduct, and his Brethren* (London, 1712), p. 17.

2 Cf. W.A. Speck, "From Principles to Practice: Swift and Party Politics", *The World of Jonathan Swift. Essays for the Tercentenary*, ed. Brian Vickers (Oxford, 1968), pp. 83-84.

3 See Swift, *Political Tracts 1711-1713*, pp. 26-27.

pamphlets of the Barrier controversy, namely *The Barrier-Treaty Vindicated*, *The Treaty Between Her Majesty and the States-General*, *Remarks upon Remarks* and *The Dutch Barrier Our's*, had to involve themselves in Swift's line of argument, which was reinforced polemically by the latter himself in *Some Remarks on the Barrier Treaty*[1]. In *The Observator*, too, the situation criticised by Swift was taken up on several occasions[2].

The third example of Swift's ability to determine the public agenda - at times it seemed almost like a monopoly - is provided by the way he shifted the focus of the debate from one nation to another. *The Conduct of the Allies* is also a text which introduced a paradigmatic change in so far as it was the first pamphlet which in the discussion of the termination of the War of the Spanish Succession named Holland considerably more frequently than France. Although this numerical preference for Holland as opposed to France was only repeated once - in fact in an increased measure - in Ferguson's anti-Dutch *Account*, the consequences of Swift's refocusing - not yet discernible in the *Examiner*[3] and probably inspired by Bolingbroke's virulent anti-Dutch posture[4] - for the continuation of the debate were unmistakable. Compared with the first phase of the turning-point debate Holland was referred to with markedly increasing frequency in Tory writings, whilst the considerably fewer references to France show that the consensus as regards the common enemy abroad, which had long been binding, no longer corresponded to the changed priorities of Government propaganda. The simultaneously reduced references to Austria also indicate that the 'new' balance-of-power rhetoric directed against Habsburg, which was to be continued only to a much lesser extent, was essentially a temporary focus of Tory propaganda and became less important after the emphasis of the polemical interaction had changed. In the Whig campaign, too, Austria received far less attention after the anti-Habsburg debate, initiated mainly by Defoe, had subsided. The fact that the Whigs, who usually firmly supported the principle of balance of power, were now giving slightly more attention to Holland than to Austria leads one to conclude that the Whigs had recognised how dangerous the topic was which Swift had brought to the boil and reacted to the Tories' campaign against the States General even more sensitively than they had to previous attacks on Austria. The fact that Dutch contours were now seen more clearly in the Whigs' nation profile than in the first phase of the turning-point debate can be recorded as a repercussion of Swift's about-turn in *The Conduct of the Allies* and at the same time as an indication of Whig determination

---

1 As in the case of *The Conduct of the Allies* (200 copies) Harley bought 100 copies of *Some Remarks on the Barrier Treaty*, in order to give these to his followers; see BL Add. MS 70351 ('Bonds and other Papers relating to Lord Oxford') with entry dated 22 February 1712. This pamphlet was one of the "commissioned" works: cf. J.A. Downie, "Swift and the Oxford Ministry: New Evidence", *Swift Studies* 1 (1986), p. 8.

2 See *inter alia* the editions of the *Observator* of 5-8, 12-15 and 26-29 December 1711, also those of 29 December-2 January, 16-19 January and 16-20 February 1712.

3 Cf. also Speck, "*The Examiner* Examined: Swift's Tory Pamphleteering", *Focus: Swift*, ed. Rawson, p. 146.

4 Cf. in this connection B.W. Hill, "Oxford, Bolingbroke, and the Peace of Utrecht", *The Historical Journal* 16 (1973), p. 244.

to ward off attacks on England's special Ally. *The Conduct of the Allies* also initiated reorientations within the nation profile which may be seen as a yardstick for the assessment of the international situation by the English public.

The polemical ingenuity developed by Swift in *The Conduct of the Allies* was manifested not only in the ability to anticipate topics of public debate, but also - and to as great an extent - in the closely linked ability to take political terrain by means of linguistic virtuosity. Swift's linguistic chutzpah has already been mentioned in the survey of the debate's time structure. Let us draw this chapter to a close by taking a particularly memorable example to illustrate Swift's striking ability to use political language in order to hold his own camp together and produce embarrassment in the enemy camp. In *The Conduct of the Allies* Swift carefully chooses the most effective point to put the question already quoted above to support his conspiracy thesis: "by what Motives, or what Management, we are thus become the *Dupes* and *Bubbles* of *Europe*?"[1] . In this question Swift clothes his contempt for the old Ministry, a contempt which is accompanied by his equally bitter outrage at the Allies' exploitation of England. Although Lord Cowper had previously used the word "bubble" to express his indignation at Tory efforts at oversimplification[2] and Trapp had already employed it to vent his disdain for appeals for moderation[3] , it was only Swift who made it a widely acknowledged opprobrious and explosive term in a clearly defined foreign-policy context. Thus he can be said to have coined an infectious catchword for the purpose of party-political propagation. Swift's use of language perhaps even followed models from top-level politics or at least lent resonance to the firm assessments of leading members of the Government. Bolingbroke, for example, wrote in a letter to Lord Peterborough on 8 January 1712: "[...] if we found that our allies persisted to make us the bubbles of the war [...]"[4] . In the ensuing period the word "bubble" - used both as a verb and as a substantive - almost became a propagandistic gem designed to show indignation at the way England was being pushed around and outwitted especially by the Dutch. Again and again, even if not with statistically predictable regularity, Tory authors of nearly all genres used this highly-charged, slightly frivolous word[5] in order to confirm their ideological harmony and later also their propagandistic superiority over the Whigs. As early as in its issue of 17-24 January 1712 the *Examiner* asked the following rhetorical question with regard to the Duke of Marlborough: "Hath he secured the Honour and Wealth of the Nation, in respect of her Allies, so as she might not be the Bubble of those whom she hath preserved from Ruin?" The evocative word was strikingly used, for example, in

---

1 Swift, *Political Tracts 1711-1713*, p. 40.

2 See Lord Cowper, *A Letter to Isaac Bickerstaff*: Boyer, *The History of the Reign of Queen Anne, Digested into Annals. Year the Ninth*, p. 83.

3 See [Joseph Trapp], *Most Faults on One Side: Or, the Shallow Politicks, Foolish Arguing, and Villanous Designs of the Author of a late Pamphlet Entitul'd Faults on Both Sides, Consider'd and Expos'd* (London, 1710), p. 24.

4 *Letters and Correspondence*, II, 141. See also *ibid.*, II, 307.

5 As one would expect, it is missing in the sermon, in which a more temperate, polite tone is required.

the terse alliterative title of the broadside *We have Been Banter'd and Bubbl'd, Banter'd and Bubbl'd* (1712) and in the prose broadside *Resolutions without doors, upon the Resolutions within doors*, which coincided chronologically with the parliamentary enquiry and demanded right at the beginning that the English seek revenge when it uttered the cry "That no Nation, no, not a petty Conquer'd Province, was ever treated with more Contempt, or more infamously Bubbl'd and Abus'd, than *Great-Britain* has been by its *Al-s*, especially the *D-h*"[1]. It is not too daring to speak of a linguistic transfusion at this point, for Swift's derision of the Dutch in *The Conduct of the Allies* is echoed here in the context of the quotation. Shortly afterwards a Whig broadside, *Poor England Bob'd at Home and Abroad* (1712), ironically proclaimed in explicit reference to parliamentary proceedings: "The Parliament having Examin'd the Case,/ Declare in their *Representation* / By whom we are Bubbl'd in every Place,/ And how we may have Reparation" (tenth stanza); in this oblique manner it testified to the polemical thrust of the omnipresent catchword. In his satirical poem *The English Foreigners: Or, the Whigs Turn'd Dutchmen* (1712) Ward denounced Marlborough as having "bubbl'd us abroad"[2]. The provocative word also appeared in a prominent position in Arbuthnot's series of allegorical tales *The History of John Bull* (1712), which was begun on 4 March. In *John Bull in his Senses*, the second part of this series published on 17 March 1712, Nicholas Frog, the personification of the deceitful Dutchman, contemptuously declares to Louis Baboon, the French King: "*He has been my Bubble these Twenty Years*"[3]. It is clear from the firm control with which Arbuthnot uses the word in this work[4] that he has as it were taken over the baton from his colleague Swift in a race which has already been run. With its caustic vividness *The History of John Bull* marked a temporary end to the ideological denigration of the Dutch, which could be revived again according to need. The prominence of *The History of John Bull* on the journalistic scene in the spring of 1712 seems to indicate that the Tories were now largely able to do without the conventional discursive pamphlet and leave it to the deft strokes of Arbuthnot's pen finally to establish in the minds of the English public the negative image of the Dutch Ally that was already gaining acceptance. Between the appearance of *The Conduct of the Allies* and that of the first three parts of *The History of John Bull* it is possible to trace how the Tories caught up and took the lead in the propaganda race and at the same time witness an impressive manifestation of the part played by specifically literary means in helping the public to come to terms with the peace problem. Two texts[5] of fictional cohesiveness - fictional consis-

---

1 Cf. above, p. 67 ("The Public Controversy about the Ending of the War of the Spanish Succession: The Main Outlines").

2 *A Collection of Historical and State Poems, Satyrs, Songs, and Epigrams. Miscellanies. By the Author of the London Spy* (London, 1717), p. 17.

3 Arbuthnot, *The History of John Bull*, ed. Bower and Erickson, p. 33.

4 See also, e.g., *ibid.*, pp. 63 and 112.

5 It is interesting that in *Who Plot best; the Whigs or the Tories. Being a Brief Account of all the Plots that have Happen'd within these Thirty Years... In a Letter to Mr. Ferguson* (London, 1712), p. 20, the same author was assumed to be responsible for *The Conduct*

tency[1] is also a feature of *The Conduct of the Allies* - mark the beginning and the end of the second phase of the turning-point debate, which led the Tories on to the road to victory. It proved useful that Swift's propagandistic catchword could be reproduced at any time, as confirmed by the reappearance of the word "bubble" in Tory propaganda writings such as the *Letter from the Famous Sir Humphry Polesworth* (1712)[2], published in the *Examiner* of 15 May 1712, and Leslie's ideologically sharp-tongued pamphlet *Salt for the Leach*[3]. In *The Fourth and Last Part of a Caveat against the Whiggs* (1712) the author reminded his readers how often "they [the Whigs] again pass'd their stale Delusions on a bubbled Nation [...]"[4], while Ward, in his crassly propagandistic poem *The English Foreigners: Or, the Whigs Turn'd Dutchmen* already mentioned above, sarcastically called his compatriots "the spendthrift Bubbles of the War"[5]. Even when the Tories used an inhabitant of the animal kingdom as a mouthpiece for their ideology, the notorious word appeared; in *The Parliament of Birds* (1712) a "learned *Swan*", no doubt Bolingbroke, lashes out at the enemies of peace and of the Queen with the following rhetorical question: "'Have not the *Jays* and chat'ring *Pyes*,/ Amus'd us with their Tales and Lyes;/ To cover from the bubbl'd Nation,/ Their Cruelties, and Depredation?'"[6] With his "And Thus the Nation *Bubbl'd* was and *Fool'd*"[7] in his poem *On the Peace* (1713), recalling the bitter chain of events leading to peace, Marshall Smith marked the end of this linguistic ploy.

The effect on the journalistic opponent was confirmed, for example, by the critical irony of the recourse to Swift's polemical usage in Maynwaring's pamphlet *Remarks on a False, Scandalous, and Seditious Libel*[8], in the broadside *Poor England Bob'd at Home and Abroad* from which we have already quoted, in *A Full Answer to The Conduct of the Allies*[9] and in the long documentary pamphlet

---

and *The History of John Bull*, an assumption which certainly does justice to the propagandistic affinity of the two works.

1 This, of course, also constitutes the main attraction of another extremely popular piece of Tory propagnada, Wagstaffe's *The Story of the St. Alb-ns Ghost*.

2 See *A Letter from the Famous Sir Humphry Polesworth, Author of the 1st, 2nd and 3rd Part of John Bull in his Senses or, Law is a Bottomless-Pit* (London, 1712), p. 3.

3 See Leslie, *Salt for the Leach*, p. 6.

4 Hornby, *The Fourth and Last Part of a Caveat against the Whiggs, etc. In a Short Historical Account of their Behaviour in the Reign of Her Majesty Queen Anne*, p. 5. See also *ibid.*, p. 101.

5 [Ned Ward], *The Poetical Entertain: Or, Tales, Satyrs, Dialogues, and Intrigues, etc.. Serious and Comical* [Numb. III] (London, 1712), p. 10 (separate pagination). See also *ibid.*, pp. 14 and 17!

6 [Edmund Stacy], *The Parliament of Birds* (London, 1712), p. 19.

7 M. Smith, *On the Peace: A Poem. Humbly Inscrib'd to the most Honourable the Earl of Oxford and Mortimer, Lord High Treasurer of Great-Britain, etc.* (London, [1713]), p. 5.

8 See [Arthur Maynwaring], *Remarks on a False, Scandalous, and Seditious Libel, Intituled, The Conduct of the Allies, and of the Late Ministry, etc.* (London, 1711) p. 36.

9 See *A Full Answer to the Conduct of the Allies*, p. 79.

The History and Defence of the Last Parliament[1], which was published in 1713. The ironic but somewhat hapless reference to the annoying word in *A Few Orthodox Remarks* (1712)[2] was also a reliable linguistic indicator of the success and staying power of Government propaganda[3]. A final indication that Swift's use of language repeatedly gave cause for polemical interaction is the unconventional use of the word by Defoe, who, in this case, too, proved to be a protean journalist and went through all the variations of linguistic usage in his application of the term to the demands of day-to-day politics. Thus, in the Whig-oriented pamphlet *A Justification of the Dutch from Several Late Scandalous Reflections* (1712) he ironically followed Tory terminology[4], whilst in *Memoirs of Count Tariff* (1713), published by Morphew, he applied the word "bubble" to the Dutch cheating the English in the sense coined by Swift and repeated throughout the whole gamut of Tory genres[5]. Proof of Defoe's quite idiosyncratic use was provided by the two issues of the *Review* of 14 February 1712, in which the word "bubble" is used to refer to the French King, and 24 June 1712, in which it is used as a warning of the Pretender's intentions with regard to Queen and country.

Altogether the word "bubble", with its considerable polemical potential, provides a perfect example of how Swift succeeded in using his verbal skill to transmit political signals which could easily be taken up by other authors and were capable, by means of propagandistic abbreviation, of stirring up collective aggression, mobilising the willingness to identify and irritating the journalistic opponent by clever simplification. The echo of the word "bubble" in Tory propaganda is an illustration in miniature of how individual linguistic aptness can initiate the establishment of quasi-official usage which then sets the pace in the struggle for domination of the public arena. At any rate, in the second phase of the turning-point debate the Whigs were no match for the Tories in this respect.

---

1 See *The History and Defence of the Last Parliament. Containing the Debates at large, on the most Important Cases in both Houses. And the Arguments pro and con, as well without doors as within* (London, 1713), p. 229.

2 See *A Few Orthodox Remarks upon a late Preface, Publish'd before some Occasional Sermons, Preach'd by the L- B- of St. Asaph* (London, 1712), p. 17.

3 Also the language in the *Medley* of 21-24 March 1712 looks like a somewhat laboured effort to counter the offensive pace with which the notorious word was used.

4 See [Daniel Defoe], *A Justification of the Dutch from Several Late Scandalous Reflections: In which is Shewn the Absolute Necessity of Preserving a Strict and Inviolable Friendship betwixt Great-Britain and the States-General. With the Fatal Consequences that must Attend a War with Holland* (London, 1712), p. 151.

5 See [Daniel Defoe], *Memoirs of Count Tariff, etc.* (London, 1713), p. 15.

III. The Treaty of Utrecht (1713) as Reflected in Peace Poems

As Defoe's remark quoted at the end of the penultimate chapter shows, everything had virtually been said on the peace issue. And yet, when in the spring of 1713 the Treaty of Utrecht was concluded, this was like a second wind for the propaganda media and for one genre in particular: peace poems. They were a kind of poetic subspecies and put the finishing touches, as it were, to the public debate over the termination of the war. What had already been exhaustively dealt with in the discursive genres like, for example, the pamphlet, was now brought up again by the parties in a renewed self-promotion effort. Once more the partisan nature of the entire debate found expression in these poems.

The Tories, of course, took the lead in the production of peace poems, not only in terms of sheer numbers. Since the conclusion of the peace treaty was a highly welcome event, it provided them with a certain vantage point from which to comment on it. But in the midst of Tory jubilations the Whigs were doing their utmost to hold their own and by no means remained silent. What the Tories did in terms of energetic self-promotion is well illustrated by Trapp's poem *Peace* (1713), which he dedicated to Lord Bolingbroke, and of which we quote the beginning in full:

> Then It is done! the wond'rous Work compleat!
> *Britain* at last is Wise, as well as Great.
> Too long have our deluded Heroes dy'd,
> For *Belgic* Avarice, and *Austrian* Pride:
> Too long have We indulg'd our Martial Flame,
> Disgrac'd by Triumphs, pillag'd into Fame.
> But now no more shall We be scorn'd, or aw'd
> By Lies at home, by Insolence abroad;
> To Foreign Nations which We sav'd, and paid,
> By our own *Native Foreigners* betray'd:
> No more shall Taxes rise, and Credit fall;
> No more, at ev'ry little Princes Call,
> Shall our resign'd, obsequious Troops advance,
> The Jest of *Europe*, while the Dread of *France*[1].

This passage reads like a pamphlet in verse; the polemical structure of discursive writing is transferred to poetry by means of oxymora and pointed antitheses.

---

1 Joseph Trapp, *Peace. A Poem: Inscribed to the Right Honourable the Lord Viscount Bolingbroke* (London, 1713), p. 1.

Against the background of past events Trapp obviously wants to confront the Whigs, the "*Native Foreigners*", once more with the catalogue of their misdeeds. He wants to take advantage of the pro-Tory mood and if possible generate fresh energy in their favour. There is a similar polemical thrust when Smith in *On the Peace* (1713) remarks on the peace envisaged by the Whigs that it "Gave our *Allies* the Profits, us the *Blows*"[1]. Trapp is so set on polarising that a common feature of all peace poems, homage to the Queen and a vision of a prosperous Britain trading with the world, becomes almost secondary:

> Her Merchants unmolested, uncontroul'd
> Enrich her Kingdoms, and import their Gold,
> Thro' all the Universe pursue their Gain,
> Secure from War, and fearless plough the Main[2].

There is a similar emphasis in most other Tory peace poems, too: in Charles Kirkham's *Philanglus and Astraea* (1712) and Ward's *Upon the Prospect of Peace* (1712)[3], both among the first of the Tory poems to appear; in Bevill Higgons' *A Poem on the Peace* (1713), William Waller's *Peace on Earth* (1713), Thomas Parnell's posthumous *On Queen Anne's Peace*, Smith's above-mentioned *On the Peace*, William Diaper's *Dryades* (1713), *Truth Discover'd; or a Short View of the Queen's Peace* (1713), *Anna Triumphans* (1713), *An Humble Offering to the Best of Queens, upon the Consummation of Peace* (1713)[4], the somewhat later *The Congress* (1714), and finally Alexander Pope's *Windsor Forest* (1713), by far the most literary of them all. In all these poems the events that led to the Treaty of Utrecht are presented once more with the obvious polemical intention of denigrating the Opposition[5] and portraying the Tory Government as a paragon of patriotism and loyalty to the Queen. This way of dealing with the past also left its imprint on the opening of Nahum Tate's *The Triumph of Peace* (1713), the Poet Laureate's contribution. To drive home their message, authors drew on a catalogue of recurring key-terms with negative political overtones like "Discord", "Rebellion", "Sedition", "Resistance", "Anarchy"[6], "Faction"[7], "Chaos", "Envy", "Fury", and "Discontent", usually with particular intensity towards the end of their poems. Each of these terms was meant to strike a propaganda blow at the Whigs, whom the Tories regarded as scheming and seditious at home and bellicose abroad. The decidedly political bias of these key-terms becomes apparent when one reads

---

1 Smith, *On the Peace*, p. 16.

2 Trapp, *Peace*, p. 17.

3 Contained in Ward 's *The Poetical Entertainer*, pp. 25-27.

4 Contained in the same author's *Collection of Historical and State Poems*.

5 *An Epistle from Sempronia to Cethegus. To which is Added Cethegus's Reply* (London, 1713) seized the opportunity to paint a lurid picture of the Duchess of Marlborough, in particular as an incorrigible evil-doer who condemned the peace (see esp. pp. 9-10).

6 Cf. also *The Canterbury Tale: Or Story of the Wandering Turtle. In Twelve Cantos* (London, 1712), pp. 8, 9, 11.

7 Cf. also Browne, *Britain's Palladium: Or, my Lord Bolingbroke's Welcome from France*, p. 8.

Samuel Wesley's non-political poem *An Hymn on Peace* (1712); it contains similar terms, but in a traditional application to describe profligate behaviour[1]. Tory peace poems were not simply yet another variation of the customary political rhetoric acclaiming the Government's policy. Their main purpose was to sustain the Government's high popularity by once more laying open the deficiencies of the Opposition and thereby giving the Tories an edge in domestic policy especially in view of the forthcoming elections. In this respect they had a complementary function with, for instance, such an aggressive prose sheet as *What Sort of Peace is this? Or, a Rod in Piss for some Body* (1713) which, voicing extreme Tory sentiment, was also an expression of the hope for retributive measures against those responsible for the former wicked war policy. These poems were more than just a rhetorical ratification of what had been achieved; in fact, any reference to past successes was intended to create a favourable climate for the Government's policy in the future.

In these poems there is a wide range of poetic gifts that authors applied to the creation of a particular Tory image. Trapp's *Peace* and Pope's *Windsor Forest* are two examples at opposite ends of the spectrum. Trapp simply clads the political reasoning of pamphlets and tracts in poetic garb. Pope in his sublime treatment of the Peace of Utrecht creates world literature, but he is different in mode only; for he, too, never loses sight of the main purpose of these poems: to propagate the Tory programme of political renewal. Thus, in the poetic genre of peace poems, too, Government propaganda showed a high degree of unity of purpose similar to that at the climax of the turning-point debate at the beginning of 1712. Individual writers' idiosyncrasies and preferences in both political personnel and content were never allowed to interfere with this objective.

Windsor Forest has received thorough treatment in several studies[2] and has also been analysed with regard to its specific form as a means of communicating political content[3]. Let it suffice here, therefore, to simply mention that the creation of this outstanding literary work coincided with the Tories' growing sense of self-assertion, which found expression in the peace poems as a general rallying-call for Conservative regeneration. *Windsor Forest*, which also gives expression to latent Jacobite sympathies, pays homage to the Sovereign and the reigning House of Stuart:

> Rich Industry sits smiling on the Plains,
> And Peace and Plenty tell, a STUART reigns[4].

---

1 See Samuel Wesley, *An Hymn on Peace. To the Prince of Peace* (London, 1713), p. 4.

2 See in particular Earl R. Wasserman, *The Subtler Language. Critical Readings of Neoclassic and Romantic Poems* (Baltimore, 1959), pp. 101-168 and Müllenbrock, *Whigs kontra Tories*, pp. 93-141.

3 See Heinz-Joachim Müllenbrock, "Alexander Pope's *Windsor Forest* (1713): Genre and Political Propaganda", *Studi Settecenteschi* 11-12 (1988-89), pp. 9-15.

4 *Windsor Forest*, ll. 41-42: Alexander Pope, *Pastoral Poetry and An Essay on Criticism*, ed. E. Audra and Aubrey Williams, *The Twickenham Edition of the Poems of Alexander Pope*, I (London and New Haven, 1961), 152.

Making consistent and ingenious use of the pastoral mode the poem indirectly unfolds the events leading to the conclusion of the peace treaty. Expression is thus given to the tenet of Tory politics, also proclaimed early in Nathaniel Castleton's *The Olive, an Ode* (1713), that the Queen freed her country from its self-destructive military engagement and pointed the more glorious way to peaceful conquests[1]. As in other peace poems, too, reference to the past is, though in a poetically sublimated manner, used for confrontation with the political opponent, as the following brief survey of recent English history shows:

> Make sacred *Charles's* Tomb for ever known,
> (Obscure the Place, and uninscrib'd the Stone)
> Oh Fact accurst! What Tears has *Albion* shed,
> Heav'ns! what new Wounds, and how her old have bled?
> She saw her Sons with purple Deaths expire,
> Her sacred Domes involv'd in rolling Fire,
> A dreadful Series of Intestine Wars,
> Inglorious Triumphs, and dishonest Scars.
> At length great ANNA said - Let Discord cease!
> She said, the World obey'd, and all was *Peace*[2] !

The subsequent oration by Father Thames, which proclaims Pope's vision of peace, culminates in the idea that England owes her present state of prosperity to Tory loyalism. The same message is conveyed in Kirkham's *Philanglus and Astraea* over several pages of 'poetic prose'. *Windsor Forest* makes short shrift of Whig principles, condensing them at the end into a catalogue of political vices[3]; at the same time it is an appeal for a Government whose loyalty to the Queen would lead to a revival of the traditional Tory concept of the unity of Church and State.

Tory peace poems with their polarisation and with hardly a trace of Harleyite moderation anticipated the tense political climate which was soon to develop. Maybe it was nostalgia which made the writers of these poems paint the ideal of a monistic state with their pronounced rhetoric of unity[4]. But on the other hand they also expressed the Tories' growing self-confidence toward the end of Queen Anne's reign, which was such an essential foundation for the future. With the benefit of historical hindsight this is not without irony; the peace poems, by harping on unity, were demanding something the Tory leaders were lacking at the conclusion of the peace and above all immediately thereafter, and which contributed sub-

---

1 The nobler character of her work for peace is also brought out in the poem that concludes the prose sheet *We are bravely Serv'd at last, by the Q-n and P-m-t* (1712), which is devoted to a polemic in home and foreign policy.

2 *Windsor Forest*, ll. 319-328: *Pastoral Poetry*, pp. 180-181.

3 See *Windsor Forest*, ll. 413-422: *ibid*., pp. 192-193.

4 "Unity, Plenty and Tranquility" and "Unity and Obedience" are the political catchwords of the peace-welcoming *Examiner* that appeared on 13 April 1713.

stantially to the accession of George I in 1714, a disaster which took the party into the political wilderness.

As regards the emerging tensions among leading Tories, Harley and Bolingbroke in particular, these were only occasionally touched upon in the peace poems, although the general tendency to polarise sharply signalled a move to the right, which was probably more to Bolingbroke's liking than to Harley's. Particular deference is shown to Bolingbroke in Trapp's polemical poem *Peace*, and in Parnell's similarly polemical *On Queen Anne's Peace* he is accorded the distinction of being the first-named politician and this even immediately after the Queen[1], but then there is praise for Harley and other politicians in both poems as well, not unlike in Elkanah Settle's *Irene Triumphans. The British Muse's Congratulatory Poem, on the Peace* (1713). Diaper's *Dryades* is not nearly as balanced: the praise is almost entirely bestowed on Bolingbroke, who is also mentioned first[2], and the final apostrophe to the arch Conservative Sir William Wyndham, who co-operated with Bolingbroke[3], shows that here the author definitely sides with a particular political grouping. No programmatic statements and no overtly personalised preferences occur in *Peace on Earth*, however, a poem by Waller, an Anglican clergyman - with High Church leanings? - who does not mention Bolingbroke at all but follows Harley's political line. There are unmistakable personal preferences, on the other hand, in Smith's *On the Peace*, which puts Harley in the centre as the antagonist of the Junto and makes him the sole architect of the peace. The emphasis is similar in the above-mentioned *The Olive* and in *The Canterbury Tale: Or Story of the Wandering Turtle*, another early manifestation of Tory peace confidence published in May 1712. Arthur Young's *Epistle to the Right Hon. George Lord Lansdowne* (1713) contains several apostrophes to Bolingbroke, whereas Harley is completely passed over. The peace poems thus also document hidden personal frictions and the politicians' efforts to capitalise on the flattery bestowed upon them. Dedicating *Windsor Forest* to Lord Lansdowne and giving him a prominent place in the poem are both indications of latent Jacobitism, albeit less conspicuous than the rhetoric in favour of the Divine Right concept. Though insiders like Swift were aware of the growing estrangement between Harley and Bolingbroke[4], which they regretted[5], this fact was - for the time being - largely 'kept under cover' in Tory peace poems, occasional references notwithstanding. Personal references could even be interpreted

1 See *Collected Poems of Thomas Parnell*, ed. Claude Rawson and F.P. Lock (Newark, London and Toronto, 1989), p. 299.

2 See *The Complete Works of William Diaper*, Edited with an Introduction by Dorothy Broughton (London, 1952), p. 68.

3 Cf. Hill, *Robert Harley*, p. 216.

4 The tension between these two politicians was mockingly alluded to in the Whig publication *The Present State of Fairy-Land. In Several Letters from Esquire Hush, an Eminent Citizen of Fickle-Borough, to the King of Slave-Onia* (London, 1713), p. 41.

5 See Swift, *Journal to Stella*, ed. Williams, I, 253, 334; II, 389, 568, 593.

as a veiled attempt to exorcise any emerging internal discord[1] when in its issue of 13 April 1713 the *Examiner* diplomatically paid its compliments on the occasion of the peace in equal measure to Oxford on the right of the throne and to Bolingbroke on the left. Although the Tory peace poems were also indicators of individual politicians' standing, the overall impression they conveyed was that of a united front vis-à-vis the political opponent. They were like so many festively dressed shop windows, but there was hardly a way to catch a glimpse of what went on behind John Bull's counter although individual decorations kept people guessing.

The authors of Whig peace poems understandably found it more difficult than those favoured by history to come to terms with an event they had long discredited and were now expected to applaud without giving up long-held convictions. Praise, the genre's distinctive mode of expression, did not come easily to them. However, instead of conceding victory by default in this short-lived but popular genre, they made an effort to face up to the occasion. A good example is Tickell's *On the Prospect of Peace*, which appeared as early as October 1712 and was favourably commented on in the *Spectator* of 30 October 1712. Since it was published before the actual conclusion of the peace it was never in danger of being drowned in the chorus of Tory jubilation, and by the time the negotiations ended it had been reprinted four times. In his poem, which is dedicated to John Robinson, Bishop of Bristol and future Bishop of London and one of the two British plenipotentiaries at the Utrecht negotiations, Tickell expressed the positive expectations that many people had, but at the same time developed a rhetoric of partial dissent. Tickell also dignifies the Queen with the compliment that it was she who pointed the way to peaceful conquest, but this is diluted by his justification of the blood toll which he places in a wider European context and which the Tories always regarded as unconscionable:

> Accept, Great ANNE, the Tears their Mem'ry draws,
> Who nobly perish'd in their Sov'raign's Cause:
> For Thou in Pity bid'st the War give o'er,
> Mourn'st thy slain Heroes, nor wilt venture more.
> Vast Price of Blood on each victorious Day!
> (But *Europe's* Freedom doth that Price repay.)
> Lamented Triumphs! when one Breath must tell
> That *Marlbrough* conquer'd, and that *Dormer* fell[2].

Praise of the Duke of Marlborough appears like a recurring theme throughout the poem: it is to him that England owes her present advantageous position. This was an interpretation of events somewhat at odds with the official Government line but one which perpetuated the Whigs' view of events. In light of the treatment that

---

[1] As early as 1712 the aggressive Tory publication *Beware of the Pretender, or, a Great Hurricane at Court: For they are Fall'n out at last* had tried to poke fun at rumours of supposed dissensions between Harley and Bolingbroke.

[2] Thomas Tickell, *A Poem, to his Excellency the Lord Privy-Seal, on the Prospect of Peace* (4th ed., London, 1713), p. 14.

Marlborough had received Tickell's poem - affirmative on the surface - was tantamount to a declaration of political misgivings.

In *A Paraphrase on the XXIXth Psalm, Occasion'd by the Prospect of Peace* (1713) the panegyric references to Marlborough were also an expression of Whig dissent. The preface is unadulterated propaganda when it states in a tone of regret that after the ground has been masterfully prepared and that after the toils of the battlefield peace has been rendered possible it is necessary "to leave it to some inferior Hand to [...] fill up the Piece"[1]. Not only in personally vituperative broadsides like *O Raree Show* (1713), *The Br-sh Embassadress's Speech to the French King* (1713) or *Nothing but Truth* (1713) did the Whigs vent their militant and uncompromising rejection[2] of what had been negotiated in Utrecht, in peace poems, too, they tried to preserve a measure of the old battle order. Their rhetoric of dissent was no doubt an attempt to keep political options open for the future in the face of present adverse circumstances. Thus the Whig peace poems also had a perspective beyond the immediacy of the occasion, and quite like those of their Tory opponents aimed at political territorial gains in the future. In poems like Tickell's *On the Prospect of Peace* and *A Paraphrase* the Whigs recorded their dissenting opinions and made themselves heard once more in spite of their disadvantaged position.

The peace poems were anything but peaceful: they were living proof, so to speak, of still unsettled political scores and thus confirmed Wesley's heartfelt sigh in *An Hymn on Peace*:

> The *Common Foe* forgot, each *Squadron* bends
> Their Arts and Arms against *Intestine Friends*[3].

The role of the peace poems in the battle for public approbation and their divisive rhetoric testify to the hunger of the public for political enlightenment and participation in the political process. In the protracted propaganda struggle over the termination of the War of the Spanish Succession the peace poems were like concluding statements in which both Government and Opposition emphatically nailed their colours to the mast.

---

1 *A Paraphrase on the XXIXth Psalm, Occasioned by the Prospect of Peace. Inscribed to Joseph Addison, Esq.* (London, 1713), p. ii (unpaginated).

2 See, as an example of unbroken Whig resistance rhetoric, "Hannibal's Speech to the People on the Peace with Rome" in the *Flying-Post* of 25-28 April 1713.

3 Wesley, *An Hymn on Peace*, p. 7.

IV. THE MAIN GENRES OF THE PUBLIC DEBATE: PROFILES AND FUNCTIONS

1. THE PAMPHLET

The pamphlet with its long tradition[1] is doubtless the number one genre in political discourse. The number of pamphlets amounts to at least half the number of all the other genres taken together. If political journalism were seen in purely quantitative terms, the significance of the pamphlet, a genre of usually considerable length, would be even more obvious, but in terms of quality, too, it occupied a prominent position in the public debate.

In the armoury of the two camps' wooing of public opinion, the pamphlets were the flagships, with smaller craft positioned around them. The authors' mutual calumnies notwithstanding, the pamphlet was the most prestigious instrument for stating one's political views with the greatest effect, and it was also the most thoroughly argumentative means of expression in the often complex process of polemical interaction. The pamphlet was the most significant medium in the public debate because it was free of any space restrictions and thus provided the necessary scope for a detailed exposition of different viewpoints, for explaining the rationale of political decisions.

Although the other genres were occasionally used as icebreakers - for example in the gradual undermining of the Duke of Marlborough's reputation in the *Examiner* - it was only through the participation of pamphlets which brought about a filtering process that any political dispute would gain stature, because only there would the essentials stand out in sharp relief. The pamphlets' detailed political analyses gave muscle to the often ramifying debates and substantially fostered the formation of partisan positions. Owing to their argumentative nature, pamphlets,

---

1 See for the period preceding the Civil War the recent work of Herbert Grabes, *Das englische Pamphlet I: Politische und religiöse Polemik am Beginn der Neuzeit (1521-1640)* (Tübingen, 1990) and Martina Mittag, *Nationale Identitätsbestrebungen und antispanische Polemik im englischen Pamphlet 1558-1630* (Frankfurt and Berne, 1992). However, the first of these studies offers no analysis of rhetorical strategies. On this compare most recently for the revolutionary period James Holstun (Ed.), *Pamphlet Wars. Prose in the English Revolution* (London, 1992) and Elizabeth Skerpan, *The Rhetoric of Politics in the English Revolution 1642-1660* (Columbia and London, 1992). Pamphlets are subjected to less detailed rhetorical examination in Nigel Smith, *Literature and Revolution in England 1640-1660* (New Haven and London, 1994). In the volume covering our period edited by Thomas N. Corns, *The Literature of Controversy. Polemical Strategy from Milton to Junius* (London, 1987), there is no treatment of the pamphlets relevant for a discussion of the War of the Spanish Succession.

at least up to a point, had the same function in the cultural environment under Queen Anne as was in the nineteenth century to be taken over by the editorial article. While to some people Defoe, the author of the *Review*, is the first leader writer, the periodical essay, although it increasingly became a platform for political debate, did not yet acquire the unique position of the later editorial. It was the function of the essay - often in well orchestrated co-operation with the pamphlet - to prepare the battle ground rather than to carry out the essential strike[1]. Other genres like the broadside and the occasional poem played a complementary though by no means insignificant role. They provided an emotional outlet during the debate, even if they did not actually promote it through sound argumentation. In the main this even applies to Arbuthnot's popular *History of John Bull* (1712), the individual parts of which were termed pamphlets, although, in the guise of fiction, they in fact emotionally exploited the change of public opinion that pamphlets had brought about. The prominent position of the pamphlet, which of course did not only rely on arguments but was also adept at stirring political resentment, is further illustrated by the fact that the public image of Whigs and Tories depended largely on how they were represented in pamphlet literature. Decreasing productivity of pamphleteers in both parties perceptively weakened the protagonists' positions in the propaganda war. Pamphlets were the pillars that supported the parties' propaganda platforms. As will be briefly outlined below, their most prominent specimens enable us to retrace the course of the debate.

The Government's intention - manifest from the beginning though not publicly stated - to end the War of the Spanish Succession by concluding a peace even without victory, was accompanied by increasingly intense journalistic activity. The Harley Ministry's long-term peace policy was reflected in the echeloned battle order of the different public genres with the pamphlet in the front line. Strategically the pamphlet became especially important for the Tories after they had taken the initiative. They did not only use the pamphlet as a clearing house for political arguments but often also as an instrument for tentatively advancing the public debate about the issue of war and peace. Through the debate initiated by the publication of *Faults on Both Sides* (1710) more serious doubts were raised for the first time about the wisdom of the war policy, though these were still marked by restraint. In the course of the election campaign of 1710 St. John's pilot publication[2] *A Letter to the Examiner* unfolded the entire range of Tory arguments to signal the impending change of policy. In the spring of 1711 Defoe's pamphlet *The Succession of Spain Consider'd* - in line with political exigencies and its author apparently conscious of the secret negotiations in progress - introduced several new arguments into the debate. Defoe adapted the balance-of-power doctrine to the new situation and directed the reproach of seeking hegemony at Austria instead of France, thereby putting an important aspect of the new Tory policy on the propaganda agenda. Then in early October 1711, before the publication of the Preliminaries, under mounting Whig pressure, it was Defoe's pamphlet *Reasons why this*

1 Cf. e.g. Owens and Furbank, "Defoe and the Dutch Alliance", p. 175.

2 This function is also noted by Laprevotte, "*The Conduct of the Allies*: contexte et originalité", p. 248.

Nation Ought to Put a Speedy End to this Expensive War that created a breakwater, partly anticipating the tide of Opposition attacks[1]. Stepping up his very personal rhetoric in support of the balance-of-power argument and adding a powerful emotional appeal, Defoe gave fresh impetus to the Government's unflagging effort to settle the question of peace on its own terms. Defoe's *Reasons Why* was a first tentative step towards taking the offensive in the public debate. Then, at the end of November 1711, with the Opposition intensifying its rhetoric of objection to the Government's political course and amid growing tension, the actual turn in the debate was initiated with the publication of Swift's *The Conduct of the Allies.* This pamphlet with its high circulation was the stimulus which Tory propaganda needed to move into top gear. Considerable polemical energy was released by *The Conduct of the Allies.* Swift's second important pamphlet of February 1712, *Some Remarks on the Barrier Treaty*, was prompted by current events in Parliament in the wake of rising anti-Dutch feelings and heightened the emotional tone that had been set by *The Conduct of the Allies.*

An analysis of the specific function of the pamphlet shows that in the Government's propaganda strategy it was used to gradually roll back the enemy's positions, to undermine the Whigs' journalistic bastions. *The Conduct of the Allies*, the Tories' most formidable weapon, virtually achieved a quantum leap in the efficiency of Government propaganda. A closer look at how certain pilot pamphlets influenced the course of the debate reveals the contribution of some outstanding personalities - in particular Defoe and Swift - to conquering territory for the Government's propaganda attacks. If the protean Defoe provided Harley with an indispensable, ever available all-purpose weapon[2], it was Swift who, with the trenchant polemical tone of *The Conduct of the Allies*, finally gave Tory propaganda the necessary clout.

On the Whig side, too, the pamphlet was the most efficient weapon in their entire propaganda arsenal. The Whigs, however, used it in a more defensive manner in order to build rhetorical barricades through the constant repetition of identical arguments and less to propagate new ideas like the Tories. The Whigs made use of the pamphlet for the purpose of lucid argumentation to lay open the unquestionable rationale of their politics. Maynwaring, the co-ordinator of Whig propaganda until 1712, employed the leading genre to fend off any signs of an emerging Tory offensive. His defensive rhetoric was intended to compensate for the fact that it was the Tories who had actually taken the initiative. As early as November 1710 Maynwaring had in the first of the so-called *Management* tracts - ascribed to Hare but revised by himself[3] - pointed to the new Government's carefully-planned formation of its propaganda forces. In June 1711 there appeared *Reflections upon the Examiner's Scandalous Peace* and *A Letter to a Member of the October-Club*;

---

1 Cf. *ibid.*, p. 248.

2 Downie is right to say: "With Defoe on his side, Harley never lacked a voice in print" (*Robert Harley and the Press*, p. 130).

3 This well-founded supposition is put forward by Snyder in "Arthur Maynwaring and the Whig Press, 1710-1712", *Literatur als Kritik des Lebens. Festschrift zum 65. Geburtstag von Ludwig Borinski*, ed. Haas, Müllenbrock and Uhlig, p. 125.

these were followed in October 1711 by *A Vindication of the Present M-y* and *Remarks on the Preliminary Articles Offer'd by the French King*, and in November 1711 by *A Letter to a High-Churchman* and *Remarks upon the Present Negotiations of Peace Begun between Britain and France*. In December of the same year there came *Remarks on a False, Scandalous and Seditious Libel, Intituled, The Conduct of the Allies* and, to support it, Hare's *The Allies and the Late Ministry Defended against France*. This well co-ordinated barrage of pamphlets, two at a time and in quick succession, with their massive rhetoric was intended to erect high obstacles in the path of the Tory propaganda campaign. Maynwaring's circumspection gave Whig pamphleteering a high degree of rhetorical coherence, which was only surpassed by the impact of *The Conduct of the Allies*. It was precisely this element of coherence which made the pamphlet the leading genre for the Whigs also. It is therefore not surprising that when the Whigs' public image was at its highest in late autumn 1711, this coincided with a particularly skilful use of the pamphlet, and when their public standing was at its lowest in the summer of 1712, the pamphlet, too, performed rather badly. When after the end of 1712 Whig propaganda was gathering pace, this was again mainly due to pamphlets such as *The Present State of Fairy-Land* (1713) and *Observations upon the State of the Nation* (1713). The course of the debate as seen from a Whig perspective shows that without vigorous use of the pamphlet their propaganda lacked its polemical thrust. It is quite revealing that on the Government side, too, it was a pamphlet - *The Testimonies of Several Citizens of Fickleborough* (1713) - which contributed effectively to neutralizing the Whigs' efforts at regaining the initiative in influencing public opinion. In the proven emotional manner this pamphlet directed the charge of complicity, which had originally been levelled at Marlborough and Godolphin, at the Whigs and the Dutch[1]. The following detailed analysis of some typical Tory and Whig pamphlets will show the genre's rhetorical potential. Precisely for the assessment of propaganda it is necessary to carry out an analysis of technique, which is often neglected by historians because of their traditional bias towards content[2].

a) Defoe, *Reasons why this Nation Ought to Put a Speedy End to this Expensive War* (1711)

Defoe was the Government's most prolific pamphleteer, and Swift its most brilliant. It seems reasonable therefore to describe the rhetorical characteristics of

---

1 See *The Testimonies of Several Citizens of Fickleborough, in the Kingdom of Fairy-Land, concerning the Life and Character of Robert Hush, commonly Called, Bob* (London, 1713), p. 18.

2 J.A. Downie notes: "[...] rhetorical analysis offers answers unavailable by other means. Historians are prone to examine simply what is said in print rather than the way in which it is said" ("The Development of the Political Press", *Britain in the First Age of Party, 1680-1750. Essays Presented to Geoffrey Holmes*, ed. Clyve Jones [London and Ronceverte, 1987], p. 123).

Reasons Why and *The Conduct of the Allies* because these pamphlets staked the journalistic ground and, although they were not published together, complemented each other in structuring the turning-point debate. It was the task of Defoe's pamphlet to contribute new arguments to the debate and set its high emotional pitch in further dealing with the war theme; his pamphlet was perhaps also intended to temporarily divert attention from the Government's true intentions by pretending to be aiming at a consensus. Swift's pamphlet on the other hand marks the beginning of the end of Whig opposition to the Government's peace policy. With its emotional aggressiveness it was a catalyst for the Government's mighty propaganda machinery.

Reasons Why played a key role in supporting the Government's peace plans by introducing new arguments into the debate and thereby overcoming the stranglehold caused by the Whigs' staccato-style insistence on retaining the status quo. The number of rejoinders - Maynwaring's *A Letter to a High-Churchman* was the most substantial response - only partly reflects this key function of Defoe's pamphlet. However, in his *A Vindication of the Present M-y, from the Clamours Rais'd against them upon Occasion of the New Preliminaries* Maynwaring saw quite clearly that the assumption of a changed political constellation after the Emperor's death - Defoe's favourite topic - had "the colour of an Argument"[1] and might bring relief to the beleaguered Government. The *Observator* of 3-7 November 1711 also pointed out the significance of *Reasons Why*. This pamphlet documents the fact that it was the Government's long-term strategy - in defensive guise in the early stages - to go through with its peace plans against all opposition. It looks as if at the beginning of the turning-point debate the Government, also with the Court Whigs in mind, was aiming for a consensus; the idea seems to have been to test whether Marlborough, too, was prepared to compromise. But then, the emotional pitch of the pamphlet left little doubt as to the Government's intention to cross the Rubicon and make its stance on the question of war and peace unmistakably clear.

The micro- and macrostructures of *Reasons Why*[2] show that by refocusing on the war theme - in the literal photographic sense - Defoe attempted both to bring about a general change of feeling towards the war and to underpin the Government's position by introducing new and convincing arguments. The pamphlet immediately sets the tone: it begins with an emotional appeal to the reader no longer to ignore "The Miseries, Sufferings and Distresses"[3] of his country. According to the author England, which used to bear any burden, was now in such a dismal plight that in his introductory pages Defoe immediately states his thesis "But *the Case is alter'd Now*"[4]. In the following months he devoted a great deal of his jour-

---

1 *A Vindication of the Present M-y*, p. 32.

2 One of the very few attempts at a rhetorical analysis of this pamphlet is made by Sutherland, *Daniel Defoe*, pp. 55-59. Harris (*A Study of the Paper War*, pp. 254-256) overemphasises similarities between Defoe's pamphlet and Mrs. Manley's *The D. of M-h's Vindication*.

3 Defoe, *Reasons why this Nation Ought to Put a Speedy End to this Expensive War*, p. 3.

4 *Ibid*., p. 5.

nalistic activity, both in his pamphlets and the *Review*, to skilful variations of this theme with an impressive display of rhetoric and considerable pertinacity. In *Reasons Why* the casuistic technique he employs to argue his case is combined with a highly effective polemical style, which - at about the same time as Mrs. Manley's rejoinders to Hare - emotionalized the debate even before Swift's *Conduct*. His argument that the situation has changed is skilfully strengthened by the antithesis that "we went out full, but are return'd empty"[1]. England's military successes are referred to by such paradoxes as "how do those very Victories ruine us?"[2] or "such Victories would vanquish the Conqueror"[3], which anticipate similar gibes in *The Conduct of the Allies* and finally lead to the question which Swift, too, was to ask the following month: "What is this to ending the War?"[4]. Such polemical similarities between *Reasons Why* and *The Conduct of the Allies* show the journalistic and strategic fine-tuning between the two pamphlets. And even if - as must be assumed - Defoe and Swift worked to a large extent independently of one another and without personal contact[5], there still seems to have been some co-ordination, possibly from above.

After a critical reminder of how the war in Flanders was conducted and of previous attempts to conclude a peace, which also anticipates similar passages in *The Conduct of the Allies*, Defoe concentrates on two points: first the particular circumstances in England and second those of her Allies[6]. It must be said, however, that, as in his other writings, non-political as well as political, Defoe is repetitive, and constantly refers back to what has been said before in order to give his argument more force[7]. As to his first point he argues that England is faced with an unacceptable alternative - "Two ruinous Extreams"[8] - if she wants to continue the war: either to levy an excise duty on food and clothing, or to pay no more interest on the war loan. This horrifiying alternative[9] is accompanied by yet another emotional reference to the plight of the poor and the ordinary people, which shows that this affective technique is one of the two fulcrums that give Defoe's pamphlet leverage.

His other point, the specific situation of the warring parties, is dealt with in the second part of his pamphlet. He uses this opportunity to concentrate on his favou-

---

1 *Ibid.*, p. 5.
2 *Ibid.*, p. 6.
3 *Ibid.*, p. 7.
4 *Ibid.*, p. 9.
5 On this cf. also Downie, *Robert Harley and the Press*, p. 129.
6 See *Reasons Why*, p. 15.
7 On Defoe's use of repetition in other genres see *inter alia* David Matchen, "Daniel Defoe's Rhetorical Art in the *Review*", *CLA Journal* 25 (1981-82), pp. 445-446 and Ulrich Suerbaum, "'I Repeat and Repeat.': Repetition as Structure in Defoe's *Robinson Crusoe*", *Telling Stories. Studies in Honour of Ulrich Broich on the Occasion of his 60th Birthday*, ed. Elmar Lehmann and Bernd Lenz (Amsterdam/Philadelphia, 1992), pp. 69-83.
8 *Reasons Why*, p. 19.
9 It immediately provoked criticism from the political opponent; cf. *The Protestant Post-Boy*, 11-13 October 1711.

rite theme: the allegedly changed circumstances in Europe after Emperor Joseph I's death, so propitious to the Government's plans[1], and the danger to the European balance of power by adopting a solution that would favour the House of Habsburg. Whereas Defoe shared with others the emotional handling of the war theme, among them the author of the broadside *Look, before You Leap, or; England Have a Care of your Candle* (1711), the elaborate thesis of the changed European circumstances was virtually his own[2]. Here he preferred a dispassionate exchange of arguments which posed as a rational approach and was intended to win over swing voters with loose party affiliations but susceptible to moderately argued positions. Like a refrain Defoe states his favourite argument: because the situation has fundamentally changed, the position of the House of Habsburg has been strengthened and England should maintain equidistance to both France and Austria. This seemingly reasonable argument marks a change of policy which is reflected in the use of "exorbitant"; this word which had again and again been applied by the Whigs to France, to which country it had exclusively referred in the past, is now applied to Austria[3]. Towards the end of the pamphlet he makes two alternative proposals for a partition to solve the Spanish question. This may be regarded as the rhetorical correlative of his opportune accommodation to the political circumstances. Thus Defoe presents this and other pamphlets like *The Ballance of Europe* (1711) as proof of his honest will to follow the dictates of reason and enter into a dialogue on the need to adapt to the changed situation with people who held different views and were not necessarily close to the Government[4]. This fits in with Harley's policy, who never directed his propaganda solely at Tory sympathisers. The emotional tone and humanitarian approach of *Reasons Why* - the very last words of the pamphlet are an outcry against "this Bloody and Expensive War", thus venting indignation at those not accessible to balanced reasoning - was typical of the initial stage of the turning-point debate in so far as there was not yet any invective against the Allies; in *A Vindication of the Present M-y* Maynwaring, recalling Mrs. Manley's *The D. of M-h's Vindication* (1711), identified this emotional appeal as the Government's latest propaganda ploy[5].

---

1 Cf. Trevelyan, *The Peace and the Protestant Succession*, p. 181.

2 Defoe and Swift doubtless divided the work between them (in this connection cf. also Poston, "Defoe and the Peace Campaign", pp. 13 and 17). Sutherland (*Daniel Defoe*, p. 55) overemphasises the similarity and overlooks the complementarity between *Reasons Why* and *The Conduct of the Allies*.

3 See *Reasons Why*, p. 41.

4 The pamphleteer Defoe as spokesman of moderation can hardly be accused of lacking rhetorical competence. The *Review*'s problems of reception after 1710, noted by J.A. Downie in "Mr. Review and His Scribbling Friends: Defoe and the Critics, 1705-1706", *The Huntington Library Quarterly* 41 (1977-78), p. 365, were largely due to the fact that Defoe had recently switched camps. Ehrenpreis (*Swift*, II: *Dr. Swift*, 419) underestimates Defoe's rhetorical abilities.

5 See *A Vindication of the Present M-y*, p. 31.

b) Swift, *The Conduct of the Allies, and of the Late Ministry, in Beginning and Carrying on the Present War* (1711)

Swift's famous "wonder-working pamphlet"[1] with its undisguised aggressiveness represents the other, increasingly dynamic, side of Harley's Janus-headed propaganda strategy. Unlike *Reasons Why*, the structure of *The Conduct of the Allies* has been analysed elsewhere[2], and the remarkable thematic and linguistic repercussions of this pamphlet have been traced in the chapter "Focus". In the present context of analysing paradigmatic examples of Whig and Tory political rhetoric, it will suffice simply to summarise the main features of Swift's text. In contrast to *Reasons Why*, the intended thrust of *The Conduct of the Allies* is conveyed even by the layout of the front page. The idea behind the front-page layout of *Reasons Why* with its confusing variety of type-faces was obviously - in spite of the italicization of the adjective "*Expensive*" - to call attention to the pamphlet's topic as early and as comprehensively as possible, whereas in *The Conduct of the Allies* the visual characteristics of the front-page clearly serve a rhetorical purpose. Its double frame gives it the appearance of an official document and in the centre the heavy lettering of "Late Ministry" puts into relief the central target around which other key-words have been arranged.

Swift's pamphlet was directed mainly at true-blue Tories to strengthen the faith of those who belonged to the flock rather than convert the unbelieving. Its essential structural feature, therefore, is polarisation. The very first sentence of the preface, which functions as an exordium, illustrates this with its ironic distinction between the majority of "Landed Men" and the minority of "Moneyed Men". Swift uses antithesis as a rhetorical device to introduce his friend-foe concept. He rigorously exploits the patterns of classical rhetoric and with a feeling for effective propaganda paints a picture of united forces whose aim has been for a long time to undermine England's position, a process that began with the Dutch King William III's policy and culminated in the deliberate exploitation of the nation by the Whig clique around the Duke of Marlborough. Although on the surface the pamphlet seems little more than a discursive commentary on the current situation, it is this central idea which gives it the unity and density of fiction[3], the memorable quality of a good story. What is presented as a mass of facts speaking for themselves[4] is in fact a subtle display of polemical propaganda. Suppression of details, distortion

1 Samuel Johnson, *Lives of the English Poets*, ed. George Birkbeck Hill, 3 vols. (repr., Hildesheim, 1968), III, 19.

2 See - also for details of further reading - esp. Müllenbrock, "Cicero and Quintilian as Mentors of British Journalism: The Rhetorical Structure of Swift's *The Conduct of the Allies*", pp. 57-66.

3 The fictional character of the pamphlet has often - rightly - been emphasised, e.g. by Eberhard Späth, "Facts and Factions: Political Pamphlets of the Time of Queen Anne", *Zeitschrift für Anglistik und Amerikanistik* 40 (1992), p. 134. This paper was originally read in a section chaired by me at the annual conference of the Canadian Society for Eighteenth-Century Studies in Kingston (Ontario) in 1990.

4 Did Laprevotte ("*The Conduct of the Allies*", p. 254) not overlook the tendentious character of Swift's so-called facts?

of facts together with emotional appeals are designed to turn the mood against the opponent on domestic as well as foreign-policy issues. In *The Conduct of the Allies* the pamphlet - the most highly regarded genre - was used to exaggerate party-political differences and foster national antagonisms by presenting the arguments with the transparency of fiction.

The Conduct of the Allies marks a considerable improvement of Tory propaganda. With the politically and socially emotive concept of the 'family' as its centrepiece the conspiracy thesis, namely that the General and Commander-in-Chief was conspiring against the nation for personal gain, attempts to discredit the Duke of Marlborough once and for all. Swift was actually exploiting for his own propaganda purposes what Harley had hinted at in his unpublished pamphlet *Plaine English* (1708)[1] , and what Boyer had also referred to in his *A Letter from a Foreign Minister in England to Monsieur Pettecum*(1710)[2] ; namely that the sinister family clan around Marlborough and Godolphin was plundering the nation. The thesis, early adumbrated in other Harleyite publications[3] and *The Examiner*[4] , culminates in the allegation that Marlborough had wanted to become King[5] . In exposing Marlborough's seemingly boundless ambition in this way Swift was bringing to its rhetorical conclusion a strand of Tory propaganda which the author of *Faults on Both Sides* had initiated by first referring - though still with self-restraint - to the Duke's request to be made Captain-General for life[6] . The 'royal' charge and lesser allegations, e.g. that Marlborough had luck on his side, will from this point be staples of Tory propaganda, *ad hoc* topoi of journalistic warfare, employed whenever needed in the ultimate aim to literally dissect the Whig hero. The relentless and unrestrained attempt to mobilise emotions in *The Conduct of the Allies* shows that the Tories had trained their sights irreversibly on Marlborough. In the immediate aftermath of *The Conduct of the Allies* Tory propaganda used this pamphlet as a platform from which its efforts to publicly dismantle Marlborough were co-ordinated, from which diverse other genres could operate effectively in close polemical interaction.

The technique of polarisation, visible in both the pamphlet's micro- and macro-structures, amounted to publicly throwing the Allies and the Dutch to the wolves. Another feature of *The Conduct of the Allies* is the new dimension of ruthlessness

---

1 See Robert Harley, *Plaine English to all who are Honest or would be so if they Knew how*, ed. W.A. Speck and J.A. Downie, *Literature and History* 3 (1976), p. 105.

2 See Boyer, *A Letter from a Foreign Minister in England, to Monsieur Pettecum*, pp. 6-7.

3 See Clement, *Faults on Both Sides*: *Or, an Essay upon the Original Cause, Progress, and Mischievous Consequences of the Factions in this Nation*, p. 36 and Boyer, *An Essay towards the History of the Last Ministry and Parliament*, p. 2.

4 Cf. Speck, "From Principles to Practice", pp. 83-84.

5 See Swift, *Political Tracts 1711-1713*, pp. 44-45. This rhetorical climax may serve as evidence that - contrary to Harris' view put forward to correct Foot's assumption (*A Study of the Paper War*, p. 302, note 30) - Marlborough was indeed "Swift's main target".

6 See Clement, *Faults on Both Sides*, p. 35. Swift himself had dealt with this request in disparaging terms in the *Examiner* of 21 December 1710.

in the denigration of the Dutch Ally, still spared by Defoe[1], inspired by satirical aggressiveness. For instance, with the intention of denouncing the Barrier Treaty the author of *The Conduct* asks whether Dutch assistance in defending the Act of Succession can be regarded as "an Equivalent to those many unreasonable exorbitant Articles in the rest of the Treaty"[2], thus applying the highly charged word "exorbitant", traditionally associated with France, to England's Ally[3]. In order to neutralize the Whigs' constant references to England's contractual obligations and loyalty towards the Dutch Ally, Swift stirs xenophobic emotions and uses them as a weapon to gain terrain in the propaganda war. By focusing his attacks on the Dutch Swift stepped up the emotionalization of the debate which Mrs. Manley and Defoe had initiated, without, however, any specific target. The nationalist tone of *The Conduct of the Allies* provides a counterpoint to the Whigs' liberal and patriotic rhetoric with its European element and ample scope for further rhetorical elaboration in the immediate future. In the guise of factual information the rhetoric in *The Conduct of the Allies* aims at the total mobilisation of the emotions. Swift's great skill at playing this game may be highlighted by the passage in which he delivers memories of Marlborough's triumphs up to bitter derision, a passage which at the same time underlines his knack of ruthless simplification: "It will, no doubt, be a mighty Comfort to our Grandchildren, when they see a few Rags hang up in *Westminster-Hall*, which cost an hundred Millions, whereof they are paying the Arrears, and boasting, as Beggars do, that their Grandfathers were Rich and Great"[4]. As the key-text of Tory political journalism *The Conduct of the Allies* fulfilled its function perfectly: it initiated a propaganda offensive and attacked the enemy head-on after pretended attempts to reach compromise and understanding had failed. Its rhetorical militancy bears witness to the Government's will to continue with its peace policy to the very end regardless of mounting resistance. It is a measure of the unique and long-term effect of *The Conduct of the Allies* that in 1713, when Whig propaganda tried to reposition itself on the journalistic scene, *The Testimonies of Several Citizens of Fickleborough* took over Swift's conspiracy thesis and applied it to the Dutch and the Whigs in yet another attempt to stifle Opposition criticism of Government policy.

---

1 On this cf. also Laprevotte, "*The Conduct of the Allies*", p. 255.

2 Swift, *Political Tracts 1711-1713*, p. 27.

3 The provocative character of this linguistic volte-face was, of course, recognised by Hare (*The Allies and the Late Ministry Defended against France, and the Present Friends of France*, part II [London, 1711], p. 8), who was approvingly 'quoted' in the *Flying-Post* of 25-27 December 1711.

4 Swift, *Political Tracts 1711-1713*, pp. 55-56. This sounds like an ironic reverberation of a passage by Hare which Swift might be assumed to have countered if a case could be made for his having gained advance knowledge of the Opposition pamphlet: "The Standards and Colours in *Westminster* and *Guild Halls*, taken from our Enemies on that Glorious Day, are Monuments of this Author's [Defoe's] Falshood, as well as of our Conquests" (*A Caveat to the Treaters*, p. 14). Swift's memorable image was taken up, for example, in the eleventh stanza of *The Flanders Ballad: Or, the D-e of Marlborough's Rare Show* (1712).

c) Maynwaring, *Reflections upon the Examiner's Scandalous Peace* (1711)

This is a perfect example of the 'factographic' pamphlet, a form which played such a prominent role in Whig propaganda. This and similar pamphlets illustrate the Opposition strategy: through endless repitition of the facts which bore witness to the nation's attitude towards the war, the Whigs underlined their demand for retaining the status quo and assumed a role not unlike that of a court of law supervising the faithful compliance with this policy. The conspicuous factualism of the *Reflections* and similar pamphlets was the rhetorical equivalent to the historical situation, namely that - contrary to circumstances under William III, who had been bound only by a secret treaty - Anne had publicly committed herself to a foreign policy sanctioned by Parliament from which the new Government could not easily extricate itself[1]. In *Reflections upon the Examiner's Scandalous Peace* Maynwaring has recourse to the whole gamut of parliamentary resolutions, addresses, royal speeches and similar texts as evidence of the Government's pro-war policy since the beginning of the War of the Spanish Succession. Such concentrated documentary evidence reflects the author's attempt at a dispassionate treatment of the facts[2].

At the same time, however, rhetoric is also skilfully employed to enhance the persuasive force of these very facts. For example, there is the occasional polemical remark like "till the beginning of the *Examiner's* M——y"[3]. Maynwaring increases the impact of the parliamentary resolutions he quotes by interpolating at the beginning of the pamphlet highly emotive words and phrases like "Liberty", "Balance of *Europe*" and "the Exorbitant Power of *France*"[4], all taken from the documents themselves, which enables him to hide his polemics behind quotations from authentic texts. By repeatedly referring to earlier manifestations of England's pro-war stance Maynwaring seeks to underline the static nature of existing facts, and his personal comments written in the present tense - interspersed at regular intervals - are intended as a stabilising factor. An example of this is his comment after quotations from the Queen's Speech on 9 November 1703; he writes: "This is the declar'd Design of all the Parties to the Grand Alliance: this is what the Queen herself declares she makes the War for; this is what both Houses of Parliament extol and bless her for, the Commons as well as the Lords"[5]. The comments show the quintessential conclusion from the passages quoted, and the present tense in which they are written reveals Maynwaring's intention to carry over the political will of the recent past into the present, to underline the continuing relevance of recent events. In *Reflections upon the Examiner's Scandalous Peace* the continual

---

1 Cf. M.A. Thomson, "Parliament and Foreign Policy 1689-1714", *History* 38 (1953), p. 241.

2 See on the express notification of this intention Maynwaring, *Reflections upon the Examiner's Scandalous Peace*, p. 5.

3 *Ibid.*, p. 6

4 *Ibid.*, p. 7.

5 *Ibid.*, p. 9.

use of the present tense indicates the author's intention to retain the validity of past consensus for the present, to stress the immutability and timelessness of a particular political position, whose reasonableness is demonstrated by repeating and thereby sanctioning the initial demand. Both Maynwaring - in this and similar pamphlets - and Hare, for example, in *The Allies and the Late Ministry Defended against France*, seem to fully trust in the power of Parliament to stem the tide of events. Such over-confident posturing seems to have been a clear misjudgment of the opponent's room for manouevre, taking for granted that progress was unstoppable and the prevailing of liberal-Protestant aims a matter of course. It is certainly not too bold to assume that such a Whig attitude shaped the rhetorical profile of Opposition journalism. This is corroborated by a remark that Maynwaring made in a letter to the Duchess of Marlborough in the summer of 1711: "[...] Folly and knavery and ingratitude, and every thing in short that is ill cannot get the better long of reason and truth and nature. For this is an unnatural Turn of Affairs, and the foundation of it is unnatural, and senseless stupid, odious Passion"[1].

After letting the facts speak for themselves, it is only towards the end of the pamphlet[2] that Maynwaring makes his own summarising comment, not, however, without striking an even more polemical note. His peroration[3] in particular is a skilful blend of objective and affective elements. With the authority of his documentary evidence of a national consensus, Maynwaring can put the challenging question to the *Examiner* at the beginning of the peroration, "when it first began to be presumptuous and criminal for a Parliament to make an Address to the Queen, that she wou'd not consent to a Peace that shou'd leave *Spain* in the Hands of the House of *Bourbon*"[4]. In the peroration Maynwaring takes up what was said in the pamphlet and once again points to the consensus in Parliament as it existed until recently. He pointedly asks what may have caused the *Examiner*'s volte-face and in the light of what had been said before he rules out any factual arguments. At the end of the pamphlet's penultimate paragraph the author uses a sequence of parallelisms, beginning with "when", to show that the circumstances are as propitious as ever for achieving the objective of the war. In the final paragraph parenthesis is used to score once again and - to convey once more the idea of continuing relevance - it is written in the present tense. This is how the author, in keeping with the pamphlet's rhetorical strategy, skilfully refers to an official political statement by the Queen, so much revered by the Tories around Swift: "(as we are assur'd in the Words of her Sacred Majesty, in her Gracious Answer to the Address of her Parliament the 23d of *Decemb. 1707*)"[5].

The pamphlet's rhetorical structure reflects the Whig strategy of constantly referring to a national political consensus agreed in Parliament in order to prevent

---

1 Letter of Arthur Maynwaring to the Duchess of Marlborough dated 15 May 1711 (?): BL Add. MS. 61461, fol. 131.

2 See *Reflections upon the Examiner's Scandalous Peace*, pp. 17ff.

3 *Ibid.*, pp. 20-22.

4 *Ibid.*, p. 20.

5 *Ibid.*, p. 22.

any Tory deviation. The factographic approach of the pamphlet must be seen as a rhetorical device intended to force the Government time and again to accept what are non-negotiable irreversible essentials of British foreign policy, any disregard of which, in view of their unambiguousness, would amount to a scandal. Like a large number of Whig pamphlets, *Reflections upon the Examiner's Scandalous Peace* aims to contain - through the impact of accumulated factual evidence - any inclination towards political change or vacillation on the Tory side, to make constancy and continuity a point of honour[1].

d) Maynwaring, *Remarks on a False, Scandalous, and Seditious Libel, Intituled, The Conduct of the Allies, and of the Late Ministry, etc.* (1711)

This text is an example of the emotion-directed type of Whig pamphlet. Its polemical nature and lack of dispassionate argumentation make it the very opposite of *Reflections upon the Examiner's Scandalous Peace*. The majority of Whig pamphlets, however, show a mixture of both extremes and blend factographic and emotional elements.

It is significant that *Remarks* is quite obviously Maynwaring's rejoinder to Swift's *The Conduct of the Allies*, which so strongly stirred the emotions, a case of answering like with like, of drawing a similarly simplistic picture to that drawn by Swift, whose pamphlet was to revolutionize the public debate. Maynwaring's *Remarks* is the first hastily written and improvised response to Swift's *The Conduct of the Allies*, even though synchronised with Hare's much more balanced reply in *The Allies and the Late Ministry Defended against France*. Both authors denigrate Swift by comparing him with Roper, and both authors, too, use highly affective phrases like "Protestant Religion" and "Liberties of Europe" to appeal to people's emotions. When at the end of the preface to *Remarks* Maynwaring says that he is not going to write any "Particular Defence of the Treaties we have made"[2], this shows quite clearly that his pamphlet was written with Hare's in mind.

After the initial appearance of emotive words such as "Constitution" and "Revolution" in the preface, there are virtual clusters of them in what follows in order to enhance the reader's readiness to identify with the text. A dense catalogue of such political key-terms at the beginning of the pamphlet addressed to authors like Swift shows the impact that *The Conduct of the Allies* had: "[...] their Business is all the same, to vilify the *Revolution, King* William, *the Protestant Succession, Credit, Trade, the* Dutch, *and all our Confederates* [...]"[3]. After the author of *The Conduct* has been depicted as a libeller and hack writer, he is denounced as a traitor and friend of the Pretender. From page four Maynwaring presents his own

---

[1] As late as the end of November or the beginning of December 1711 Hare considered it reasonable to suppose that the Ministry would honour "*the repeated Advices of Parliament* [...]" (*A Caveat to the Treaters*, pp. 40-41) in order to secure British interests.

[2] Maynwaring, *Remarks on a False, Scandalous, and Seditious Libel, Intituled, The Conduct of the Allies, and of the Late Ministry, etc.*, p. iii (no page numbers in original).

[3] *Ibid.*, p. 3.

conspiracy thesis, which determines the character of the entire pamphlet and counters Swift's with one not less simplistic although by no means original. The main point of Maynwaring's thesis is that those who advocate a peace that would favour France are in league with the Pretender and want to overthrow the post-revolutionary order in Britain. It is this antithetical structure, the Whigs' peace policy seen as supportive of Britain's liberal constitution and the Tory policy of Jacobitism, that determines the character of the pamphlet and manipulates the reader's sympathies. Maynwaring parries Swift's attack on Marlborough, namely that he favours his own family, by pointing to the Tory Jacobites, who support the family of the Pretender[1]. And with regard to the passage in *The Conduct of the Allies* where Swift plays down the power of the Pretender's followers in England[2], Maynwaring pointedly remarks: "The Lessening the Interest of the Pretender at the same time that he writes for him, is one of the cunningest Parts he is to act"[3].

Remarks is not a well-organized pamphlet, its purpose is not to invalidate Swift's criticism of the Allies' policy by reasoned argument. *Remarks* is intended to keep the Opposition on the alert, strengthen its ranks in the face of the Government's allegedly anti-Revolution policy and its departure from consensus with the Allies, especially the Dutch. To achieve this, the strokes of Maynwaring's brush are somewhat bold, his language is sloganising and bellicose. *Remarks* is a militant appeal to rally round the flag, and only rarely are there signs of Maynwaring's characteristic rhetorical sophistication, for example when his exposure of alleged Dutch misdemeanours borders on the grotesque in an effort to neutralize Swift's attacks[4]. As the first response to *The Conduct of the Allies*, *Remarks* aims at instant polarisation and massive bombardment of the enemy with highly charged language. It does this in a less disciplined polemical manner than another similarly emotional Whig pamphlet of 1713, *The Present State of Fairy-Land. In Several Letters from Esquire Hush, an Eminent Citizen of Fickle-Borough, to the King of Slave-Onia*. Unlike the restrained polemics of this pamphlet and the matter-of-fact tone of *A Full Answer to the Conduct of the Allies* (1712), Maynwaring virtually throws his invectives and slogans about, repeating his conspiracy thesis "The friends of *France* cannot love whom *France* hates"[5] like a refrain and firing salvos of affective language to drive home his point: liberal order versus slavery and tyranny[6]. There is not much reasoning and what little there is is sometimes ill-placed[7]. The pamphlet seems somewhat haphazard, an immediate tit-for-tat, erratic in places as if all the author had in mind was a quick rejoinder to Swift's pamphlet. The end is actually not bad. There the author settles his personal account with his opponent, and to direct attention to the latter's dubious position he

---

1 *Ibid.*, p. 5.
2 See Swift, *Political Tracts 1711-1713*, p. 27.
3 *Remarks*, p. 6.
4 *Ibid.*, p. 37.
5 *Ibid.*, p. 38.
6 See e.g. *ibid.*, p. 34.
7 *Ibid.*, pp. 24-25.

asks several rhetorical questions: "Is it enough to pretend a Zeal for the Church, and a hatred of Indulgence; a concern for Land, and a contempt of Credit; an Inclination to *France*, and an Aversion to the *Dutch*?"[1].

Remarks shows the Whigs' political will to hold their own, it employs rhetoric for the purpose of instant and rather crude retribution. This is why Maynwaring makes such generous use of emotive and thus polarising terms popularized through Whig propaganda. It is one of the flaws of *Remarks*, however, that, its militant tone notwithstanding, references to leading Government politicians remain rather vague - obviously a deliberate device of Whig journalism - and that Maynwaring hardly goes beyond an ironical jibe at the men behind Swift and other Tory writers. In several places the raving repartees seem uncontrolled and indicate the degree of perplexity that *The Conduct of the Allies* caused in the ranks of the Opposition. *Remarks* is an extreme example of emotional rhetoric, of polarisation and the massive use of politically manipulative language. And yet it is representative of all Whig pamphlet literature, which in its fight to swing the public mood in its favour never relied on the power of facts alone.

Reflections upon the Examiner's Scandalous Peace and *Remarks on a False, Scandalous, and Seditious Libel* are two extremes between which the subtle nuances of rhetoric in Whig pamphlet literature unfolded.

2. THE POLITICAL ESSAY

Although the pamphlet was the established genre for serious political discourse, the significance of the essay increased under Queen Anne. Political essays appeared in weekly periodicals and similar publications, which specialised in commenting on political events that had been reported elsewhere, particularly in the daily papers. During Queen Anne's reign the opinion-forming periodicals concentrating on the political essay had a perceptible influence on the public debate[2]. John Tutchin's *Observator*, which still used the dialogue format, had been founded as far back as 1702; this had been followed in 1704 by Defoe's *Review*, which introduced the 'leader' article into contemporary journalism. When the *Examiner* appeared in 1710 - immediately after the new Government had established itself - the significance of the political essay was further enhanced, and it was to become a serious rival of the pamphlet as the hitherto leading genre.

One of the characteristics of journalism under Queen Anne is the fact that the leading political authors of the day - Swift and Defoe on the Tory side, Maynwaring, Ridpath and, before him, Tutchin on the Whig side - were essayists as well as pamphleteers. This shows how closely connected the two genres were in the struggle to shape public opinion. Especially during the turning-point debate essayists and pamphleteers worked together in propagating specific political views.

---

1 *Ibid.*, p. 40.

2 Cf. De Beer, "The English Newspapers from 1695 to 1702", p. 127.

Such co-operation took place in October 1711[1], when Defoe's *Review* and some of his own pamphlets like *Reasons why this Nation Ought to Put a Speedy End to this Expensive War* pursued a common strategy in order to inform the public about how the existing political balance would be disturbed if Austria were to gain the Spanish throne. A similar relationship developed between *The Conduct of the Allies* and the revived *Examiner*, whose function it was to propagate Swift's propaganda first disseminated in his pamphlet. And as long as Opposition propaganda was co-ordinated by Maynwaring, it was the *Medley* and several Opposition pamphlets which jointly addressed readers to strengthen Whig positions. In these cases pamphlets and essays were like communicating tubes.

That the political essay was the most important newcomer on the propaganda stage is shown by - among other things - the new genre's role as a catalyst in bringing about long-term swings of the public mood. During the period of transition from the old Government to the new the *Examiner* was the spearhead of the Harley Ministry and was outstandingly efficient in the ongoing effort to change the public's perception. Beginning in the late autumn of 1710, Swift's *Examiner* persistently undermined Marlborough's prestige to prepare the terrain from which the final attack to annihilate the Whig hero was to be launched at the politically most favourable moment. At the end of April 1711 Swift broke the 'No peace without Spain' taboo in his weekly paper. This was a comparatively inconspicuous attempt to test public reaction to the Government's intended volte-face in its war policy[2]. The otherwise tight rhetorical structure of Swift's political papers was neglected in this case in favour of the essay genre's traditional task of heretically calling into question seemingly undisputed positions! The *Examiner* thus enabled the Government to cross another threshold without as yet risking open confrontation. Although the *Medley* succeeded quite well in its self-imposed task of countering the arguments of the *Examiner*, the latter, as the Government's propaganda spearhead, performed extremely well in eroding the residual prestige of the preceding Ministry by launching vitriolic attacks on leading Whig politicians and at the same time opening new perspectives. In a manner similar to Swift's, and also at the same time, Defoe used the political essay to break the ice, as it were. As in *The Succession of Spain Consider'd*, he has some critical thoughts on Austria in the wake of the Emperor's death in the *Review* of 28 April 1711, where he points to the possible future consequences for the European balance of power.

The essay was not only a quick and easy way to spread Government-inspired political messages but was also a very adequate instrument for keeping certain topics alive in the public mind and thereby strengthening the Government's role as the leading force in shaping public opinion. As a propaganda weapon the political essay could be used for short flashes as well as for sustained fire. In October 1711, for example, Defoe used his *Review* to systematically strengthen the Government's position vis-à-vis the Whigs' rhetoric of protest by painting the looming danger of hegemony on the European Continent, making Austria the culprit

---

1 Cf. Poston, "Defoe and the Peace Campaign", p. 111.
2 See *Examiner* 39, 26 April 1711.

instead of France[1]. The reaction of the *Observator*, which devoted a whole series of issues to refuting Defoe[2], who had switched camps and virtually assumed the role of a Government journalist, shows to what extent he had in fact succeeded in regaining the initiative for the Government and in binding enemy forces.

On the Tory side pamphlets and other genres took advantage of the *Examiner's* force and prestige, often used it as a point of reference and acknowledged it as an authority. On the Whig side it was rather the opposite. It was the periodicals which often referred back to the pamphlets to strengthen their own version of Whig policy. This trend changed of course when *The Conduct of the Allies* was published, which henceforth became the principal reference point for all other publications.

Towards the end of Queen Anne's reign it was the periodical essay that created an environment in which the political essay could flourish. This is why, after he had taken over the *Examiner*, Swift 's initial format was similar to that of the periodical essayists[3]. The immediate success of the *Tatler* brought additional motivation to the political periodicals, although as propagators of party propaganda they could not be as courteous in tone and manner.

But overall, the leading political weeklies did profit in different measures from the esteem in which the public held the periodical essay because of its literary qualities. Like the periodical essay, the political essay had little in common with the fact-oriented newspapers and the ponderous and somewhat long-winded style of the regular pamphlets. The political essay steered clear of both superficiality and pedantry. It offered a skilful combination of immediate reaction to and detailed comment on political issues. As to rhetorical sophistication and effect the political essay was often second to none. The political weeklies combined the dailies' topicality with the pamphlets' discursive method, which gave them a middle status of enviable flexibility between reporting news and commenting on it. Such flexibility had already been displayed by the *Tatler*, which, during the peace negotiations in 1709, had skilfully arranged the facts in a manner that turned news items into commentaries[4].

The political essay was a discursive genre whose purpose was to create political awareness, stir public emotions and sustain them over long periods. This it did with greater frequency and ease than any of the other genres at the time. It was indispensable as an instrument for keeping certain issues alive in the public consciousness and exerting constant pressure on the political opponent. Through all this it contributed to the diversity of the journalistic scene under Queen Anne

---

1 See details in "Focus", p. 89, note 3.

2 See details in "Focus", p. 90, note 3.

3 See on this Heinz-Joachim Müllenbrock, "Swift as a Political Essayist: The Strained Medium", *Reading Swift: Papers from The Second Münster Symposium on Jonathan Swift*, ed. Richard H. Rodino and Hermann J. Real (Munich, 1993), pp. 151-158.

4 See on this Edward A. Bloom and Lillian D. Bloom, "Steele and his Answerers: May 1709 - February 1714", *The Dress of Words. Essays on Restoration and Eighteenth Century Literature in Honor of Richmond P. Bond*, ed. Robert B. White, Jr. (University of Kansas Libraries, 1978), p. 172.

compared to that under her predecessor. To use a metaphor - not entirely inappropriate in view of the militancy of polemical exchanges - the pamphlets were the battleships in the journalistic armoury, some occasionally even serving as the flagship, whereas most political essays were the light cruisers with only some in the heavy cruiser class. The following brief analysis of the rhetorical features of the more important political weeklies[1] will reveal the particular configuration of forces putting their impact on this genre during the debate about war and peace at the end of Queen Anne's reign.

The Rhetorical Profile of the Main Political Periodicals

a) *The Examiner*

The Harley Ministry's demand for a foreign-policy change was nowhere more clearly expressed than in the *Examiner*. From the moment Swift took over the journal it became a weapon whose rhetoric was employed with one objective in mind: polarisation. The prevailing rhetorical device to serve this purpose in both style and argument was antithesis, which created straight front lines. Polemical antithesis was used both as a micro- and macrostructural element, sometimes dominating a whole series of issues as the predominant rhetorical feature. Swift wanted to make the *Examiner* the journalistic focus in his campaign to discredit the previous Government and in particular its war policy. This intention became quite obvious in the self-assured manner in which he signalled a new beginning and virtually ignored his opponents. He was no doubt convinced that distancing himself from others and passing over what they had to say - especially the author of the *Medley* - would contribute to the intended effect. And in the rare cases where he did react[2] it was probably to enhance the effect of his own statements, whereas the snide attacks of his opponents suffered from attrition through overuse. The authoritative pose[3] that Swift adopted in the *Examiner*, occasionally provoking ironic comments from his adversaries, but more often wry smiles, was part and parcel of the *Examiner's* technique.

Swift's approach of introducing a persona and adopting a moderate easy-going style was obviously intended to capitalise on the favourable public image of the essay periodicals - the *Tatler* was an instant success from the start. But he soon dis-

1 Although De Krey, *A Fractured Society. The Politics of London in the First Age of Party 1688-1715*, p. 215 realises the importance of the political essay, he does not attempt any analysis of the function of such papers (cf. pp. 218-219). A description of the function of the most important essay-sheets at the end of the Seven Years' War is given by Robert D. Spector, *Political Controversy. A Study in Eighteenth-Century Propaganda* (New York: Greenwood Press, 1992), although not much is said on the rhetorical profile.

2 See, e.g., *Examiner* 42 (17 May 1711) in reply to the *Medley*.

3 On this cf. also Frank H. Ellis, "Arthur Mainwaring as Reader of Swift's *Examiner*", *The Yearbook of English Studies* 11 (1981), pp. 65-66.

continued the persona device and chose a disembodied voice instead. Gradually he also changed his tone and style, and his very own rhetoric of polarisation became the hallmark of his periodical, while at the same time retaining some of the periodical essayists' moderate stance[1]. In all this Swift displayed considerable cunning, as a few examples will show. In numbers 17 (23 November 1710), 18 (30 November 1710) and 28 (8 February 1711) Swift castigated the seeming lack of gratitude towards the Duke of Marlborough, exposed the Earl of Wharton, thinly disguised as Verres, and in a letter to Crassus drew up the Duke of Marlborough's catalogue of misdeeds yet again[2]. In these issues the author begins on the moderate note of a periodical essayist and then develops the antithesis between the previous Government's corruption and the new Government's sense of responsibility. In these carefully structured articles he adapts classical rhetorical devices to suit his polemical and satirical style[3]. In the *Examiner* Swift resorted to stinging satire because the new Tory Government would only enjoy public approval if the previous Government's prestige could be destroyed through systematic attacks on the Duke of Marlborough.

Swift created the impression that his sharp-tongued appeals were directed at the entire nation[4], but it was really the landed gentry he addressed, because unlike the Whig-oriented moneyed men, parvenus of the 1688 Revolution, they were to him the backbone of the nation and the heart of the Tories. In his propaganda campaign for the new Government Swift relentlessly made use of polarisation and through sheer linguistic chutzpah succeeded in breaking through the solid bulwark of his opponents' defences. Hyperbole such as his allegation in *Examiner* 18 (30 November 1710) that "Nine Parts in ten of the Kingdom"[5] support Harley's political course was supposed to show the authority and strength of the new Government, whereas the Whig opposition was reduced to and stigmatised as "a routed Cabal of hated Politicians"[6]. Time and again he presented his antithesis of the new Ministry serving Queen and Country and the old Ministry with the family clique around Marlborough and Godolphin as its nucleus, who for reasons of self-interest had prolonged the war. Swift's staccato style ensured that his antitheses were etched on the public mind, preparing the terrain for the massive propagada strike of *The Conduct of the Allies* late in November 1711.

With his sloganising rhetoric[7] - directing his acid ad hominem attacks consistently at leading Whig politicians, while sparing his journalist colleagues in the Opposition camp[8] - he kept up the pressure on the political foe and gradually set

---

1 Cf. Müllenbrock, "Swift as a Political Essayist", pp. 153-156.

2 Harris' statement that "Swift was careful to maintain his own impartial stance" (*A Study of the Paper War*, p. 164) is only valid in a legal sense; his rhetorical strategy made his partisanship all the more conspicuous.

3 See Müllenbrock, pp. 156-157 for Swift's procedure in *Examiner* 28.

4 See Ellis, "Arthur Mainwaring as Reader of Swift's *Examiner*", p. 73.

5 Swift, *The Examiner and Other Pieces Written in 1710-11*, p. 26. See also the almost identical formulation in number 27 (1 February 1711).

6 *Ibid.*, p. 78.

7 Cf. Ellis, "Arthur Mainwaring as Reader of Swift's *Examiner*", p. 64.

8 On this strategy see also Speck, "*The Examiner* Examined", pp. 147-148.

the Harley Ministry's offensive in motion. Number 39 (26 April 1711) of the *Examiner* illustrates Swift's technique of using rhetoric in order to skilfully tap into political issues, even if sometimes only tentatively. It is here that he performs a salto mortale by distancing himself from the 'No peace without Spain' policy while at the same time having the effrontery to denounce the policy sanctioned by the House of Lords Address of 1707 as a "monstrous Step in Politicks". Perhaps such exaggeration was meant to contain any emerging self-doubt among the Tories, but Swift's main intention, of course, was to shift the responsibility to the Whigs in the forthcoming debate on the Spanish question. By denouncing the past policy towards Spain he puts the ball in the court of the Whigs, whom he accuses of steering a perverse course, thereby forcing them to justify themselves. Swift's overdoses of rhetoric enhanced the publicity of his statements. Although the *Medley*, specialising in polemical rejoinders to the *Examiner*, gave no quarter and finally became a thorn in the latter's flesh, Swift had caused the Opposition considerable loss of terrain whilst at the same time amassing vast propaganda capital which was to yield rich interest when at the decisive stage of the debate *The Conduct of the Allies* was published.

When the *Examiner* reappeared early in December 1711, it lacked Swift's rhetorical brilliance, but it was still a skilfully edited propaganda medium. The revived *Examiner* was to *The Conduct of the Allies* what the cushion of a billiards table is to the balls. The pamphlet provided the periodical with multiple opportunities for its polemical arguments to rebound. Thus the periodical helped in its more modest way to bring about a change in the war policy debate and - a measure of its efficacy - was constantly in the Opposition's sights.

b) *A Review*

The second pillar on which the new Administration's propaganda rested was Defoe's *Review*, whose rhetorical profile ideally complemented that of the *Examiner*. The latter was to attack the Opposition head-on. The *Review*, however, in addition to addressing moderate Tories, was above all to seek assent to the Government's peace policy among those still undecided in the Opposition camp, which led Defoe to adopt a well-balanced rhetoric that considered alternative options and in an obliging tone suggested that readers do the same. The *Review* was the soft-spoken advocate of the Government's new policy. Determined and yet conciliatory it tried to win the support and acclaim of the sceptics. Its rhetoric was that of consensus, not polarisation. Aimed at advancing Harley's political objective of a broader political base, it took into account the diverse political leanings among the Government's possible supporters.

The *Review* of 13 October 1711 executed the turnaround on the Spanish question, the justification being that reason demanded that a distinction be made between "The whole undivided monarchy of *Spain*" and "*Old Spain*". From now on the *Review* followed a course of equidistance to France and Austria, neither of which, as was explained in great detail, was to be allowed to increase its power to the point of unsettling the political balance in Europe. The issues of 25 October

1711 and 6 March 1712 are good examples of the rhetorical technique that was the *Review's* hallmark: arguments are well-balanced, opposing views are carefully weighed, positions are considered from a seemingly non-partisan point of view and the middle-of-the-road solutions that the Harley Ministry would be prepared to go along with are presented. The typical structure of an issue of the *Review* reflects a way of thinking aloud which considers both sides of a coin. Repetition[1] is used to create the impression of painstaking thoroughness and openness, which may even include the readiness to admit errors. After the policy change on the Spanish question the prevailing technique of the *Review* consisted in translating into rhetoric Defoe's central point after the death of Emperor Joseph I: "The case is altered now". Defoe's manifest aversion to the "exorbitance" of any one power, no matter which, finds its structural equivalent in his balanced rhetoric, which in turn shows his readiness to follow the dictate of reason and avoid extremes. The insistence on the danger which any strengthening of Austria would create illustrates the kind of labour-sharing relationship between Defoe and Swift as pamphleteers and also as essayists; while the *Review* played the Austrian card in the run-up to the Government's propaganda offensive, Swift shortly afterwards gave the go-ahead for the calumnious polemics against the Dutch, whom Defoe had spared. The need for a change of attitude towards Austria in the wake of changed circumstances remained the *Review's* staple argument until the spring of 1713. The aim was to increase the periodical's credibility and lend conviction to its author, who had deviated from the Whig course, a step which forced him on to a somewhat tortuous path[2].

Defoe's conciliatory rhetoric, which sought consensus even with those who held opposing views, embraced everything to do with the peace issue, e.g. on 30 October 1711, when he denounced the parties' extreme positions, or on 21 February 1712, when he attacked an altogether too narrow interpretation of the commitment that the alliance imposed on its members. Unlike Swift in the *Examiner* and Maynwaring in the *Medley*, Defoe only rarely used party-political labels for polemical ends. The *Review* seemed so balanced in tone because the critical element regarding opposing views only slightly outweighed the author's aim to state his own position clearly. Direct attacks were rare, ad hominem assaults almost absent. This shows Defoe's effort to maintain a tone of disciplined reasoning. However, beginning in October 1711, he introduced an emotional element into the hitherto matter-of-fact presentation of the war and peace issue. He thus adapted his consensus rhetoric to the increasingly heated debate between Whigs and Tories. In this, too, Defoe the essayist made a concerted effort with Defoe the pamphleteer.

From approximately mid-October 1711, the *Review* fulfilled an important complementary function; together with *Reasons Why* and others of Defoe's pamphlets it helped to establish a bridgehead for the Government to prepare the ground for

---

1 In this way Defoe remained true to himself both as political essayist and pamphleteer; cf. also references on page 128, note 7.

2 This task is described by Downie ("Mr. Review and His Scribbling Friends", p. 365) over-harshly, but with some justification, as "dirty work".

its forthcoming propaganda offensive. After his about-turn on the Spanish question, the author of the *Review* found it decidedly more difficult to sound convincing in his protestations of independence than, for instance, in his earlier rejoinder to the *Examiner* on 14 December 1710, and the *Observator*'s continual attacks on the renegade were not without effect. He was noticeably ill at ease having to unequivocally come out on the Government's side in an atmosphere of increasing polarisation. During the Government's head-on attack on Marlborough and the Whig Opposition in the first quarter of 1712, the *Review's* performance was less impressive and less self-assured than before. During the mud-slinging campaign against Marlborough, of which Defoe, who had been generous in his praise of the General, disapproved[1], it was difficult for the periodical to make itself heard. Significantly it was only in the pamphlet that Defoe, who had a public past as the author of the *Review*, was able to adopt a sometimes aggressive tone towards Marlborough from the security of comparative anonymity.

c) *The Medley*

It soon became apparent that the *Whig-Examiner* was ineffective. Therefore, to counter the impact of the *Examiner*, a new periodical was launched whose tone was belligerent right from the beginning. By pitting Maynwaring against Swift, the new Whig mouthpiece was committed to a style of personalised antagonism. As Ellis has shown[2], Maynwaring was sharp-witted and sarcastic, always eager to read what his opponent had to say. Maynwaring's strategy may be described as 'meticulous response'. He would normally deal with those of his opponent's arguments which were particularly vulnerable. But since Swift usually chose to remain silent, there was not much of a 'dialogue'. What mostly happened is illustrated in number 37 of *The Medley* (11 June 1711). After quoting from the *Examiner*, the specific argument brought forward by Swift is refuted step by step, following which Maynwaring deals with the topic in question from his own point of view.

This fault-finding approach, not unlike an accountant's, enabled Maynwaring to present Swift as "The Blunderer"[3]. And on several occasions he did indeed succeed in exposing a number of errors, sometimes on important points of fact, as for example in number 37 of the *Medley*, where he corrects Swift with the help of a reader's letter to the editor. In *Medley* 10 (4 December 1710), which deals with the obligation to show gratitude towards the Duke of Marlborough, Maynwaring shows with skilful rhetoric that *Examiner* 17 (23 November 1710) offers a good example of what Swift must have had in mind when in *Examiner* 15 (9 November 1710) he wrote about the deliberate telling of lies in political matters. *Medley* 19 (5 February 1710) advises the Tories not to credit the Whigs with any part in the Revolution of 1688/89, in which only good churchmen had a share. Towards the end of this issue Maynwaring wittily takes a dig at Swift's preference for landed

---

1 See the *Review* of 22 January 1712.

2 See "Arthur Mainwaring as Reader of Swift's *Examiner*", pp. 49-66.

3 Cf. *ibid.*, p. 65.

men by pointing out that the financially potent Dutch hardly count "because they have a Trading Interest only; no Landed Interest, no Church Interest, in which we have a great advantage over them"[1].

But were such sallies, though admittedly witty, sufficient to neutralize the belligerent Tory periodical? The latter's authoritative pose, noted, for example, in issues 13 (25 December 1710) and 19 (5 February 1711) of Maynwaring's periodical, and much resented by the *Medley* in spite of its own self-assured repartees, was based on the claim that what it had to say was so unprecedented, so important that any criticism of detail was simply beside the point. Maynwaring's (and occasionally Oldmixon's) casuistry verged on the pedantic[2] and did more damage to the personal image of their opponent than to the political substance of his periodical[3]. The *Medley* remained defensive, the initiative was always on the side of its opponent, who might at times prove vulnerable on individual points of fact but could hardly be seriously harmed in his general approach. The *Medley's* technique of being doggedly reactive, of fragmentizing the issues, its lack of vision[4], led to personal skirmishes instead of parrying the opponent's challenges and concentrated more on fault-finding than on offering political alternatives. In *Medley* 20 (12 February 1711) Maynwaring's cutting remark that the *Examiner* "differs with his own Majority of Nine Parts in Ten of the Kingdom"[5], is really nothing but cheap repartee. The *Medley*'s persistent but somehow mulish personal attacks and at the same time its failure to offer the public a more positive perspective amounted to a serious fault in its overall strategy. The *Protestant Post-Boy*, whose author treated Roper ("my Friend Abel") in the same condescending way as Swift had been treated by Maynwaring, found it much easier to project such an image. It was also typical of the *Medley* to launch personal attacks almost exclusively at Swift, the ersatz target in a somewhat anaemic war, whose own ad hominem sorties were nearly always directed at Whig politicians.

The *Medley* never started a big counter-offensive, seeking engagement in separate theatres of war instead. Like the Whig pamphlets, its aim was to narrow the enemy's scope for political change by constant reference to binding parliamentary

---

1 *Swift vs. Mainwaring: 'The Examiner' and 'The Medley'*, ed. Ellis, p. 226.

2 A contemporary opponent, Clement, ironically and quite openly referred to Maynwaring's somewhat laboured polemics, pointing to the "Scholastick Conceits" of "his flashy wit" (*A Vindication of the Faults on Both Sides, from the Reflections of the Medley, the Specimen-Maker, and a Pamphlet, Entituled, Most Faults on One Side* [London, 1710], p. 5).

3 One of the very few who unequivocally point out that applying pedantic logical standards did not take any wind out of Swift's journalistic sails is Guy Laprevotte: see "*Examiner* et *Medley*: La Référence à l'Antiquité dans le Débat Politique", *Bulletin de la Société d'Etudes Anglo-Américaines des XVIIe et XVIIIe Siècles* 27 (November 1988), p. 133.

4 L.S. Horsley, "Rogues or Honest Gentlemen: The Public Characters of Queen Anne Journalists", *Texas Studies in Literature and Language* 18 (1976), p. 220 correctly states: "The role of Maynwaring and his colleagues as writers opposed to the *Examiner* led them to define their own identity in a peculiarly negative way".

5 *Swift vs. Mainwaring*, pp. 233-234.

resolutions and similar decisions. Hardly ever did the *Medley* come forward with any position of its own. A rare exception is number 30 of 23 April 1711, which was prompted by the appointment of new Governors of the Bank of England. Unlike Whig pamphlets, especially in the second half of 1711, the *Medley* lacked the drive to successfully promote its policy of preserving the status quo. Stylistically its defensive method of simply reacting to the enemy's moves is apparent in the sparing use of charged words like "Jacobite" and "Pretender". Not even "Revolution" appears anywhere near as often as in the *Examiner*. Number 31 (30 April 1711) illustrates the periodical's self-imposed restraint in being purely reactive. Swift's comparatively inconspicuous presentation of his policy change on the Spanish question is immediately noticed but then, in the *Medley's* fragmentising technique, the author quietly passes on to other topics and never takes it up again in subsequent issues. On whatever topic the *Medley* scored points, its successes were always partial and never amounted to a substantial territorial gain that would have forced back the enemy. The *Medley* never propagated any uplifting political message, its sometimes almost scholastic rhetoric was the expression of a pedantic and cavelling mindset[1] .

In the spring of 1712 the *Medley* returned - although too late - twice weekly, and this time without Maynwaring's participation. Right from the first issue (3 March 1712) it was clear that henceforth it would not limit its activities to responding to individual opponents but would broaden its scope to provide a platform for its own version of political truth. There was less verbal wit in the new *Medley*, but more thrust in its rhetoric, which focused uncompromisingly on the deep and principled disagreement on war policy between the Government and the Opposition. Number 3 (10 March 1712) lucidly described the Government's long-term and successful strategy to lend plausibility to its volte-face on war policy, thus at the same time highlighting the territorial gains of Tory propaganda. Occasionally the *Medley* adopted Maynwaring's and Hare's technique of fact-oriented refutation of enemy positions - e.g. in the above-mentioned third issue - but by and large the political situation, favourable to the Tories, forced it to make ad hoc responses in order to penetrate enemy lines wherever there was an opening in order to regain some lost territory. However, as late as the summer of 1712 the new *Medley* had not gained any rhetorical profile which would have enabled it to seriously embarrass the Tories.

d) *The Observator*

Alongside the *The Protestant Post-Boy* and the *Flying-Post* - which did not fit the usual pattern since, despite being newspapers, they devoted large sections to commentary -, the *Observator* - praised by Swift as the best Opposition paper in *Examiner* 42 (17 May 1711) - was the only opinion-forming Whig periodical between the late autumn of 1711 and the spring of 1712, that is during the decisive

---

1 Laprevotte rightly speaks of an "érudition fertile, certes, en rapprochements heureux, mais parfois vétilleuse et pédante" ("*Examiner* et *Medley*", p. 136).

period of the turning-point debate. The *Observator*'s structural approach followed the question-and-answer format which pre-dated the periodical essay proper and which was typical of the early stages of journalism. But even so, the rather unsophisticated *Observator*, though lacking stylistic refinement, attained a fairly high level of rhetorical competence. Ample use of repetition led to frequently redundant information as, for instance, in the issue of 21-24 March 1711. But under Ridpath's[1] prudent editorship the *Observator*'s arguments were usually clear and easy to follow. This was partly due to the regular use of emotive words in order to underscore the political polarisation. Unlike the *Medley*, which tried to emulate the intellectual standard of the *Examiner*, the *Observator* was aimed at a lower social stratum, but its clear-cut unequivocal rhetoric showed what the genre - an essay-style weekly - was able to achieve.

The *Observator* came into its own particularly after the war-and-peace debate intensified, following the publication of the Preliminaries in mid-October 1711, and during the ensuing polemical exchanges it became an unmistakable feature on the journalistic landscape. It was quite characteristic that in its issue of 13-17 October 1711 the *Observator* immediately chose as its target Roper's radical *Post Boy* in order to attack the Government's political volte-face on the question of peace. During the following period of intensifying propaganda it was through its sheer persistence that the *Observator* contributed to increasing and stabilizing Whig pressure. Thus, between 20-24 October and 7-10 November 1711 there was an uninterrupted series of comments on the Tory argument that the threat of hegemony had shifted, a point that had been dealt with in previous issues and was to be taken up again later. In its summarising headlines the *Observator* made regular prominent use of the word "exorbitant", which Defoe had launched against Austria, thus presenting familiar content in a familiar form. The *Observator* had frequent recourse to rhetorical questions in order to avoid any ambiguity and - as illustrated in its issue of 17-21 November 1711 - largely dispensed with irony, the effect of which could never be calculated with certainty. It stood up to its rivals with considerable journalistic skill and gave its Whig clientele something to identify with. This in turn led to an excessive number of references to France, the denounced enemy, never more so than in the last quarter of 1711.

The *Observator* sent unmistakable signals of Whig perseverance and, from the issue of 24-28 November 1711, began to expose the author of the *Review* as a turncoat, causing him considerable discomfort, as is shown by Defoe's reaction in the *Review*[2]. Beginning with the issue of 1-5 December 1711, which by way of introduction cites at length Maynwaring's pamphlet *Remarks upon the Present Negotiations of Peace Begun between Britain and France* as an authority, the *Observator* now trained its guns on *The Conduct of the Allies*. The key position of *The Conduct of the Allies*, like previously that of Defoe's *Reasons Why*[3], did not go unnoticed. However, the immediate and intense attacks on Swift, accusing

---

[1] Ridpath can be assumed to have taken an active interest in the continuation of the *Observator* soon after Tutchin's death.

[2] See e.g. the *Review* dated 29 November 1711.

[3] See the *Observator* of 20-24 October 1711.

him, as might have been expected, of being a Jacobite[1], show that one serious danger posed by Swift's pamphlet had escaped the *Observator*, namely the snowballing effect of continually stirring anti-Dutch emotions, which finally resulted in a virtual avalanche of anti-Dutch sentiment.

The *Observator's* uncompromising collision course, aimed at directly engaging the enemy, gave Whig propaganda an idiosyncratic touch of militant perseverance. The *Observator's* straightforward rhetoric exposed very convincingly to what extent the Tories had deviated from essential Whig positions which had once been theirs as well. Repetition became the *Observator's* hallmark, a kind of didactic 'recycling' of arguments, which turned out to be more efficient than the *Medley's* fragmentizing method, which squandered rhetorical energy instead of focusing it. Occasionally, the *Observator* used forceful imagery, as for example in the issue of 12-15 March 1712, where its opponents are accused of having tried everything "to Mohawk the Union and Barrier-Treatys, the Empire, and the *Dutch* Commonwealth". In this case the *Observator*, in retorting to Tory authors who had calumniated the Whigs as Mohocks[2], seems almost to have coined a new verb; in Johnson's *Dictionary*, at any rate, "mohawk" is only a noun[3]. Like the Whig pamphlets, the *Observator* incessantly pointed to the factual evidence of parliamentary resolutions and similar texts[4]. On every possible occasion it brandished the accusation of Jacobite leanings and pro-French feelings like a cudgel against the peace faction in the Government camp[5]. With its strong didactic streak the defiant *Observator* came close to the Opposition's most important newspaper, the *Flying-Post*, which even in difficult times loudly sounded the Whig trumpet[6].

3. THE NEWSPAPER

Newspapers and periodicals were different in both function and structure. The 'news' papers provided the public with basic factual information, the kind of raw material that the periodicals used for detailed discussion[7]. Only on very few occa-

---

1 See the editions of 5-8 December and 12-15 December 1711 of the *Observator*.

2 See, for instance, Hoffman's broadside *Vulpoon in the Snare; or, a Hue and Cry after Eight and Twenty Millions Sunk by the Hawkubite Crew* (1712).

3 In the broadside mentioned in the preceding footnote, however, the gerund "*Mohocking*" had already occurred in the twelfth stanza.

4 See e.g. the *Observator* of 17-20 October 1711.

5 See e.g. the editions of 5-8 December and 12-15 December 1711 of the *Observator*.

6 That Ridpath's militant journals went strongly against the Tory grain becomes especially apparent in the acrimonious denunciation contained in *The Rattle-Snake, or, a Bastonado for a Whigg* (London, 1712), a poem by William Forbes of Disblair.

7 Ellis has correctly described this relationship with reference to the two Tory organs of polemic thus: "Generically, *The Examiner* constitutes the editorial page (complete with

sions did the functions of the two genres overlap so that one did the job of the other or both did the same. Carrying news was the job of the newspaper, with news from abroad as their first property and domestic news in second place. This was the format of the official *London Gazette*, the *Daily Courant*, the first daily paper, the *Evening Post*, the first evening paper, and the *British Mercury*.

Although reporting news was the first priority, our concern is the occasional merging of news items and opinion-forming comment. Thus the *London Gazette* of 6-8 December 1711 first informed its readers about the Queen's Speech in Parliament of 7 December, which, printed in full, was directed against "the Arts of those who delight in War". This was tantamount to a partisan comment and set a precedent for further attempts to influence public opinion. Sermons and other genres not long afterwards also referred to the Queen's Speech, which gave Government propaganda some respite at a critical moment and shortly afterwards gave impetus to the Government media when these went on the offensive[1]. Sometimes mere information was demonstrably not the papers' prime objective. Especially foreign news was interspersed with rumours, moods, interpretation and guesses; the *Flying-Post* of 6-9 December 1712, for example, mingled opinion and news. Although details of places and dates were supposed to create the impression of authenticity, the reader - especially with news from abroad - was often hardly able to distinguish between the opinions of people concerned, the opinion of the correspondent or even that of the editor. A good example is the *Post Boy* of 26-28 April 1711. Home news was usually more neutral, especially when official announcements were printed. But even here there was a concomitant partisan note as for example in the *Flying-Post* and the *Post Boy*, which regularly followed up reporting - already tainted by party bias - with aggressive polemics.

Opinion-forming was not limited to odd bits of polemical comment mixed with news but was done even more deliberately with particular targets in view. To demonstrate this form of participation in the polemical interaction of the time, we shall take a look at the parties' two ideologically most outspoken papers, the Tory *Post Boy* and the Whig *Flying-Post*. The *Post Boy* usually had a number of news items, both from abroad and at home, on military and diplomatic matters with occasionally some information on trade and finance, as its issues of 14-17 April 1711 and 15-17 April 1712 illustrate. Such seemingly neutral reporting would at times have a partisan slant. In its issue of 26-28 April 1711, for example, there was a report from The Hague in which it became apparent that the paper advocated putting out feelers with a view to negotiating a peace. In a paper committed to straightforward reporting without any argumentative interpretation such interpolation of opinion posing as information could act as a stimulus in the process of

---

letters to the editor also written by Swift) of a weekly newspaper of which Abel Roper's *Post-Boy* is the news section" (*Swift vs. Mainwaring*, p. xxi).

1 In his broadside *A New-Years Gift for the Plunderers of the World* Hoffman prays: "Good GOD of PEACE hence scatter far/ Those Plunderers that delight in War!" The selfsame couplet can be found at the end of another broadside by this author, *The True Copy of a Paper Stuck upon the D. of M-'s Gate at St. James's, on Saturday last, Being the Day of Her Majesty's Accession to the Crown* (1712).

shaping public opinion. In fact the Tories regularly used Roper's *Post Boy* to fly a kite. The issue of 26-28 April 1711, for instance, reported on French objections to ceding Spain but declared the alleged beginning of peace talks a mere chimera. Together with Swift's pilot essay in the *Examiner*[1] this must be seen as a synchronised effort to test the public's reaction to new political steps. Taboos were thus broken and a long-term process of changing public opinion was initiated. That the *Post Boy* was simply acting on cue from the Government is shown by the fact that Swift never distanced himself from it, whereas in number 16 of the *Examiner* (16 November 1710) he characterized Leslie's *Rehearsal* as extremist only to present himself as moderate and reasonable.

On rare occasions, which duly attracted public attention, the *Post Boy* went beyond inserting the odd political dig into otherwise neutral reporting and crossed into the territory of the genuinely opinion-forming periodicals. The *Post Boy* of 13-16 October 1711 carried the text of the French Preliminaries and preceded it with a lengthy essay-style commentary which supported the Government's peace campaign. The issue of 8-10 November 1711 contained an essay-like summary of the Tories' strongest arguments in favour of ending the war and accordingly aroused the attention of the Opposition press[2]. The fact that Roper used the essay form at a critical stage of the debate to address his partisan readers even more directly shows that the role of the newspaper was that of complementing other genres in their journalistic function. The examples cited fit into the larger pattern of a Tory propaganda campaign in which pamphlets and periodicals were the main participants and to which the newspapers made a co-ordinated contribution. The *Post Boy* of 13-16 October 1711 emotionalized the war theme in the manner of Defoe, stressing the heavy toll of lives and the financial burden and offering a new view of the balance-of-power principle with regard to France and Austria. The *Post Boy* of 8-10 November 1711 contained the charge of war profiteering and must be seen in connection with the imminent publication of *The Conduct of the Allies*. When right at the beginning Roper disparagingly speaks of "a Sett of Men", for example those opposed to ending the war, this anticipates Swift's later "a sort of Men" on the first page of *The Conduct of the Allies*. And Roper's rhetorical question whether "the Sober, and Impartial Part of Mankind would not censure his Conduct"[3] if the Emperor were to remain adamant also points ahead to *The Conduct of the Allies* by even mentioning the word "conduct". Actually, Roper had used the ominous word before in the issue of 13-16 October 1711 with reference to the Duke of Marlborough, the true target of Tory propaganda. The *Post Boy*'s strategy to influence public opinion becomes evident also in the issues between 8-11 November and 20-22 November 1712. In the guise of a reply to *The Sighs of Europe* (1712), which contains a dramatic appeal never to back down on the Habsburg solution to the Spanish question, the *Post Boy* obviously sought to

---

1 Number 39 (26 April 1711); cf. on this pp. 51 and 142 of this book.

2 See the editions of 17-21 November and 1-5 December 1711 of the *Observator* as well as the *Protestant Post-Boy* of 10-13, 13-15 and 15-17 November 1711, and also the *Flying-Post* of 10-13 November 1711.

3 *The Post Boy*, 8-10 November 1711.

neutralize the impact of the Whig publication. Having previously - in the autumn of 1711 - imitated the essay, the *Post Boy* in this particular case slipped into the role of pamphleteer.

Whereas the *Post Boy* showed considerable versatility in its occasional adaptations of different genre-formats, the pugnacious *Flying-Post* was always a hybrid, mixing news and opinion. It hovered between tendentious reporting and aggressive polemics. With its use of various journalistic sub-genres it offered its readers considerable variation[1], whereas at the same time its strident polemical tone lent it unmistakable political contours. The issue of 17-19 July 1712, for example, contains Whig propaganda expressed in different forms, variations on the theme of the High Church-Jacobite threat. The *Flying-Post* made generous use of the formal scope of the essay-form, which gave it its unique position among the newspapers. Because of its polemical intrepidity it was closely observed in the enemy camp. The wide range of journalistic techniques[2] was meant to attract attention, and the unconventional paper became the stormy petrel of Whig propaganda.

Our survey would be incomplete without mentioning the newspapers' role as convenient instruments for the publication of diplomatic statements alongside more usual propaganda, which was how in particular the Allied governments tried to put a tight rein on the Harley Ministry. It was thus the Whig Opposition which profited most from the role of the newspapers as a means of expanding the scope of diplomacy into the public sphere. The *Daily Courant*, for example, which had a Whig bias, published in its issue of 5 December 1711 the so-called *Hanover Memorial* or *Bothmer Memorial*[3], in which the Elector of Hanover opposes the Government's peace policy. Apart from the usual advertisements this issue contained no other news besides this foreign intervention. The use of the highly emotive word "Slavery" in the fourth paragraph of the *Memorial* seems to indicate that the document was conceived from the beginning with a view to publishing it. The *Hanover Memorial* was printed in the *Flying-Post* of 4-6 December 1711, too, and also featured prominently in the *Evening Post* of 4-6 December 1711 and the *Protestant Post-Boy* of 8-11 and 11-13 December 1711. Publication of the document by the *Daily Courant* and other papers lifted morale among the Whigs and annoyed the Tories[4]. The influence of the publication on the further course of the debate is shown by the Tories' rejoinder *A Letter from a Whig-Gentleman in the Country to his Friend in Town* (1712)[5]. Through the publication of the *Memorial*

---

1 In the wide variety of ways it couched political contents, the *Flying-Post* ignored the austere demands of a major Whig apologist who had pronounced in the context of reviewing hostile writings: "Fiction and Ornament are of no Advantage, but when they serve a Cause, that can't bear to be seen in its true Light" (Hare, *The Management of the War in Four Letters to a Tory-Member*, p. 1).

2 See, for instance, the issue of 22-24 November 1711 where - at a crucial stage of the public debate - two poems celebrating the Elector of Hanover and the Duke of Marlborough precede the more regular reporting of news.

3 On this cf. also Coxe, *Memoirs of John Duke of Marlborough*, VI, 134.

4 See Churchill, *Marlborough*, VI, 488.

5 Cf. Boyer, *Quadriennium Annae Postremum; or the Political State of Great Britain*, 2nd ed., vol. I and II for the Year 1711, 678-679.

the House of Hanover made known its long-term party-political leanings, thereby sending signals that did not go unnoticed among politicians in Britain[1]. When Samuel Buckley, the editor of the *Daily Courant*, printed the *Memorial* of the States General in April 1712, this angered the Government so much that legal proceedings were initiated[2]. This particular kind of journalism, which produced classified material[3] for prophylactic purposes, and which even the Queen officially called a nuisance[4], reflected the Whig policy of containment and was the Opposition's counterpart to the practice of the *Post Boy*, which moved to the frontiers of journalism to explore the terrain for the Government. In her reply to the *Letter* of the States General the Queen rightly remarked that its publication in the *Daily Courant* had turned it into a "Remonstrance instead of a Representation, and an Appeal to the People instead of an Address to the Sovereign"[5], which illustrates how the Opposition deliberately used the press to reinforce diplomatic pressure.

Apart from such exceptions the newspapers were usually not able to deal with political issues in an argumentative way and, unlike pamphlets and essays, contributed little to their elucidation. And yet, although news reporting was their domain, they always found a way to bring particular issues before the public forum and thereby stimulated the political debate. Even in military matters pertaining to statistics the news-covering media managed to take on party-political colouring. During and after the Bouchain campaign, for example, each of the contending papers printed biased reports from sources friendly or hostile to their respective views. Thus the *Supplement* of 19-21 September 1711 presented its readers with exaggerated figures of English losses in French accounts. These were immediately refuted by the *Flying-Post* in its issue of 20-22 September 1711. The papers were not only on the receiving end acting simply as conduits for the news of the day. They played an active role in shaping public opinion, a process which, circumstances permitting, they could effectively re-direct, speed up and intensify. Although the papers did not see this as their primary function, it was nevertheless the sphere where they made considerable contributions. News reporting remained their first priority but it influenced the environment for political debate. Though there were differences in degree, news was hardly ever passed on as bare facts, the denotative topic was enriched with connotative trimmings. Via its reporting of news from Vienna, for example, a partisan paper such as the *Flying-Post* regularly conveyed the undisguised message of resolute Austrian resistance to a premature peace, as its issues of 27-29 November and 27-29 December 1711 illustrate. In its issue of 17-19 September 1711 the non-partisan *British Mercury*, for instance, reported from Holland on rumours about the Dutch attitude to the peace question and thus probably raised expectations in spite of the matter-of-fact style.

---

1 See also Hill, *Robert Harley*, p. 170.

2 See Boyer, *Quadriennium Annae Postremum*, III, 233-234.

3 See also the publication of the Emperor's *Letter* to the States General in the *Flying-Post* of 11-13 December 1711.

4 See Boyer, III, 359.

5 *Ibid.*, p. 360.

The Whig *Daily Courant*, on the other hand, in its issue of 21 April 1711 presented the *Resolution* of the States General after the death of Emperor Joseph I in such openly positive terms that this could be interpreted as signalling agreement, which turned the reporting of mere facts into an act of stimulating and guiding public reaction. Somewhere between the *British Mercury* and the *Daily Courant* belongs the *Evening Post*, with its issue of 15-18 December 1711, which informed its readers from The Hague about co-ordinating steps among the Allies. The fact that news reporting never took place in an emotional vacuum made the newspapers instruments - sometimes knowingly, sometimes unwittingly - in the opinion-forming process.

4. THE BROADSIDE

Any survey of the public genres under Queen Anne must include the broadside[1]. It was the shortest and literally the most spectacular of the propaganda media and the fastest to react. It testified to the fact that the sharing of party-political convictions led to a cultural interchange between 'high' and 'low'. The 'noisy' broadside was the tabloid of its age, whose sensational propagation of messages reached right across the social spectrum[2]. A contemporary pamphleteer remarked explicitly with regard to the impact of the cheap broadside material that "this is what the Rabble hear daily bawl'd about the Street, and greedily they suck in the Poison: These *Scriptions* reaching those who cannot buy above a Half pennyworth of Scandal at a Time; and as they make up the Numbers, the Mischief they do is the more pernicious"[3]. The broadside was the medium par excellence for spreading political messages. Its zippy presentation of controversial political views, which gave the genre a high entertainment value, made it the ideal instrument for instant polarisation. For Whigs and Tories alike it was a welcome completion of their propaganda armoury. The broadside gained its significance because the political print was only just developing and therefore played almost no part in the media dispute over the right peace.

In the wake of the publication of the Preliminaries on 13 October 1711 and Marlborough's dismissal early in 1712, the number of Whig and Tory broadsides increased considerably, which illustrates this genre's particular dependence on specific current events. The broadside needed something to react to, something that invited a quick response and thus provided an opportunity to whip up emo-

---

1 Only single sheets should be classified as broadsides. Regarding this customary classification cf. e.g. Paul Denzer, *Ideologie und literarische Strategie. Die politische Flugblattlyrik der englischen Bürgerkriegszeit 1639-1661* (Tübingen, 1991), p. 16. Cf. on this also *Illustrierte Flugblätter des Barock. Eine Auswahl*, ed. Wolfgang Harms *et al.* (Tübingen, 1983), p. vii.

2 Cf. also Speck, *Tory and Whig. The Struggle in the Constituencies 1701-1715*, p. 92.

3 *Who Plot Best; the Whigs or the Tories*, p. 16.

tions along party lines, which it did like no other genre. Spectacular events worked like a fuse igniting the broadside's potential for stirring emotions, boosting trends, and giving explosive issues adequate publicity. Here is an example: After the publication of the Preliminaries, Maynwaring's *An Excellent New Song, Called Mat's Peace* (1711) evidently played a key role in rekindling public awareness of the still unsolved Spanish question. Other broadsides like *The Procession* (1711) took a similar rhetorical approach. The genre's imagery and other deliberately emotional stylistic features enabled it to arouse feelings and create moods. A good example of the genre's potential for aggressiveness is the Whigs' *The Br-sh Embassadress's Speech to the French King* of March 1713. As instruments of party propaganda the broadsides made generous use of emotive words, key-terms in the parties' propaganda war, originally introduced by more substantial genres but readily utilised for their own ends. *The Procession's* use of "Pope", "Pretender" and related words characterizes the genre's endeavour, albeit to differing degrees, to make the public aware of certain political dangers - in this case the latent threat of Jacobitism - not by arguing a specific case but simply by taking up biased buzz words, thereby prejudicing the public's judgment[1]. Especially the broadsides' polarising language, their preference for ideologically charged terms, made them the ideal instrument for drumming into the public mind the parties' easily memorised political slogans. Their staccato style made them a high-decibel amplifier on the journalistic stage.

The broadside mostly sailed in the wake of other, more discursive genres, taking up their political language and arguments[2] and turning them into powerful weapons in its own arsenal of scandal-mongering rhetoric. Just as Whig broadsides adopted the term "Scandalous Peace" in - for instance - *An Excellent New Song* (1711), so Tory ones borrowed some of the reproaches against the Duke of Marlborough. Disconnected from their discursive context these borrowings were simplifications intended for a less educated or even uneducated readership. Thus the broadsides intensified what had emerged as the essential points in the other genres' discursive argumentation. Otherwise they had little to contribute to the solution of political controversies. Thus their aim was not to convert the political opponent but to encourage their own side[3]. The genre was essentially a secondary medium, serving as the primary media's amplifier. But there were exceptions. Occasionally the broadside played a more independent part, sending out well-calculated signals. In the early autumn of 1710 the genre seems to have taken on the task of sensitizing people to the implications of Godolphin's dismissal. Shaking up

---

1 H.T. Dickinson's description of how political prints operated in the later eighteenth century also applies to the broadsides of the early eighteenth century: "Political prints argued by assertion, appealed to authority and prejudice, and relied heavily upon shibboleths and rhetoric" (*Caricatures and the Constitution 1760-1832* [Cambridge, 1986], p. 20).

2 The following formulation by Roy Porter applies particularly to the broadside in the light of the fact that it was a genre whose train of thought relied heavily on other genres: "prints mirrored rather than made opinion" ("Seeing the Past", *Past and Present* 118 [1988], p. 191).

3 See also Denzer, *Ideologie und literarische Strategie*, p. 261.

the public was no doubt part of its domain. A more interesting example of occasional independence is Swift's *The Fable of a Widow and her Cat*, which appeared in January 1712. Taking advantage of the changed political situation this broadside assumed a pilot function in so far as the final appeal "Do him [Marlborough] Justice" was intended to goad the Commons, who were to meet shortly afterwards in order to assess the findings of the select committee, into assuming an uncompromising attitude. The well-timed publication of this broadside shows the Tories' skill in utilising the genre during the turning-point debate in order to accelerate the dismantling of the General. These examples, by the way, also illustrate the broadsides' usefulness as historiographic source material because they provide snapshots of the political mood and record contemporary events like a seismograph.

Any analysis of the broadside's contribution to party propaganda must not omit the fact that - rather surprisingly - it appeared in different strengths at different stages during the critical debate about the termination of the War of the Spanish Succession. Thus practically only Whig broadsides were published between the autumn and the end of November 1711, whereas Tory broadsides did not appear before the very end of that year or the beginning of the next[1]. These had been all but non-existent before December 1711! But then the scene changed and by January 1712 Tory broadsides outnumbered Whig ones. One reason for this might be that the genre needs a propaganda offensive to pull it along in its wake, which, - until Swift's *The Conduct of the Allies* - was only the case on the side of the Whigs, however. It is true that Whig propaganda offered brave resistance to the Tories well into the first quarter of 1712, but to unfold its entire potential of aggressive personalised rhetoric and reach mass circulation, the broadside needs a clearly defined target. Until November 1711 it was Defoe, pamphleteer and political essayist, who set the pace in Government journalism. His moderate tone and discursive method in dealing with the balance-of-power issue did not mobilise sufficient vituperative energy to spark off the production of broadsides. Only after the end of 1711, following Marlborough's dismissal and the opening of the emotional anti-Dutch campaign - which, interestingly, was largely ignored by the broadside -, did the Tories have a clearly defined target. It is not surprising, therefore, that this was the time when Tory broadside production and its impact reached a climax.

Only by this time had pamphlets and periodicals sufficiently popularized a number of key-words and slogans on which the broadside as a responsive follow-up genre usually depended[2]. Its linguistic dependence on the more sophisticated genres is illustrated by the fact that 'hard words' would only be used after they had gained currency through frequent application elsewhere. An example of this is the

---

1 One notable exception seems to have been Hoffman's *A Wonderful New Prophecy: Giving a Certain and True Account when the Church Ills will be Great again* (1711), which, however, is not as aggressive as the author's other examples of the genre.

2 Its capacity to inform - with regard to prints see Porter, "Seeing the Past", p. 200 - should not be denied in principle, but is nevertheless based on the resources of other, leading genres.

use of "perquisite" with reference to the Duke of Marlborough in broadsides like *The Grand Enquiry, or, What's to be done with Him?* (1712), Swift 's *A Fable of the Widow and her Cat* or *The Description of Dunkirk with Squash's and Dismal's Opinion* (1712). It was Swift who had already given the word an especially ominous ring in the famous *Examiner* essay about British ingratitude (23 November 1710). Shortly afterwards, in a pamphlet referring to the reproachful *Examiner* of 21 December 1710, the portentous word was there again, for instance, in a highly polemical passage incriminating Marlborough in the thin disguise of classical analogy[1]. More recently - and significantly - Swift had again used the term with disparaging intent in a crucial part of *The Conduct of the Allies*[2] and thus prepared for its further dissemination. This shows once again that the broadside's main function as a secondary medium was to intensify political statements and appeals and not primarily to elucidate and explain them. Political concepts like Britain's equidistance to France and Austria, Defoe's favourite topic since the autumn of 1711, which did not lend themselves easily to polemical presentation, were not taken up by the broadsides at all or - as in the prose broadside *Look, before You Leap* - only briefly raised as a question. There was nothing in this concept that could be translated into polemical wit or personalised calumny, which shows that only if there was room for sloganizing rhetoric did the broadside come into its own as a torchbearer of propaganda.

After the first confrontation of Tory and Whig broadsides in December 1711, it was in January 1712 that the polemical exchanges between Whigs and Tories included an unprecedented number of broadsides. This bears witness to the hitherto unknown intensity of the public debate, which employed the full range of political rhetoric including - on both sides - the fast sermons. The participation of all genres in the propaganda process at this time shows that this was the high point of the debate about the termination of the War of the Spanish Succession.

Since the turn of the year 1712 the co-ordination of Tory propaganda had taken a qualitative leap, which is illustrated not least by the multiple use to which the broadside was put[3]. The genre's principal function of sounding the trumpet for certain political issues was expanded, and for the first time broadsides concentrated on individual aspects of a specific issue, presenting a mosaic of views which formed a coherent picture of the rationale of Government propaganda. Thus, the thrust of the genre was intensified by virtually dismantling the dismissed General and Commander-in-Chief. This was facilitated by the fact that the broadsides' various points of attack had previously been put at the genre's disposal by Tory pamphlets and periodicals. This strategy of vociferously proclaiming Marlbo-

---

1 See *Reasons why a Certain Great G-l has not yet Receiv'd the Thanks of either of the two Houses of P-nt.... In a Letter to the Mayor of St. Albans* (*s.l.*, 1710), pp. 14-15.

2 See Swift, *Political Tracts 1711-1713*, ed. Davis, p. 42.

3 The remarkable thing here is the Government's determined will to mobilise; nevertheless ballads were still regarded in the later eighteenth century, for example during the Seven Years' War, as primarily a weapon of the Opposition; cf. on this John Brewer, *Party Ideology and Popular Politics at the Accession of George III* (Cambridge, 1976), p. 156.

rough's sins was intended to convince the public of the seriousness of the Whig leader's misdemeanours. After Marlborough had officially lost the Queen's confidence, this political decision found its extension in the joint propaganda chorus of broadsides and the other - more discursive - genres, which together held forth on the General, listing the stereotype catalogue of his alleged sins: aspiring to the crown, striving for personal gains and, besides, having simply had luck on his side. These skilfully orchestrated propaganda efforts, which publicly exposed Marlborough like on an X-ray screen, gave Tory propaganda an astonishing degree of coherence. Marlborough's dismissal by the Queen - a defensive measure - and the creation of twelve new Peers were both exploited by the Tories for their propaganda purposes in order to regain the offensive and raise the tone of the ongoing debate to a high polemical pitch. The Tory offensive, initiated by the publication of *The Conduct of the Allies*, reached its climax with the barrage of volleys that the broadsides launched against the Whigs' leading figure. Provided with ammunition by other genres, the broadsides displayed the Tories' aggressiveness in its most concentrated form and also their determination to bring about a change in the public debate. The broadside was an important instrument in the hands of the Tories in their effort to paint the public image of both the opponents and the supporters of peace in more clearly contrasting colours. The genre is a telling example of the inherent strength of Government propaganda.

5. THE SERMON

Among the main genres taking part in the debate about the War of the Spanish Succession the sermon was something special. In terms of numbers it ranked lowest, because sermons needed a special occasion, like commemorating the Queen's accession, or the death of Charles I[1]. They followed the rhythm of the ecclesiastical year, which restricted their discursive adaptability. Sermons would refer to certain current events but would not directly react to them like pamphlets, periodicals or broadsides. An exception is Hare's *The Charge of God to Joshua*, preached in September 1711 on the occasion of a victorious battle and subsequently published. But usually sermons were slower to take up political events owing to their dependence on the church calendar. Compared with the other genres of political rhetoric, sermons were rather inflexible.

Their comparatively rigid structure did not lend itself easily to treating political topics. Exordium, explicatio and peroratio usually formed the framework of a ser-

[1] On this compare most recently George Watson, "The Augustan Civil War", *The Review of English Studies*, N.S., XXXVI (1985), pp. 331-334. See also Robert E. Sullivan, *John Toland and the Deist Controversy. A Study in Adaptations* (Cambridge, Mass., and London, 1982), p. 309, note 28.

mon, and argumentatio and applicatio its centre[1]. Any reference to contemporary matters and any comment would normally be restricted to the applicatio, that part of a sermon where the application of theological reasoning to concrete situations had its place.

But this structural handicap notwithstanding, the political sermon, which disappeared from the scene immediately after 1715[2], had its place in the debate about the War of the Spanish Succession[3]. Sermons profited from the high esteem in which spiritual literature was held at the time, and consequently many of them were printed almost immediately[4]. Alongside the other genres the sermon's role was no doubt modest - with occasional exceptions - and yet, as a medium of political communication, it was employed regularly if cautiously. The specific strength of the genre was its ability to exploit for political purposes deep-rooted and universally accepted ideas and concepts. The sermon's commitment to the exegesis of the Bible along typological lines hardly admitted of any detailed comment on complex contemporary issues. The genre's characteristics could only be used to full advantage where an undifferentiated political groundswell could be intensified by religious reference. But in an era where claims to political power were still based on religious concepts - for the last time in English history[5] - such opportunities abounded. The sermon was quite inadequate for a detailed ratiocinative refutation of a particular argument or a presentation of original views; it was rather the appropriate medium for lending general support to widespread political sentiment by exploiting religious susceptibilities. The sermon occupied a middle position in the spectrum of the propaganda genres. Its potential for influencing public opinion through its very specific kind of rhetoric puts it halfway between the discursive pamphlet and analytical essay on the one hand and the emotional broadside and occasional poem on the other.

In a certain way, however, the sermon was itself 'occasional' owing to its dependence on specific religious events in the course of the year. An exception is Hare's above-mentioned sermon *The Charge of God to Joshua* (September 1711). It puts a religious interpretation on the capture of Bouchain by the Duke of Marlborough, thererby contributing to initiate a debate on this particular event within the wider context of the ongoing general political debate[6]. Incidentally, the Gen-

---

1 Regarding the structural conventions of the sermon see e.g. Rolf P. Lessenich, *Elements of Pulpit Oratory in Eighteenth-Century England (1660-1800)* (Cologne and Vienna, 1972).

2 Cf. Downie, *Robert Harley and the Press*, p. 15.

3 Cf. F.G. James, "The Bishops in Politics, 1688-1714", *Conflict in Stuart England. Essays in Honour of Wallace Notestein*, ed. William Appleton Aiken and Basil Duke Henning (London, 1960), p. 251.

4 Of course an even larger number remained unpublished; see on this Françoise Deconinck-Brossard, *Vie Politique, Sociale et Religieuse en Grande-Bretagne d'après les Sermons Prêchés ou Publiés dans le Nord de l'Angleterre 1738-1760* (Paris, 1984), p. 11.

5 Cf. G.V. Bennett, "Conflict in the Church", *Britain after the Glorious Revolution 1689-1714*, ed. Holmes, p. 155.

6 See Snyder, "Arthur Maynwaring and the Whig Press, 1710-1712", p. 130.

eral - likened to Moses in Hare's sermon - was the most gratifying and most frequently used Whig figure for biblical analogies. By raising political matters to a religious level, Hare's sermon gave a short-term boost to Whig morale. And the idea that God's providence favoured England[1] no doubt flattered the ordinary people as well. Hare probably regarded it as an inherent advantage of the genre that the biblical context in which he developed his political analogies spared him the arduous task of presenting a detailed peace plan. The Tories tried at once to neutralize the effect of Hare's emotional and persuasive appeal to religious feelings. Mrs. Manley's rejoinder *A Learned Comment upon Dr. Hare's Excellent Sermon Preach'd before the D. of Marlborough, on the Surrender of Bouchain by an Enemy to Peace* (1711), in which Swift most certainly had a part[2], shows this quite clearly. Her disillusioning down-to-earth approach was obviously meant to steal Hare's thunder. But then Hare's spectacular and courageous exploitation of a military feat that so uplifted the Whigs was in itself enough to show quite plainly the limits of the genre. The sermon's inherent typological approach, namely to equate England with God's chosen people, admitted of no detailed consideration of the debate about war and peace, because the biblical event, the taking of Palestinian land by the Isrealite tribes led by Joshua, would have implied the taking of the whole of France under the leadership of Marlborough. Hare's identification of Marlborough with Moses boomeranged when Mrs. Manley, in a pamphlet whose sole purpose was to reply to Hare's sermon and which was a rare specimen of journalism even by the standards of the time, asked pointedly whether England would now have to wait forty years before a peace could be concluded[3]!

In general - not counting such an outstanding and exceptional sermon as Sacheverell's *The Perils of False Brethren* (1709) - sermons played a less conspicuous role in the propaganda battle. Their chief function was perhaps twofold: first, to comment on political issues, precisely within the genre's formal limits, and thus influence the political climate and create a degree of awareness of new political developments. For example, in his sermon *Noah's Dove. An Earnest Exhortation to Peace*, preached on 7 November 1710 and dedicated to Harley, which expressed gratitude for the military successes in the summer, Thomas Swift had discreetly suggested adopting a moderate political course[4]. The function outlined above was performed in particular by sermons delivered in the Commons on special occasions, e.g. those by Bisse (March 1710), Snape (March 1711), Altham (January 1712) and Ayerst (February 1712). To the extent that their rhetoric deviated from the traditional and prevalent non-partisan style which addressed Government and Opposition, Tories and Whigs alike, these sermons sometimes set a new tone and were an indicator of new political positions. A good example of this

---

1 This patriotic attitude was also employed by the preachers during the Seven Years' War; see on this D. Napthine and W.A. Speck, "Clergymen and Conflict 1660-1763", *The Church and War*, ed. W.J. Sheils (Oxford, 1983), pp. 238-239.

2 See Woolley, "The Canon of Swift's Prose Pamphleteering, 1710-1714", p. 104.

3 See *A Learned Comment*, p. 9.

4 See on this Phyllis J. Guskin, "Political Implications of Thomas Swift's Sermon *Noah's Dove* (1710)", *Eighteenth Century Life* 1 (1974-75), pp. 46-50.

is Altham's fast sermon before the Commons. It is a well-balanced political homily in which High Church key-terminology like "Rebellion", "Submission" or "Unity" and "Concord"[1] is not employed with the aim of immediate political or even polemical reference but remains embedded in the religious context of the occasion. The sermon presents the war against Louis XIV, who poses a threat to freedom, as a just war, but at the same time underlines the need to conclude a peace to put an end to the human drain from which the nation is suffering. Altham's sermon, which even includes the Allies in its prayer[2], aims at consensus but also points out the Government's position and the new facts it has to consider. These sermons quite effectively carried political messages within the genre's - rarely overstepped - strict limits that forbade overtly partisan polemics. Gradually, and more deliberately, the Government seems to have used the House of Commons sermons with their quasi official aura as an instrument to state its own political objectives. These sermons, which in their own way are a discursive complement to other genres, may therefore also be read as historical documents which provide evidence of the Government's cautious but unequivocal way of sending out signals as to its long-term intentions and political course.

The second function of the sermon was, albeit less frequently, to participate in undisguised partisan propaganda. This second function put the sermon in line with the other genres, overtly completing the political parties' propaganda activities. Here are two examples, one from each party, and it is probably not mere coincidence that both are fast sermons of 1712. Trapp's sermon[3] openly sides with the Tories and the Government, and its polarisation makes it an exception within the genre. Trapp tries to create a sense of a common political cause, and he attacks Whig arguments with increasing vigour in the manner of a pamphleteer. His sermon is intensely political. The leitmotiv-like reference to the human cost of a continued war adopts Defoe's emotive approach, but the sermon also uses Swift's antithesis of the Sovereign and the nation on the one hand and Marlborough and a selfish Whig clique on the other from his recently published *The Conduct of the Allies*. Trapp's use of emotive political terms shows that his purpose was purely ideological. But in spite of his unusually vigorous pace he stops short of actually referring to the parties by name, which is the only feature that still distinguishes his sermon from a pamphlet. Interestingly, Trapp also avoids the key-word "perquisite", which would not in itself have been out of place in a sermon but which - as current in all genres of Tory propaganda - was extremely politicised and could appropriately be replaced with the more general terms of condemnation "Avarice or Ambition"[4]. Even *The Quaker's Sermon: Or, a Holding-Forth concerning Barabbas* (1711), which still poses as a sermon although it is in fact a pamphlet,

---

1 See Altham, *A Sermon Preach'd before the Honourable House of Commons at the Church of St. Margaret Westminster, on Wednesday, Jan. 16.1711/12*, pp. 11, 12-13, 15, 16, 18.

2 *Ibid.*, pp. 18 and 21.

3 Joseph Trapp, *A Sermon Preach'd at the Parish-Church of St. Martin in the Fields; January the 16th, 1711* (London, 1712).

4 *Ibid.*, p. 11.

shows restraint in the use of party names; actually, there is only one - although polemical - reference to the Tories[1]. Trapp's sermon[2] was an integral part of the Tory propaganda network, intensifying in a religious context the general tenor since the turn of the year 1711-1712, namely the Harley Administration's determination, ubiquitous in political writing, to end the war. Such a sermon was a militant political homily and, like the dissenter Mayo's *Pray for the Peace of Jerusalem* (1712), its rhetoric was the closest approximation to that of the secular genres.

But even where there was more professional self-restraint than Trapp chose to exercise, the pro-Government fast sermons of January 1712, like Altham's and Smalridge's, followed the Tory propaganda line that the continuing bloodshed could no longer be tolerated[3]. Their tone, however, remained consistent with the genre's own technique of affective language. They were able to dispense with the highly charged phrases of pamphlets and essays. Instead of polemical key-words there were catalogues of specific vices or - on the Tory side - references to the hitherto "just and necessary" war as "bloody, cruel and expensive". Those of the clergy who sympathised with the Government were unanimous in the emotionalization of the war in their sermons, quite in tune with Tory propaganda but strictly within the limits of the genre. The emotionalization of the war, with its immense loss of human life, was supported by theological and secular arguments alike and bore the seal of Christian mercy. Thus a general political message was spread even further through a particular genre's rather narrow scope for expression. In particular the fast sermons of 1712 show the qualitative leap executed by the Tory propaganda campaign, aiming at identical targets though different in tone. In the autumn of 1711 the sermon had occasionally been used for propaganda purposes by the Whigs, and the Tories had not used it at all from September to December of that year. The change in the stand-off between the Government and the Opposition did not occur until January 1712. Only then did the fast sermons signal the Tories' resolve to take the lead in the propaganda contest to shape public opinion. During the decisive stage of the turning-point debate the sermon - previously only used sparingly for the promulgation of political intentions - was fully integrated into the parties' armoury. Especially at the beginning of 1712, more so than at any time before or later, the sermon was used to recharge the Government's propaganda batteries.

The Whigs tried as best they could to ward off this Tory offensive. A good example is Fleetwood's rhetorically highly sophisticated fast sermon of 16 January 1712, the Whigs' rejoinder to Trapp's politically committed pulpit oratory. Fleetwood's party bias becomes apparent if one reads his sermon alongside Wright's

---

1 See *The Quaker's Sermon: Or, a Holding-Forth concerning Barabbas* (London, 1711), p. 18.

2 For its controversial character see *Mesech and Kedar. Or, Reflections on a Scurrilous Pamphlet, Entitl'd, Mr. Trapp's Sermon, Preach'd at the Parish-Church of St. Martin in the Fields, on the General Fast, etc.* (London, 1712), esp. pp. 11 and 18.

3 In her Speech on 7 December 1711 the Queen had pointedly referred to "a War which has cost so much Blood and Treasure [...]" (*Journals of the House of Lords*, XIX, 336).

Sermon Preach'd at Black-Fryars of the same day. Wright's sermon, despite its express condemnation of Louis XIV, is conservative in as much as the political theme is presented in theological guise with its general moralising remarks about the depravity of the time. Fleetwood, on the other hand, presents his political topic without such circumlocution. Right from the beginning his sermon is delivered "against such as delight in War", which directly takes up the theme of the Queen's Speech in Parliament[1]. Fleetwood's, and thus Whig, strategy consists in diverting the Tories' reproach of "delight in war" away from the Whigs and applying it to France. Originally directed by the Queen at those opposed to peace in her Speech of 7 December 1711[2], the "delight in war" slogan is now directed at the French King, who, as the public are reminded, was notorious for breaking promises as well as treaties[3]. Fleetwood thus capitalised on a slogan that was originally intended to calumniate the Whigs. But for all his skill, there remains a feeling of tit-for-tat, of improvised Whig self-defence. To make his political position unequivocally clear, Fleetwood gives his sermon a very effective ending. Although his support for the continuation of a just war is obvious from the beginning, it remains restrained, and only towards the end does he adopt the polemical tone in which it had become fashionable to discuss the question of war and peace. Only then, on the last two and a half pages, does he unleash Whig key-words like "Liberties", "Slavery" and "Protestant Succession". But even when his rhetoric reaches its climax the party names are never mentioned; even the traditional Whig accusation of Jacobitism is never made. The polemical section of Fleetwood's sermon begins with the succinct remark: "And therefore they who now tell us, that we entered *wrong into it*, are those I doubt, who would have us go *wrong out of it*"[4]. The preceding exegesis of a passage from the Bible has prepared the ground for this final onslaught and lends it conviction. In spite of its courageous refutation of the "delight" reproach[5], Fleetwood's sermon, the main passages of which[6] were cited with approval in the *Protestant Post-Boy* of 5-7 February 1712, had a decidedly defensive note, as is shown by the subtle rhetoric which effectively refutes the argument, which was being used with ever increasing intensity, that the Duke of Marlborough had simply had luck on his side. Labelling him "*a General, wise*, and *brave*, and *fortunate*, as was our last"[7] is a pointed reaction to the increasingly derogatory attacks by the Tories, but it avoids cheap invective and is moderate and detached enough in tone not to affect Fleetwood's position as a preacher. The defence of the Duke of Marlborough at the end of the peroratio is a con-

---

1 See *The London Gazette*, 6-8 December 1711.

2 This Speech was promptly exploited by Government journalists, for instance by Defoe in *No Queen: Or, no General*, p. 2.

3 See [William Fleetwood], *A Sermon on the Fast-Day, January the Sixteenth, 1711/12. Against such as Delight in War. By a Divine of the Church of England* (London, 1712), p. 19.

4 *Ibid.*, p. 21.

5 *Ibid.*, p. 17.

6 *Ibid.*, pp. 21ff.

7 *Ibid.*, p. 23.

vincing example of how a sermon could assume the function of a political manifesto without violating the genre's dignity. With its renewed emphasis on the justness of the war Fleetwood's sermon was typical of the Whigs' reaction to the Tory propaganda offensive. That the Tories had indeed gained the offensive is shown by Mayo's polemical fast sermon *Pray for the Peace of Jerusalem*, in which the author - mimicry-like - resorts to Tory terminology like "sedition" to parry the Government's own rhetoric, which was to rally the nation round the Tory cause; in other words, Mayo tried to beat the Tories at their own game.

Alongside Hoadly it was Fleetwood who was the most effective ecclesiastical advocate of Whig policies. The impact of his sermons can be inferred from the Preface to the edition of *Four Sermons* in May 1712. This Preface appeared in the *Spectator* of 21 May 1712, a fact which was still favourably commented on in the pamphlet *Revolution-Principles: Being a Full Defence of the Bishop of St. Asaph's Preface to his Four Sermons* (1713)[1] , the last item to deal with Fleetwood's provocative publication. With its use of key-terms of Whig propaganda like "Arbitrary Power" and "Popery"[2] the Preface takes on an aggressive tone which distinguishes it from the disciplined rhetoric of Fleetwood's fast sermon. His militant and programmatic Preface was probably intended to close ranks among the Whigs, who had recently appeared somewhat disconcerted in their journalistic performance. Thanks to the publicity that the *Spectator* gave it[3], this seems indeed to have been its effect. Swift's replies in *A Letter of Thanks from my Lord W-n to the Lord Bp of S. Asaph, in the Name of the Kit-Cat-Club* (1712) and the *Examiner* of 17-24 July 1712 show how the Government felt pricked by it. But in the context of the genre as such, Fleetwood's stimulating Preface remained an exception. The publicity it gained[4] indicated that Whig propaganda was on the decline. In the summer of 1712 it was at its lowest and desperately needed such a stimulus to make itself heard at all. After this the sermon played an increasingly insignificant role in the debate on the war, sometimes to the point of oblivion, and had to concede pre-eminence to the other forms of political rhetoric.

1 See *Revolution-Principles: Being a Full Defence of the Bishop of St. Asaph's Preface to his Four Sermons: In Answer to the Objections which have been Made against it proving them to be all Groundless, by Scripture, Law, and Reason* (London, 1713), p. 3. Cf. also the detailed appreciation of foreword and sermons by Kennett, *The Wisdom of Looking Backward*, pp. 230-235.

2 William Fleetwood, *Four Sermons* (London, 1712), p. v.

3 The book containing it was also publicized in that periodical in its issues of 26, 28 and 31 May and on 3 and 5 June 1712.

4 See also *A Letter to the B-p of St A-ph, on Burning his Preface by the Hands of the Common Hangman, on Thursday the 12th of June, 1712* (London, 1712).

V. Public Discourse: Whig and Tory Rhetoric

In our macro- and microstructural analyses we have traced the development of the public debate and the role of individual genres. Naturally, Government and Opposition alike drew on a set stock of linguistic strategies in their efforts to influence public opinion. The use of highly charged words to put their own position into relief, and a repertoire of defamatory phrases and personal invective to denigrate the political opponent, these were common features of Government and Opposition rhetoric. Recurring polemical codes gave the political debate of the time its unmistakable characteristics. However, as we have pointed out, the parties' polemical interaction was also marked by obvious differences owing to their political positions. It is these differences between Whig and Tory rhetoric that this chapter deals with. We will look at three main aspects: argumentative strategy, key-terminology and imagery. We will show that, irrespective of individual genres, certain recurring techniques are discernible, although in different degree and not necessarily verifiable in each text.

1. Whig Rhetoric

a) Argumentative Strategies

From the summer of 1710 the political situation made it seem expedient to the Whigs to insist on maintaining the status quo and preventing the new Government from withdrawing from the hitherto binding national consensus on the issue of war and peace. Conversely, the secretive politics of the Harley Ministry made it likewise a matter of expediency for the Tories to undermine the public image of the previous Government, without as yet openly abandoning their common war policy, which was not to happen until the all-out confrontation beginning in December 1711. The pamphlet as the leading genre conveys a first impression of the characteristic features of Whig journalism. The pamphlet blends ratiocinative with polemical and affective elements. And it is this feature that the Whigs used for their purposes in a manner very much their own. Their technique, which one might call the 'rhetoric of documented recourse', consisted in the regular use of official statements from the parliamentary process which demonstrated Britain's determination to continue the war until it was brought to a victorious end. In a matter of national urgency the Government was thus confronted with a national consensus which it could not ignore with impunity. In this context Whig rhetoric made ample use of *probationes inartificiales* calling attention to bipartisan resolutions. Maynwaring's *Reflections upon the Examiner's Scandalous Peace* (1711) is a good example. Maynwaring also employed this technique in the *Medley*. In view of the existing facts, which favoured their own position, the Whigs' strategy displayed the 'rhetoric of factual accumulation'. Thus the Whigs could appeal to the Government's sense of honour and call to mind that there was a national consensus; Maynwaring's ironic *A Vindication of the Present M-y* (1711) provides a good example, as do most of his other pamphlets. During the Whig propaganda offensive up to December 1711 this factual approach was complemented by considerable polemical aggressiveness. Whereas Maynwaring skilfully blended factualism and polemics, Hare's even more pronounced, at times almost 'antiquarian' factualism coexisted awkwardly with his regular and irksome berating of his political opponents. From the beginning of 1712 political invective became less frequent and was soon virtually replaced with a less forceful strategy in Whig pamphlets: merely to point out and correct the opponent's factual errors. This was an indication of Whig embarrassment vis-à-vis the Tory strategy of whipping up emotions, which they obviously found difficult to counter, hence their conspicuous, rhetorically less vigorous recourse to parliamentary resolutions and especially to historical evidence. This particular Whig predicament in the spring of 1712 is well illustrated by Hare's pamphlets *The Barrier-Treaty Vindicated* and *The Treaty between Her Majesty and the States-General* as well as Burnet's *Our Ancestors as Wise as We* and is still noticeable in such a publication as *The Secret History of the Geertruydenbergh Negociation*.

The Whigs' insistence on, and presentation of, what counted as officially sanctioned policy made them appear in a favourable light on the public stage for quite some time, particularly because on several occasions they professed confidence in the Government, which enabled them to discredit Tory positions all the more effectively. This is well documented in pamphlets like Maynwaring's *A Vindication of the Present M-y*, *Reflections upon the Present Posture of Affairs* (1712) and *Observations upon the State of the Nation* (1713). A Whig pamphleteer, who wanted to exorcize the threatening Anglo-Dutch estrangement, stated with feigned assurance at the end of his preface "*that we are under no Apprehensions of such a Ministry*"[1] as England suffered from under Charles II. It was, by the way, common practice for Whig pamphleteers like, for example, Hoadly in *The Thoughts of an Honest Tory* (1710) and Hare in his dialogue-pamphlet *Bouchain* (1711), to assume a particular role to gain more room for their arguments. The above-mentioned strategy of making the 'No peace without Spain' demand non-negotiable was an expression of the Whigs' policy of containment pursued since the summer of 1710. As we said earlier, the rhetorical utilization of the 'No peace without Spain' issue gave the Whigs the necessary leverage to articulate their expectation that the Government abide by at least some principles of a bipartisan war policy. The Whigs had always adhered to the view that the parties should retain a modicum of consensus and therefore avoided any undifferentiated attack on

1 *The History of the Peace with France and War with Holland in the Year 1672*, p. vii.

the Government. Instead, their criticism of Government policy was mostly directed at individuals with extreme views. The title of Maynwaring's often quoted pamphlet *A Letter to a Member of the October-Club* (1711) illustrates this technique of concentrating on the fringe of the political spectrum. The Whigs' expectation - as it was at least rhetorically professed - that there remain a minimum of consensus found expression also in their sparse use of the name "Tories", whereas their own name was used without any inhibition by their political opponents to discredit the previous Ministry. Maynwaring's *Remarks on a False, Scandalous, and Seditious Libel* (1711) is a notable exception that arose from a specific situation. Another reason why the Whigs refrained from all-out Tory bashing was that they apparently did not want to be criticised for lack of national solidarity. Appropriately, in Maynwaring's *Remarks on the Preliminary Articles Offer'd by the French King* (1711) "Tory" does not appear at all; instead, "a certain Party among us"[1] and "A Party among our selves"[2] are used, which could easily be associated with extreme forces in the Government camp. And where "Tories" does appear, as in *The Whigs Appeal to the Tories* (1711), it can even have a positive connotation in so far as the pamphlet appeals to the party moderates not to make common cause with extremist elements[3]. These features, typical of pamphlet literature, are absent in the usually less sophisticated broadsides, where the tone is unequivocally aggressive and where the parties use each other's names with almost equal frequency. Although, among periodicals, the mettlesome Whig *Observator* is an exception in this regard and the pro-Government *Review's* use of party names is somewhat more discerning than that of other Tory organs, it may yet be said that the use of party labels was a political marker. The Whigs' modest use of the opponent's party name must be seen in connection with one of their propaganda objectives, namely to aim at the entire Tory spectrum and play off one group against the other in order to strengthen the centre. Besides, whenever the Whigs wanted to adopt a polarising tone, there were substitutes they could use like, for example, "High Church Party", "High-Fliers" or - in a foreign-policy context - "Friends of France". The latter was used by Maynwaring in *A Letter to a Member of the October-Club* and by Hare in *The Allies and the Late Ministry Defended* (1711), though more sparingly than "Tories".

Another conspicuous difference between Whig and Tory rhetoric is the use of ad hominem attacks, which the Whigs directed almost exclusively at journalists and the Tories mainly at politicians. But again, broadsides do not quite fit into this pattern. Whigs and Tories alike, although the Whigs less often, used this genre for attacks on politicians, not journalists; after all, aggressiveness is the broadside's most conspicuous characteristic. Good examples of the above-mentioned distinction are provided by Maynwaring's *Medley* and Swift's *Examiner*. In both pamphlets and periodicals the Whigs concentrated on journalists who could easily be denigrated because they held extreme views, with Roper as their prime target.

---

1 Maynwaring, *Remarks on the Preliminary Articles Offer'd by the French King*, p. 8.

2 *Ibid.*, p. 12.

3 See *The Whigs Appeal to the Tories. In a Letter to Sir T-H-. With a Postscript concerning the Proceedings in P-t* (London, 1711), p. 15.

To quote but one relevant example, the latter was stigmatized as "that Prostituted TOOL of a Frenchify'd Party" in the *Protestant Post-Boy* of 30 October-1 November 1711. Although the pugnacious *Flying-Post* persistently put the question as to who had commissioned Roper[1], it stopped short of actually mentioning names. Roper, Leslie and Swift were the whipping boys who bore the brunt of Whig attacks, substitutes, as it were, for the Government. The reason why the Whigs spared Government politicians and attacked Tory journalists instead, was probably less the fear of legal consequences and of the Government's machinery of repression - a motive which of course must not be underestimated - than the political aim of demonstrating their sense of responsibility.

b) Political Key-Terms

More than thirty years ago Donald J. Greene found that it was not possible to prove a correlation in prose between "certain patterns of political thinking and certain patterns of linguistic behaviour"[2]. In political rhetoric, however, such a link can indeed be shown to exist[3]. Their respective ideologies led the parties to adopt a specific terminology and to develop a particular use of imagery which in the context of public debate defined their political orientation much more clearly than was consistent with political reality, where the dividing lines were often less distinct. The Whigs saw the War of the Spanish Succession as an opportunity to consolidate the post-revolutionary order in Britain and placed it in the wider European context of Protestant liberty versus Louis XIV's tyranny. Hare, for instance, declared himself unambiguously in favour of "preserving the Liberty and Balance of *Europe*, and reducing the exorbitant Power of *France*"[4]. At home the Whigs[5] were the party that advocated a liberal constitution and had welcomed the Revolution of 1688/89, and abroad they were the party of European commitment - at least by comparison with the Tories. Their idea of freedom, which blended aspects of both domestic and foreign policy, was to some extent based on concepts of natural law[6]. Thus a Whig pamphleteer in 1712 reminded the public of the noble project of restoring in Europe "the Primitive Rights of Human Nature"[7] violated

---

1 See - as a representative example - the issues of 3-6 and 10-13 November 1711.

2 Donald J. Greene, "Is there a 'Tory' Prose Style?", *Bulletin of the New York Public Library* 66 (1962), p. 449.

3 Sullivan in *John Toland and the Deist Controversy. A Study in Adaptations* even talks of "two families of political discourse" (p. 147) and states: "One was Tory and the other, Whig" (p. 147).

4 *A Caveat to the Treaters*, p. 41.

5 On their ideological positions cf. Müllenbrock, *Whigs kontra Tories*, pp. 19-45.

6 See e.g. Toland's pamphlet *Anglia Libera* (1701). Cf. on this aspect Sullivan, *John Toland and the Deist Controversy*, pp. 159-160.

7 *The Secret History of the Geertruydenbergh Negociation*, p. 21. - The Tories sometimes countered such language by pointing to natural obligations at least as fundamental, "the Law of Nature, the Right of Blood" (*The Queen, the Present Ministry, Lewis XIV and Philip V Unanswerably Vindicated*, p. 17).

by Louis XIV. An advocate of Bishop Fleetwood stressed that the latter was merely standing up for "the LIBERTY of Mankind"[1].

In their political propaganda this ideological bent was translated into a set of recurring key-terms which became the hallmark of their rhetoric. The use of highly charged words in their frequent and intense appeals to the public made up for the restraint which the Whigs exercised in the use of ad hominem attacks on prominent politicians. Their comparatively modest recourse to personal invective directed at Government politicians was offset by a number of politically charged terms which they sounded like clarion calls. Of these "France/French" was the most frequent word pair because it could be used in foreign- and domestic-policy contexts alike. Roper, for example, was continually denounced as a tool of "the French Faction" in British politics, as for instance in the *Flying-Post* of 1-3 November 1711. "Allies" and related terms were also used, all with a positive connotation and not, as in the case of the Tories, as mere lip service or even pejoratively. The frequency of the emotive pair "France/French" in all genres explains the comparatively rare occurrence of such terms as "Catholic", "Jacobite" and "Popery", which were all automatically associated with each reference to the French enemy or his English friends. Another politically charged term was "Liberty", usually appearing in combinations like "Religion and Liberty", "Civil and Religious Liberties", "Religious Laws and Liberties" or "Liberty of Europe". The idea of liberty was suggested by such terms as "Protestant Succession" and "Hanoverian Succession", which, for their part, evoked the association of "Popery/Pretender". Terms like "Protestant Succession"[2] were almost exclusively used by the Whigs, although the Tories never failed to pledge their loyalty to the Act of Settlement. Among the periodicals the *Observator* shows the typical application of such charged terms, especially during the first stage of the turning-point debate. It is characteristic of Whig propaganda in all genres that these terms occur in clusters to enhance their polemical thrust, which is supposed to demonstrate fighting spirit. Such clusters[3] aim at rhetorical impact through redundancy of information. Towards the end of the main part of a substantial pamphlet Hare, for example, called on those who were "for the *Hanover* Succession, the Protestant Religion, and the Liberties of *Great Britain*"[4] to oppose plans to put the Duke of Anjou in possession of Spain and the West Indies. In *A New Protestant Litany* (1712), a Whig broadside with a high frequency of charged terms, Maynwaring used "France", "Catholic", "Pretender" and "Popery" to evoke merely by association a danger to the Protestant Succession. And in *Remarks on a False, Scandalous, and*

---

1 *Revolution-Principles: Being a Full Defence of the Bishop of St. Asaph's Preface to his Four Sermons*, p. 1.

2 See, for instance, the *Flying-Post* of 22-25 September 1711, which even speaks of "the Revolution and Protestant Succession".

3 On the formation of key-word clusters see also Fritz-Wilhelm Neumann, "The Semantic Subsystems of ECCOP (The Eighteenth-Century Corpus of Pamphlets); or, the future of the toys for the boys critique", *Anglistentag 1992 Stuttgart: Proceedings*, ed. Hans-Ulrich Seeber and Walter Göbel (Tübingen, 1993), pp. 423-424.

4 *A Caveat to the Treaters*, p. 76.

Seditious Libel Maynwaring drew heavily on this formidable ideological arsenal when he accused the author of *The Conduct of the Allies* (1711): "But this Writer does not look on the Safety of our Religion and Liberty, the Guarantee of the *Dutch* Barrier, and the Protestant Succession, as *Things of moment* [...]"[1]. Similarly, and significantly, the reply which the author of *A Full Answer to the Conduct of the Allies* (1712) gave his opponents mixes positive and negative key-terms: "What *Englishman* that has these Things at Heart, and dreads the Mischiefs of *Popery*, and *Arbitrary Power*, but must look on the *Conducter* with the utmost Indignation, while he sees him treating the Care of the *Protestant Succession* with so much contempt"[2].

The Whigs'[3] constant use of politically emotive terms with Protestant connotations gave their own followers something to identify with, and their opponents something to challenge. However, the near automatism of these propaganda slogans[4], their almost reflex-like use[5], carried the danger of attrition. When from the end of 1711 Tory propaganda played the Dutch card, this to a certain degree caught the Whigs by surprise, and their traditional slogans proved a rather blunt weapon. The Tories had soon stirred emotions to such a point that the Whigs' usual alarm rhetoric proved inadequate to stem the ensuing tide of aggressiveness. Whig journalism showed the first unmistakable signs of fatigue in the face of the Tories' reinvigorated propaganda.

c) Metaphors and Images

Whig propaganda language made only sparse use of metaphors. This is partly due to the sociological composition of the reading public, which in the case of the *Observator*, for example, was Nonconformist. However, there is a stock of every-day metaphorical language, including common proverbs, which both parties drew on to express their political views. Thus the familiar image of the wolf in sheep's clothing appeared in publications of both sides, and illness and fire were often used in connection with war. Broadsides in particular made ample use of such common linguistic material with a special predilection for proverbs and adages, and with journalists and politicians as their preferred targets. For this purpose

---

1 Maynwaring, *Remarks on a False, Scandalous, and Seditious Libel*, pp. 33-34.

2 *A Full Answer to the Conduct of the Allies*, p. 29.

3 The *Protestant Post-Boy* of 15-18 September 1711 defined a Whig as "one who is against POPERY, SLAVERY, ARBITRARY POWER, absolute NON-RESISTANCE, and DIVINE HEREDITARY RICHT [sic]".

4 Citing "*France* and the *Pretender*" and "*Popery* and *Slavery*" as examples, a Tory pamphleteer quite adequately points out to his Whig opponent that the latter "upon most Occasions" uses such terms "without farther shew of Reason" (*An Examination of the Management of the War*, p. 40).

5 Linda Colley writes: "[...] Britons reminded themselves of their embattled Protestantism in what often seems a wearyingly repetitive fashion precisely because they had good cause to feel uncertain about its security and about their own" (*Britons. Forging the Nation 1707-1837* [New Haven and London, 1992], p. 23).

they also turned animal imagery to good rhetorical account; thus, for instance, the broadside *The Tr-us Treaty* (1712) illustrated the dangers of a Tory peace in the guise of the fable of the wolves and the sheep, with Harley figuring as Robin[1]. In other genres Whig propaganda aimed less at individuals, particularly politicians, and used metaphorical language more for a general characterisation of the political opponent. Hare, for example, in the first part of *The Allies and the Late Ministry Defended against France* extended Swift's metaphor of a conflagration in *The Conduct of the Allies*[2], and the author of *Reflections upon the Present Posture of Affairs* referred to Leslie as an 'incendiary'[3]. These examples illustrate the particular characteristic of Whig rhetoric which we mentioned earlier, namely to limit personal attacks to the inner circle of fellow journalists.

Another striking feature of Whig rhetoric is the fact that, unlike the Tories, they almost never used images to gain public support for their main political ideas. Instead they preferred more abstract concepts, sometimes borrowed from natural law. In Samuel Garth's *A Poem to the Earl of Godolphin* (1710), the state is even likened to a smoothly running engine. Concepts from natural law were especially appropriate in a foreign-policy context, such as for example Louis XIV epitomizing the disdain for the basic human impulse for freedom. They were less adequate at home as a means of countering attacks from a political opponent who resorted to traditional ideas of kingship and governance to exploit their populist potential.

2. TORY RHETORIC

a) Argumentative Strategies

In pamphlet literature - to begin again with the leading genre - the Tories, too, combined ratiocinative and affective elements within a wide range of rhetorical techniques. But beyond the features common to practically all political rhetoric the Tories offered more variation and complexity, whereas the impression of Whig pamphleteering is one of greater uniformity in spite of some authors' individual differences. The main reason for this is the 'twin-track' strategy pursued unwaveringly by Government propaganda. It reflected the personal idiosyncrasy and political orientation of the Prime Minister, circumspect and also open to the demands of expediency. On the one hand, the Harley Ministry tried to win public support by projecting an orthodox Tory image, but on the other, it pursued a line which seemed to be keeping the door open for consensus with moderate Whigs. The task of translating this latter policy into political rhetoric was assigned to De-

1 References to Harley as Robin had almost become proverbial, especially in broadsides; see also *Poor England Bob'd at Home and Abroad* (1712).

2 See *The Allies and the Late Ministry Defended against France* [part I], pp. 24-27.

3 See *Reflections upon the Present Posture of Affairs*, p. 31.

foe, who consequently addressed Whig readers in a conciliatory tone reflecting the flexibility of Harley's approach.

This dual-track course produced the characteristic dichotomy of Tory pamphlets and periodicals: the 'hard and soft' approach. The uncompromisingly aggressive variety is represented by authors like St. John, Mrs. Manley, Swift, Wagstaffe and Leslie and tends almost immediately to cross the threshold from argumentation to polemics. Their polemical harassment of the political opponent was complemented by the frequent use - in nearly all genres - of the antagonist's party name. The *Examiner* and the *Review* adopted a different political approach and consequently differed in their rhetorical techniques. The *Examiner* concentrated more on exposing the opponent's political position and therefore contains a higher proportion of relevant political terminology, whereas the *Review* aimed primarily at defining its own position. Similar in their polarising purpose to the polemical citation of the opponent's party name were the personal attacks on Marlborough and Whig politicians like Godolphin, Wharton and Lord Townshend. Generally, these techniques were applied regardless of genre. The sermon, however, was naturally committed to more restraint and hardly indulged in personal invective against politicians at all.

Defoe, on the other hand, aiming at a Whig clientele and eager to win over voters, made lengthy argumentation the hallmark of his pamphlets. He was much more cautious in the use of overt polemics, and where it did occur it posed as an expression of the author's disappointment at his readers' intransigence. Thus, *The Ballance of Europe* (1711) consists largely of sound, matter-of-fact arguments, and only towards the end - after preparatory hints at the beginning - does Defoe openly appeal to his readers' emotions by copiously citing examples of Habsburg tyranny in Protestant countries in order to lend polemical support to his argument against Spain under Austrian rule[1]. To demonstrate his readiness for consensus Defoe's rhetoric concentrates very much on facts, and his casuistic argumentation in favour of adaptation to political change anticipates in a certain way his procedure in *Moll Flanders*, here applied to politics. Defoe's persevering efforts to convince his readers by the force of his argument were especially apparent in pamphlets like *Reasons Why* (1711), *The Ballance of Europe*, *An Essay at a Plain Exposition of that Difficult Phrase a Good Peace* (1711) - and also the *Review*, all published by Baker. On the other hand, pamphlets like *No Queen: Or, no General* (1712) and *Peace, Or Poverty* (1712), published by Morphew, used historical references more for purely illustrative purposes. The reasoned approach of the Baker pamphlets with regard to historical precedents is thus similar to that of some Whig pamphlets.

In Defoe's conciliatory variant of Government propaganda the party label "Whig" with its negative connotations appears only rarely. This was especially so in the Baker pamphlets, whereas those of 1712 by other publishers moved closer towards the new confrontational style. While there is not a single reference to "Whigs" in *The Succession of Spain Consider'd* (1711), *The Ballance of Europe*, *An Essay at a Plain Exposition* and *The Felonious Treaty* (1711), there are four in

---

1 See Defoe, *The Ballance of Europe*, pp. 35ff.

the more polemical *No Queen: Or, no General* and five in *A Farther Search into the Conduct of the Allies* (1712), published by Morphew, but - surprisingly - there is no mention in the emotional *Peace, Or Poverty*. Strikingly, "Whigs" appears only once even in *Reasons why this Nation Ought to Put a Speedy End to this Expensive War*, a pamphlet which was crucial for the further course of Government propaganda. In *Armageddon* (1711) on the other hand, where "Whigs" occurs with unprecedented frequency, Defoe strikes a propitiatory note; in fact he is making advances to the Opposition. In *The Present Negotiations of Peace Vindicated from the Imputation of Trifling* (1712) the party name turns up rather frequently with hostile connotations, which one might feel inclined to regard as exceptional at first, but then there may be a simple explanation. At this stage the Whigs had lost considerable public terrain and apparently Defoe no longer saw any need for his usual consensus rhetoric. By and large, however, Defoe's use of the Opposition party label was demonstrably chary for the simple reason that he wanted to retain a chance, however slight, for Government policies to find acceptance in the Opposition camp. This is corroborated by the *Review*. In the issue of 13 November 1711, for example, Defoe unequivocally criticises the Whigs for their one-sided and partisan position on the Spanish question, but he never even once refers to them by name, to demonstrate his preference for sound argument instead of for polemics. In the *Review* of 20 May 1712 "Whig" and "Tory" are used quite frequently in what may be regarded as a laboured attempt at balanced rhetoric, if for no other purpose than to prove his often claimed commitment to a middle course dictated purely by reason.

b) Political Key-Terms

The Tories, too, made consistent use of ideology-based terminology, their hardline application outstripping Defoe's partly more moderate approach. On certain essentials they adhered to retrograde views like, for example, the unity of Church and State (hence the label "Church party") and loyalty to the monarch, views which culminated under Queen Anne in a renaissance of the concept of Divine Right[1]. Tory traditionalism also became apparent in their often guarded reservations about the new order after the Revolution of 1688/89 and their preference for landed over commercial interests. In foreign policy the Tories - with a strong High Church and Jacobite element but also a Hanoverian wing - inclined towards isolationism[2] and advocated a stronger military engagement at sea instead of on land. Their foreign policy lacked the Whigs' European dimension and in relation to other nations was often overtly xenophobic[3].

In the Tories' political terminology emotionally charged words with positive connotations were fewer than in Whig rhetoric. The hard core of charged terms,

---

1 On the ideological positions of the Tories cf. Müllenbrock, *Whigs kontra Tories*, pp. 46-50.

2 Cf. Holmes, *British Politics in the Age of Anne*, p. 64.

3 See *ibid.*, pp. 64 and 69.

however, occurred with great regularity in the Tories' orthodox and aggressive propaganda to define their political position, often in antithetical reference to their opponents. Central to Tory ideology were such terms as "Queen" and "Prerogative", which were contrasted - spectacularly for the first time by St. John in his pilot publication *A Letter to the Examiner* (1710) - with the deplorable lack of loyalty on the Whig side. "Church and Nation" and also "Queen and Nation"[1] offered further opportunity for positive identification. In its subtitle *The Flanders Ballad: Or, the D-e of Marlborough's Rare Show* (1712) promised to discover "all his Covetous Actions again [sic] his Q-n and Country". "Queen and Nation" in particular was used in simplistic contrast to "Family and Faction", the negative label being applied to the Whigs. The *Examiner*, for example, employed the convenient "Family" label, which had already assumed an ominous ring in a pamphlet[2] of August 1710 still appeasing Marlborough, and which had previously also been used in the pamphlet *A Letter from a Foreign Minister in England, to Monsieur Pettecum* (1710) by Boyer[3], who at that time was still trying to ingratiate himself with Harley, in its issues of 23 November and 14 December 1710 to point to the undermining of the interests of Queen and nation by the political cronyism of the Marlborough clan. The negative connotation of "Family" was relentlessly exploited in *The Conduct of the Allies*[4], and propagated further in Ferguson's *Account* (1711)[5]. Even in Defoe's *No Queen: Or, no General* it occurred four times[6]. Further contrastive pairs were "landed men" and "moneyed men" or "landed interest" and "moneyed interest" as well as the often used antithesis of concord and discord. Besides, the Whigs were frequently denigrated as atheists and republicans just as they in turn concentrated their propaganda activities on the extremist fringe in the Tory party. In spite of its determinedly emotive terminology Tory rhetoric remained vague in outlining the party's ideological position with regard to constitutional orthodoxy because only sparse use was made of the term "Protestant Succession", which Defoe, however, used as a positive referent in his own writing. In late 1711 Tory propaganda came truly into its own by also focusing on the Dutch and making "Dutch" a staple of the emotive vocabulary, whose aggressive element was thus further enhanced.

The strategy behind the Tory use of positive and negative key-terms was to present their own policy as 'natural' and that of the Whigs as 'unnatural', a strategy underlined by a corresponding emphasis prevailing in Tory imagery. The language clearly reflected the prevailing concepts of party ideology. In a letter to the Earl of Strafford of 8 January 1712 Bolingbroke, for example, spoke of the Whig faction's "unnatural proceedings"[7]. There are frequent references to the natural

---

1 Thus already Clement, *Faults on Both Sides*, p. 36.

2 See *Reasons why the Duke of Marlborough Cannot Lay down his Commands*, p. 3.

3 See *A Letter from a Foreign Minister in England, to Monsieur Pettecum*, p. 6.

4 See Swift, *Political Tracts 1711-1713*, p. 41.

5 See Ferguson, *An Account of the Obligations the States of Holland Have to Great-Britain*, p. 6.

6 See Defoe, *No Queen: Or, no General*, pp. 10, 11, 17.

7 Bolingbroke, *Letters and Correspondence*, II, 145. - Cf. on the related stigmatisation of

order at home having been upset by upstarts and their rebellious behaviour towards the Queen. Similarly, with regard to foreign policy, it was pointed out how unfavourably Britain's financial burden compared with that of the Dutch. This polemical strategy led to the frequent use of "monstrous" in all genres to qualify the political opponent. In *Examiner* 38 (19 April 1711) Swift spoke of "monstrous Encroachments of exorbitant Avarice and Ambition"[1] with regard to the Whigs and in *Examiner* 39 (26 April 1711), referring to the Lords' address of December 1707 concerning Spain, of "this monstrous Step in Politicks"[2]. The word "monster" was fired in an exceptionally dense barrage at Marlborough in Hoffman's broadside *The Portraiture of Oliverus Secundus, the Modern Protector in Body and Conscience* (1712). In the broadside *The Story of Typhon* (1711), too, there were several references to Marlborough's "monstrous" greatness, and Wharton was stigmatised as a "monster" at the end of *The Character of a Certain Whigg* (1712), another broadside; and in *The Epilogue to His Grace James Duke of Ormond's Last Speech to Her Majesty, at his Departure for Flanders* (1712), also a broadside, we read with reference to the Whig Junto, which had so pressurized the Queen: "But Providence, the Guardian of the Just,/Baffled, and laid their monstrous Schemes in Dust". The same abusive language was regularly employed in Ward's poem *The English Foreigners: Or, the Whigs Turn'd Dutchmen. A Satyr* (1712), where a perplexed contemporary observer puts the following indignant question to Britannia: "What Monsters hast thou suckl'd at thy Breast?/ What upstart Traytors cherish'd and caress'd?"[3]. In his anti-Austrian campaign even Defoe resorted to this emotional and simplistic way of passing political judgment. In *The Succession of Spain Consider'd*, for example, he warned his readers of a "monstrous increase"[4] of Habsburg power, and in *The Ballance of Europe* cautioned not "to raise again such a Monster in *Europe*"[5]. Thus we can again observe the concerted use of politically inflaming language over the entire gamut of genres as an instrument of Tory propaganda, which thereby achieved a high degree of persistence. On the whole, the Tories inclined more strongly towards emotional language than the Whigs and fully utilised its potential for polarisation.

But thanks to Defoe the presentation of Government propaganda did not - even in its language - lack balancing elements, his rhetoric being very much the same in the *Review* and his pamphlets during the turning-point debate, i.e., between the autumn of 1711 and the spring of 1712. Even in Defoe's characterisation of the political opponent certain key-terms do occur, but where he outlines his own position the style is more discursive so that by and large the tone of the *Review* and of the pamphlets came close to being conciliatory. Defoe's original Whig convictions and Harley's policy of also aiming at a Whig clientele led to the continued use

---

this much-used term also Pat Rogers, "Swift and Bolingbroke on Faction", *The Journal of British Studies* 9 (1970), p. 98.

1 Swift, *The Examiner and Other Pieces Written in 1710-11*, p. 133.

2 *Ibid.*, p. 140.

3 *The Poetical Entertainer*, Number III, p. 7. See also pp. 3 and 14.

4 Defoe, *The Succession of Spain Consider'd*, p. 31.

5 Defoe, *The Ballance of Europe*, p. 36.

even during the turning-point debate of a particular set of terms around "Protestant" and "Protestantism" and the concepts of the Protestant Succession and a liberal constitution. The positive connotations that such language evoked indicated to the Opposition that there remained forces in the Government camp with views similar to theirs. Even at a time of increasing confrontation this breadth of terminology was meant to signal that a modicum of consensus still existed with a chance, be it ever so slight, of bridging political differences.

c) Metaphors and Images

Large sections of Government propaganda are phrased in a language whose imagery reflects the Tories' traditionalism. Like the Whigs they used negative metaphors of illness and arson to denounce particular policies. They had, however, a special preference for animal metaphors, more so than the Whigs. This can be observed, for example, in the use of bird imagery to evoke Jacobite sympathies[1]. On this linguistic plane, too, there was a high degree of interrelatedness between the various media. In Kirkham's thoroughly Tory poem *Philanglus and Astraea* (1712) the precursors of the Whigs at the time of the Civil War are branded as "Birds of Prey, and [...] Devouring Beasts"[2]. A pamphleteer summarily denounces the Whigs as "these Serpents"[3]. In *A Farther Search into the Conduct of the Allies* even Defoe resorts to some aggressive animal comparisons to direct public indignation at the political opponent. To a far larger degree than in Whig propaganda the main function of these metaphors was to concentrate Tory criticism on individuals in the Opposition camp, as for example in King's *Rufinus* (1712). In *Oliver's Pocket Looking-Glass* (1711) Marlborough is compared to a viper which the deceived Queen has nursed in her bosom[4]. In Leslie's *Salt for the Leach* (1712), which, like earlier Tory pamphlets critically mirrored in *The Re-Representation: Or, a Modest Search after the Great Plunderers of the Nation* (1711), abounds in animal imagery[5], the bellicose Whigs are likened to leeches. The ironic albeit forced references to such language in the second and fourth stanzas of the Whig broadside *Poor England Bob'd at Home and Abroad* (1712) were an indirect acknowledgement of the punch of Tory propaganda. Broadside literature, with its popular appeal, was especially rich in animal metaphors whose aim it was to stigmatise the political opponent, as *Advice to the True Representatives of Old England* (1710?), *The Grand Enquiry, Or, What's to be Done with Him* (1712), *The Fable of the Cocks and Ganders* (1712) and *The Description of Dunkirk with Squash's and Dismal's Opinion* (1712) demonstrate, to mention only a few. In *The*

1 See with reference to this Tomoko Hanazaki, "A New Parliament of Birds: Aesop, Fiction, and Jacobite Rhetoric", *Eighteenth-Century Studies* 27 (1993-94), pp. 235-254.

2 [Charles Kirkham], *Philanglus and Astraea: Or, the Loyal Poem* (Stamford, 1712), p. 8.

3 Hornby, *The Fourth and Last Part of a Caveat against the Whiggs*, p. 34.

4 See *Oliver's Pocket Looking-Glass*, p. 23.

5 Cf. also the poem "Rufinus" appended to King's pamphlet of the same title (1712).

Whigs No Plunderers (1711) Godolphin, the previous Prime Minister, is referred to as a "sly fox" or "Volpone", and in Swift's *A Fable of the Widow and her Cat* (1712) Marlborough's behaviour is compared to a cat's. Quite in line with the Tories' practice of lending the idea of monarchy some ideological lustre, such animal metaphors[1] were sometimes combined with religious concepts, which led to a kind of biblical populism[2] that stirred people's emotions. The following two lines from Hoffman's broadside *The True Copy of a Paper Stuck upon the D. of M-'s Gate at St. James's, on Saturday last, Being the Day of Her Majesty's Accession to the Crown* (1712) provide a good example: they are directed against Marlborough and combine positive and negative elements in a single pithy antithesis: "But God who guards our Gracious ANNE,/ Will smite the great *Leviathan*". This occurs again in the same author's broadside *A New-Years Gift for the Plunderers of the World: With an Ancient Prophecy* (1712). In another broadside, *The Portraiture of Oliverus Secundus*, Hoffman refers to Marlborough as "In Mind more Monster than *Leviathan*". By that time the portentous epithet could be applied to Marlborough - presenting him as a wicked and exorbitant war-profiteer - on the very title page of the hastily composed poem *The Land-Leviathan. Or, Modern Hydra: In Burlesque Verse, by way of Letter to a Friend* (1712). And in the retrospective peace poem *Anna Triumphans* (1713) the foreign enemy is also referred to by this name[3]. The Whigs' presumptuous aspirations were also expressed through mythological comparisons; thus Leslie likened them to Phaethon, adding: "but [they] have only shewn their own Folly, set the World on Fire, and fallen from the Chariot they were not able to Guide"[4]. In this way the preordained course of history could be objectified in a mythical form.

The Tories liked analogies between politics and nature because they could thus set unequivocal value standards with which people could identify. An expression of this is their habitual emphasis on the protective nature of the monarchy, which evoked the traditional concept of a patriarchal ruler. Demanding gratitude and loyalty towards the Queen amounted to an attempt to define the conditions of political life in terms of bonds that are natural to man. The Whigs, in spite of regularly pointing to the ingratitude of their opponents towards Marlborough, did not have at their disposal such an arsenal of affective language - inflammable material which the Tories fully utilised to kindle the feelings of their political base; the latter's need for easy identification was gratified by a propaganda strategy which translated complex issues of power politics into the familiar sphere of personal relationships. Characteristically, this technique was refined by a religious veneer in the wake of a revival of the concept of Divine Right during the final years of Queen Anne's reign reminiscent of the medieval world view with its strong sense

---

1 Even as late as in the *Examiner* of 27 March 1713 the Whigs, who were intent upon thwarting the peace, are dismissed as "Viper".

2 Leviathan, the personification of evil in the following examples, was the most popular of biblical monsters; cf. Mary K. Wakeman, *God's Battle with the Monster. A Study in Biblical Imagery* (Leiden, 1973), p. 64.

3 See *Anna Triumphans. A Congratulary Poem on the Peace* (London, 1713), p. 10.

4 *Salt for the Leach*, p. 7.

of hierarchy. Such use of metaphors[1], expressing a traditional understanding of the State and of politics, was common to all Government propaganda and gave all genres a positive note.

There were certain time-honoured formulas with which Tories and Whigs alike - although in different degree - used to refer to Queen and monarchy. Thus the phrase "Nursing Mother of the (our) Church" was employed with reference to Queen Anne in the sermon preached on the occasion of the victory at Oudenaarde by the Whig Thomas Knaggs on 19 August 1708 at St. Margaret's, Westminster, and also in the High Church sermon *The Wise Man's Counsel upon the Test* by the Tory Richard Welton on 19 November 1710 with its particular emphasis on the monarch's authority[2]. Significantly, the same metaphor, which Defoe would not want to do without, either[3], was also used in the *Post Boy* of 5-7 February 1712, which shows that it was particularly well received by the Tories. In Ward's poem *The English Foreigners*, which gives expression to an ideology both Tory and Royalist, Queen Anne is referred to as "Our Royal Nursing Mother"[4]. In *A Poem Dedicated to the Queen, and Presented to the Congress at Utrecht, upon Declaration of the Peace* (1713) the epithet "tender Parent"[5] is applied to the reigning sovereign. Smith in his poem *On the Peace* (1713), which is a vindication of Tory politics, credits the Queen with " [...] *Maternal Passion* for Your Subject's *Due*"[6]. Similar expressions like "Parent of Plenty" and "fountain of Riches and Happiness", politically applied with reference to the Queen or the monarchy, were staple elements of Tory rhetoric[7] giving expression to their traditional concept of submission to the will and authority of the sovereign. The author of *The English Foreigners*, for instance, addresses Harley thus: "Give *England* Peace, beneath bless'd ANNA's Care,/ And put a Glorious Period to the War"[8]. This rhetoric, of course, implied criticism of the Whigs' lack of loyalty to the Queen. Thus a belligerent Tory pamphleteer declares with regard to alleged plots of the

---

1 See for the wider context Dietmar Peil, *Untersuchungen zur Staats- und Herrschaftsmetaphorik in literarischen Zeugnissen von der Antike bis zur Gegenwart* (Munich, 1983). Cf. also Alexander Demandt, *Metaphern für Geschichte. Sprachbilder und Gleichnisse im historisch-politischen Denken* (Munich, 1978) and, most recently, Francesca Rigotti, *Die Macht und ihre Metaphern. Über die sprachlichen Bilder der Politik* (Frankfurt/ New York, 1994).

2 See Thomas Knaggs, *A Sermon Preach'd at St. Margarets, Westminster, August the 19th. 1708* (London, 1708), p. 16 and Richard Welton, *The Wise Man's Counsel upon the Test. In a Sermon Preach'd before the Honourable the Lieutenancy of the City of London* ... (London, 1710), p. 14.

3 See *Reasons why this Nation Ought to Put a Speedy End to this Expensive War*, where Anne is called "a true Nursing Mother" (p. 25).

4 *The Poetical Entertainer*, Number III, p. 9.

5 (London, 1713), p. 5.

6 *On the Peace: A Poem*, p. 16.

7 With the following comparison a pamphleteer surely went too far, even for Tory taste: "Our Queen is as the Breath of our Nostrils [...]" (*No Punishment, no Government: And no Danger even in the Worst Designs*, p. 12)!

8 *The Poetical Entertainer*, Number III, p. 23.

irreverent Whigs against their Sovereign: "[...] the first Blow is ever directed at our Head, to smite the Shepherd, and then devour the Sheep"[1]. As early as 1710, St. John in his trend-setting *A Letter to the Examiner* had satirically spoken of Queen Anne as surrendering to the will of the Junto and also contrasted the Duchess of Marlborough, the scourge of God, with the Queen, the fountain and instrument of his mercy[2]. Political metaphors aiming at a religious transfiguration of the monarchy were especially frequent in the *Examiner* after Swift; time and again a bright light was cast on Tory ideology, which made it stand out like a shining example against the dark background of Whig attitudes and policies. In the *Examiner* of 13 April 1713, for example, in which the Peace of Utrecht was welcomed, the Queen is called "the *Guardian Angel* of our Island". Of course the time-honoured view of the monarchy could also be put to polemical use in a foreign-policy context; thus a Tory author reproachfully refers to the Dutch as "a People who have slighted a Queen who hath been their Nursing-Mother [...]"[3]. Like a signature tune the Tories' presentation of the monarchy evoked patriarchal and religious connotations among their supporters, who were thus incited to condemn the Whigs' unnatural irreverence. Through their metaphorical political language the Tories projected a traditional, almost old-fashioned party image, though its propagation through a whole range of streamlined genres strikes one as almost modern.

An interesting independent variety of the use of political metaphors is found in Defoe, who, as pamphleteer and also as essayist in the *Review*, created his very own and unmistakable imagery to put across his cherished political topics, among them his staple, the political balance in Europe, which, quite in line with the Harley Ministry's policy, he wanted to see sustained. In five issues of the *Review* between November 1711 and July 1712 Defoe made skilful use of the traditional scales metaphor in this connection in order to state his case as strikingly as possible[4]. In the *Review* of 1 November 1711, for example, where he launched a rhetorical attack on Austria, we read: "This however may be a useful Hint to such as are willing, blindfold to throw the Weight of *Europe's* Strength into the Imperial Scale, and out-Ballance the rest, by the same Hand which once bid fair to devour the whole [...]"[5]. Here Defoe criticises the intention to hand the Spanish crown to the House of Habsburg, whose sphere of influence had on past occasions proved a threat to freedom. The latter argument in particular gave Defoe an opportunity to appease his political conscience after joining the Government camp. Besides, his combination of "blindfold" and "Scale" evokes the image of Justitia, which is of course intended: it is Defoe's personal political message. Any abstract solution to

---

1 *A Vindication of Oliver Cromwell, and the Whiggs of Forty-One*, pp. 13-14. An almost identical formulation can be found in the same author's *No Punishment, no Government: And no Danger even in the Worst Designs*, p. 13.

2 See *A Letter to the Examiner*, pp. 12-13.

3 *The Speech of a Noble Peer* (London, 1712), p. 22.

4 See the editions of the *Review* dated 1 November 1711, 13 November 1711, 17 November 1711, 3 July 1712 and 12 July 1712.

5 *Defoe's Review*, VIII, 383.

the Spanish Succession which simply followed the contractual stipulations of the Grand Alliance to the letter would not do justice to the concrete political situation, dominated by power politics; thus his use of a traditional metaphor is a plea for a pragmatic solution which takes existing facts into account. This was also Defoe's method in the *Review* of 12 July 1712, where he again emphasised the need for Britain's role as arbiter: "[...] *Britain* now holds the Ballance, and will turn the Scale [...]"[1]. Here the traditional metaphor expresses Defoe's political message that it is England's historic mission to keep the European balance of power in place, if necessary through cautious intervention. Through the seasonable use of the balance-of-power rhetoric Defoe rejects both the orthodox Whigs' support of the Emperor, whom they would like to see gain the Spanish crown, and traditional isolationist tendencies in Tory foreign policy.

By and large Defoe used metaphors sparingly[2], which is hardly surprising given his dissenting readership. But he used them regularly to give his balance-of-power rhetoric the necessary impact. In the *Review* of 20 May 1712 he expressed his demand that Britain maintain equidistance from France and Austria thus: "[...] the middle Way between both, is the safe, the just, the most Reasonable; as clipping the Wings of both, that neither the *French* with his *Meridian Sun* may scorch us, nor the Voracious *Roman Eagle* may devour us"[3]. Although in terms of stylistic purity the metaphors are somewhat mixed, Defoe achieves his aim: an unmistakable contribution to the balance-of-power issue. The word "clipping" expresses the idea of containment of power, and the plural "Wings" suggests the evenness and symmetry of such a policy. Finally, Defoe's reference to the Imperial eagle, Austria's heraldic bird, makes use of the traditional bird-of-prey metaphor and aptly applies it to the threat that Austria posed. Comparing Austria to a live creature lends particular force to his admonition that vis-à-vis this great power which actively threatens others the utmost caution must be exercised, whereas the scorching sun metaphor is more static, thus presenting France as a more predictable danger, similar perhaps to that which Icarus fell victim to, but only after climbing too high. This rhetoric gives apt expression to Defoe's line of argumentation, which aims at balance and compromise - the hallmark of his journalism -, and yet, his use of metaphor is like putting an exclamation mark, as it were, behind the danger posed by Austria. In the same issue of the *Review* Defoe very appropriately used the 'rocks' metaphor to strengthen his argument in favour of a balance-of-power policy. Should the Spanish crown pass to the all-powerful Emperor, then - so runs his argument - this would pose a lasting threat to the Protestant interests in Europe, a concern which is succinctly expressed towards the end: "Splitting the Cause of God upon *German Scylla*, to avoid *French Charybdis*?"[4]

1 *Ibid.*, p. 817.

2 This tendency is however overemphasised by E. Anthony James, *Daniel Defoe's Many Voices. A Rhetorical Study of Prose Style and Literary Method* (Amsterdam, 1972), p. 9.

3 *Defoe's Review*, VIII, 726.

4 *Ibid.*, p. 728.

Defoe also used metaphors referring to every-day life with which his addressees were no doubt familiar. The Utrecht horse-fair metaphor is a good example. It is one of the most widely employed metaphors in the *Review*, for example, in the issues of 14 February 1712 and 1 March of the same year, the first offering a particularly instructive example of Defoe's rhetorical technique. Because of his outrageous demands Louis XIV is compared to a skilful horse trader. By likening French negotiating tactics to established business practices Defoe probably hoped to pander to Whig susceptibilities. In the *Review* of 14 February 1712 he pointed out that, being aware of France's deceitfulness, the Allies were well able to defend themselves against any attempt to make them pay through the nose. Besides, it was a well-known fact that France desperately needed a peace agreement and would therefore soon be ready to make concessions. After all, both the Allies and France knew what was in their best interest: "And do you think we do not know how to set a Price upon our Horse, as well as the King of *France* does upon his?"[1] . It is the function of the elaborate horse-fair metaphor to carefully consider all aspects of the peace negotiations and point towards a viable solution. Defoe's imagery thus pays tribute to Harley's realpolitik with its flexibility and clearsightedness. That this kind of rhetoric was also intended to mitigate England's confrontation with her Allies becomes clear from a humorous passage in the *Review* of 1 March 1712: the Dutch have suggested providing 40,000 riding crops to drive Louis XIV out of Spain and let England pay three quarters of the cost. Nobody was outraged, everybody was amused.

Defoe also used some elaborate comparisons from every-day life to characterize England's relationship with the Dutch, the deterioration of which was of some concern to him. In the *Reviews* of 9 February and 12 July 1712 the cooling off between the two countries was expressed in terms of a marital quarrel. He blames the Dutch Ally's negligent behaviour for the present predicament of the Protestant family[2] in the first-named issue, but then it is for Britannia, the spouse, to avert further damage, as the second issue makes clear: "The Man begins it [the quarrel], but the Woman, who by Prudence and Temper should have mov'd him to Reform, or at least, might have restrain'd his Extravagancies, she makes the Destruction unavoidable to them both"[3] . Thus Defoe, while blaming Holland, is at the same time appealing to England to exercise restraint in her own interest. The Anglo-Dutch relationship was also the topic of the *Review* of 10 June 1712. On their way to York Jack and Tom are quarrelling over which route to take, an obvious allusion to the two countries' difficulties in agreeing on a joint political course. The arguments in the two travellers' quarrel correspond to those of the Anglo-Dutch controversy, with Defoe taking sides by suggesting that it is up to Britain to make

1 *Ibid.*, p. 562.

2 The family metaphor was, by the way, a means of bringing internal friction dramatically to the surface in the late eighteenth century as the Anglo-American conflict loomed closer: see J. Vernon Jensen, "British Voices on the Eve of the American Revolution: Trapped by the Family Metaphor", *The Quarterly Journal of Speech* 63 (1977), pp. 43-50.

3 *Defoe's Review*, VIII, 820.

its wayward companion listen to reason. Similar criticism had previously appeared in *Reasons Why*: "the *Dutch* were the Mint in which every Article of Peace must be coined, or else it could not be Current in the Confederacy"[1]. What characterizes Defoe's imagery in connection with the Anglo-Dutch relationship is the fact that it was anchored in his readers' every-day experience. This enabled him to heighten their perception of the regrettable differences between the two Protestant countries so closely allied[2].

1 *Reasons why this Nation Ought to Put a Speedy End to this Expensive War*, p. 37.

2 On Defoe's use of pictorical language see also Hans Lohrengel's study *Politische Metaphorik in Defoes 'Review'* (Staatsexamensarbeit, University of Göttingen, 1992).

VI. Some Aspects of Authorship and Readership

1. Social Background and Denominational Allegiance of Authors; Genres and Party-Political Orientation

It is a well-known fact of general literary history that English writers of the eighteenth century came from a broad social spectrum, including the aristocracy. So Goethe's complaint about the lack of aristocratic writers in Germany does not apply to the England of the Enlightenment, where the Earl of Halifax, Lord Lyttelton, Lord Chesterfield and others were active men of letters[1]. There were noblemen among the political authors, too. St. John, the later Lord Bolingbroke, for instance, wrote the pioneering *A Letter to the Examiner* (1710), and the pamphlet *Observations upon the State of the Nation, in January 1712/13* (1713) has been attributed to the Earl of Nottingham. As was the case with belles-lettres, however, the vast majority of authors of political writings belonged to the middle class, particularly the upper middle class. And just as with belles-lettres, political authors from the lowest classes, if there were any at all, were the exception. Within the broad complex of the middle class the proportion of members of the professions with an Anglican background and education was very high. Against the Anglican predominance Nonconformists and also autodidacts were rare among authors although more frequent among the Whigs than among the Tories, Roper being, of course, a Tory autodidact. Examples of Whig authors belonging to non-Anglican denominations are Ridpath and Oldmixon. It is well-known that Defoe, too, who never completely denied his Whig origins, was a Dissenter. The fact that political authors, irrespective of their social and educational background, were generally more or less automatically discredited as hirelings and mercenary scribblers by their opponents has to do with the lack of theoretical legitimisation of both the press and the party system, which was frequently still considered pathological.

Besides denominational differences, there were also certain professional constellations which manifested clear distinctions as regards genre and party-political allegiance. Members of the professional classes were of paramount importance for political writing, and a large number of them belonged to the lower clergy - this likewise confirms the not insignificant role played, as is well known, by the clergy in eighteenth-century literature, for instance in novels and nature poetry[2]. The

---

1 See Müllenbrock, "Einleitung: Die politisch-gesellschaftlichen Grundlagen der englischen Aufklärung", Müllenbrock (Ed.), *Europäische Aufklärung II*, pp. 22-23.

2 See esp. Herbert Schöffler, *Protestantismus und Literatur. Neue Wege zur englischen Literatur des 18. Jahrhunderts* (2nd ed., Göttingen, 1958).

prominent part played by the lower clergy was not only reflected in their own particular domain, the sermon, where the majority of the clergy were on the Tory side; it is significant that there was a slight Whig overbalance in sermons preached by the higher clergy. The lower clergy also had the largest share in the production of pamphlets and poems - note especially the rich variety of peace poems. There are some quite interesting party-political correlations between professional groups and genres. There was, for instance, an unusual concentration on the Tory side of poems written by the lower clergy - the Whigs produced only a fraction of the number produced by the Tories. Other genres were more under Whig influence. In particular the major public genre, the pamphlet, was - in numerical terms - more the domain of the Whigs. So more pamphlets were written by Whig politicians than by Tory ones, and, surprisingly, there were more Whig pamphlets even among those by the lower clergy. An examination of pamphlets by authors occupying senior administrative posts reveals that the Whigs in fact had a virtual monopoly! The majority of documentary publications, too, came from the Whig camp, if we leave aside Boyer's contribution, which was a special case. The longer prose romance in the style of Mrs. Manley's *The New Atalantis* (1709) seems to have been used exclusively by the Tories; Oldmixon's *The Court of Atalantis* (1714), which employs this medium to take a critical look at members of the Tory Ministry but which did not appear until after the completion of the Utrecht peace debate, can be classified as a belated response to Tory variations on this genre.

Although it is difficult to distinguish between these features strictly along party lines, it can be said that the traditional genres like sermons, poems and prose romances were more often than not written by Tory sympathisers. Altogether the 'narrative slant' in important Tory propaganda, which is also seen in the widespread use of time-honoured verse fables such as Stacy's *Parliament of Birds* (1712), is quite remarkable. Texts like Swift's *The Conduct of the Allies* (1711), Arbuthnot's *The History of John Bull* (1712) and Wagstaffe's *The Story of the St. Alb-ns Ghost* (1712), to name but a few, characterized by what one could call the 'spell of fictional consistency', released tremendous polemical energy. Significantly, all these appeared during the Tory offensive of the turning-point debate, when the Tories staked everything on emotional mobilization. On the other hand authors who preferred the 'professional' genres like pamphlets or documentary writings tended to be Whigs. It can be said without exaggeration that until well into 1710, the year when the government changed, Whig propaganda appeared more professional than its Tory counterpart. The particular agility of the Whigs in their use of the pamphlet, incidentally, does not conflict with the fact that, at least until 1710, the Whigs also made full use of the drama, a powerful medium for propaganda purposes[1], because the political promotion of the drama by some members of the Kit-Cat Club with their own vested interests had a strong profes-

1 Cf., regarding the political instrumentalisation of this genre, Loftis, *The Politics of Drama in Augustan England* and Müllenbrock, *Whigs konta Tories*, chapter II.

sional touch[1]. It is Harley's achievement that the greater propagandistic effectiveness of the Whigs over a considerable period was systematically broken; the chapter focusing on the turning-point debate has shown in its description of the process of polemical interaction how the thrust of Tory propaganda eventually outdid that of the Whigs at the beginning of 1712. Besides, political writers hardly ever concentrated on just one genre, but were as a rule productive in several. This was particularly true of the most prominent authors, those mainly responsible for determining the broad polemical lines such as Swift, Defoe and Maynwaring. Their share in the production of broadsides was disproportionately high. There was a particularly high rate of anonymity in this genre, but a considerable number of the broadsides which can be attributed to a particular author were actually written by Swift, Defoe or Maynwaring, although these did not, of course, match the productivity of a specialist like Hoffman. The strikingly intensive use of the broadside by influential political commentators also shows with how much careful consideration this genre was integrated into the polemical interaction.

An interesting and in many respects representative group stands out among those authors who were responsible for the most important opinion-forming periodicals - *The Examiner*, *A Review*, *The Medley* and *The Observator* -, a group that was mainly instrumental in maintaining the uninterrupted progress of the political debate. Swift, Defoe, Maynwaring and Ridpath, all belonging to the generation born during the Restoration, had consciously witnessed the Revolution of 1688/89 or even played an active part in it. It is a remarkable fact that three of them - Swift, Defoe and Maynwaring - changed party at some time in their lives, or at least had a change of political views, which points to a certain fluctuation in the political life of the time and a corresponding adaptability of the authors who helped to shape it. Moreover, all four authors, who not only wrote essays but were productive in other genres, too, channelled most if not all of their literary energy into journalistic activities during the period from 1710 until 1713. This can be seen as an indication of the increasing significance and professionalisation of political propaganda in the ongoing debate between the Government and the Opposition.

2. ASPECTS OF A GENRE (THE POLITICAL ESSAY) AND ITS READERSHIP

Our examination of the sociological aspects of readership focuses on the four periodicals mentioned above, which followed a clear party-political line, sought to shape public opinion and - for the most part - simultaneously developed a conscious appeal to a specific audience. Although the main emphasis will be on the opinion-forming journals, sociological aspects of readership concerning other genres will be briefly considered in order to complete the picture. At the beginning it

[1] Cf. Müllenbrock, *op.cit.*, pp. 52-53.

is appropriate to recall some remarks made in the introduction, namely that - like belles-lettres - political writing, too, was addressed almost exclusively to the middle and upper classes, and this although more and more sections of the population were being drawn into the process of public political communication and despite the fact that via the oral presentation of broadsides even the lowest classes were from time to time mobilised by political propaganda. Within the vast complex of the middle and upper classes it is possible to make some quite clear sociological distinctions among the readership, especially since in the early eighteenth century - in contrast to the Victorian age - there was no collective readership yet which was addressed in its entirety by the literature produced, as by Dickens' novels, for example; the various literary genres were still rather tailored to specific strata of the reading public. To give an example, Richardson's novels were intended primarily for a lower to middle bourgeoisie whose expectations were met first of all by didactically effective instruction in questions of moral conduct and religious edification rather than being combined with classical educational ideals. Comic epic poems like Pope's *The Rape of the Lock*, on the other hand, were addressed to a public comprising the aristocracy and the upper middle class, both with a classical education and more interested in formal brilliance than moral instruction[1]. Such sociological distinctions can also be seen in the way political writers communicated with their public. In order to describe the sociological framework as objectively as possible, the following criteria will be applied: first of all, the degree of classical education (a measure of which is the use of Latin texts and references to classical literature, history and mythology); secondly, references to other areas of knowledge, especially to English history to illustrate political positions; and thirdly, linguistic aspects, especially vocabulary, but also imagery and syntax.

a) *The Examiner*

Among the four opinion-forming periodicals the intended readership[2] of the *Examiner* occupies the top position in the socio-cultural hierarchy. In the form of prefaced mottoes[3] and passages inserted into the text the *Examiner* makes the most extensive use of Latin. The thirty-three issues written by Swift between November 1710 and June 1711 contain fifteen Latin quotations. Although translations or paraphrases are provided at essential points in the argument, as numbers 14 (2 November 1710) and 17 (23 November 1710) show, Swift relies to a certain

1 See e.g. Ulrich Broich, *Studien zum komischen Epos. Ein Beitrag zur Deutung, Typologie und Geschichte des komischen Epos im englischen Klassizismus 1680-1800* (Tübingen, 1968), pp. 159-162.

2 For Swift's audience cf. also Richard I. Cook, *Jonathan Swift as a Tory Pamphleteer* (Seattle, Wash., and London, 1967), second chapter.

3 On mottoes as indicators of addressee awareness for the periodicals during the Seven Years' War see Spector, *Political Controversy. A Study in Eighteenth-Century Propaganda*, p. 7.

extent on his readers' own ability to understand Latin. The degree of difficulty is thus somewhat higher than that of the *Medley*, which does without prefaced mottoes and uses practically no Latin quotations, always working with paraphrases instead. So it is only in the *Examiner* that the Latin language plays any real role as a vehicle for classical education. In keeping with this orientation is the exceptionally frequent recourse to ancient history for historical examples; ancient history accounts for about eighty per cent of these (Fig. 1)[1] , and it is complemented by numerous allusions to classical mythology. Incidentally, the later *Examiner*, which was revived in December 1711, made considerably less use of Latin, which earned it an ironical note in the *Observator* of 12-15 December 1711 and demonstrated a slight shift in its attitude to its readers. The cultural component of the *Examiner* is matched by its comparatively select vocabulary, the most extensive of the four periodicals under consideration (Fig. 5). This includes a clearly discernible though not over-conspicuous proportion of foreign words, particularly hard words; but there is a noticeable paucity of abstract nouns, so that Swift does not lapse into Johnsonese in this respect, either. Rather the *Examiner* is at pains to present political facts as clearly as possible with the aid of numerous down-to-earth images with sometimes decidedly popular appeal - it is quite a remarkable fact that the *Examiner*, which appears the most intellectual of the four opinion-forming periodicals, uses a comparatively wide variety of images. Thus in the *Examiner* the prestige-enhancing recourse to the classics combines with the desire to lend vigour to the political message; despite its love of the classics and a traditionalism that must have appealed to the gentry - primarily its intended readership - the *Examiner* was clearly determined to avoid dryness. Structurally, too, the *Examiner* meets relatively superior standards; the altogether unmistakable cultural elitism of this periodical is underlined by the frequent borrowing of classical rhetorical patterns[2] and also by genuine classical imitations, as in the Verres issue of 30 November 1710.

Swift's syntax is characterized by an unobtrusive structure that ensures intellectual clarity, but without Defoe's overt didactic care. For instance, the *Examiner* lacks explicit repetitive elements, and Swift only uses the paratactic constructions favoured by Defoe for rhetorical emphasis, which does not detract from the lightness and elegance of his prose, which aspires to the ideal of easy and familiar style[3] for the upper class and thus leaves no doubt as to its audience. The language of the *Examiner* and *The Conduct of the Allies*, though more rhetorical,

---

1 See end of chapter for graphs.

2 Cf. on this Müllenbrock, "Swift as a Political Essayist", pp. 151-158. *The Conduct of the Allies*, too, is firmly based on the divisions prescribed by the classical scheme of disposition: see Müllenbrock, "Cicero and Quintilian as Mentors of British Journalism: The Rhetorical Structure of Swift's *The Conduct of the Allies*".

3 Cf. on this stylistic ideal Gerd Stratmann, "'*Easy and Familiar*' - Zur klassizistischen Theorie des Prosastils", Rüdiger Ahrens and Erwin Wolff (Eds.), *Englische und amerikanische Literaturtheorie. Studien zu ihrer historischen Entwicklung*, I (Heidelberg, 1978), 237-251. See also Beate Wackwitz, *Die Theorie des Prosastils im England des 18. Jahrhunderts* (Hamburg, 1962), pp. 12-13.

flows in part as naturally as that of *Gulliver's Travels*. Never falling into uncontrolled long-windedness, it at the same time avoids the all-too smooth style characteristic of the *Spectator*. Swift's prose in the *Examiner*[1] is urbane, but it also allows something of the author's roughness to show through. Thus there is a kind of unpolished politeness about it which presumably appealed to the landed gentry, who made up the larger part of the readership. The *Examiner* was tailored to reach this audience above all. Although it took no account of the lower or lowest social strata, it nevertheless repeatedly introduced key-words which became current in all Tory propaganda and reached the entire social spectrum. The word "perquisite", for instance, which was early and conspicuously applied to Marlborough in *Examiner* 17 (23 November 1710), became de rigueur throughout Tory writings and was taken up especially by numerous broadsides[2], which relied on such linguistic pacemakers and, in a kind of propagandistic recycling process, made Swift's political lunges accessible to a wider circle of readers[3]. Although particularly aimed at the gentry, the *Examiner* was able to initiate new linguistic trends throughout the social spectrum, and the provocative style it employed in its treatment of the political opponent made it a very effective propaganda tool.

b) *A Review*

The *Review* was the ideal complement to the *Examiner*, with regard to both its ideology and its readership. The strikingly small part played by the classics shows that its readers were to be found at the opposite end of the social scale. Of the four opinion-forming periodicals the *Review* makes by far the fewest references to ancient history; they account for only about a fifth of the historical examples selected (Fig. 2). On the other hand, the high percentage of references to English and European history - the Stuart period receives the most attention in the *Review* - indicates a middle-class readership interested in practical information. It is quite obvious that in the *Review* Defoe was laying emphasis on the non-classical curriculum customary at the dissenting academies, as is confirmed by the frequent inclusion of knowledge taken from the natural sciences or geography. Whilst the classics are practically absent in the *Review*, the fact that religion - apart, of course, from a politically conceived Protestantism[4] - plays no more than a minor role in-

---

1 See also Müllenbrock, "Swift as a Political Essayist".

2 See e.g. *The Queen's and the Duke of Ormond's New Toast* (1712), *The Grand Enquiry, Or, What's to be Done with Him?* (1712), *The Description of Dunkirk with Squash's and Dismal's Opinion* (1712) and Swift's own broadsides *The Fable of Midas* (1712) and *A Fable of the Widow and her Cat* (1712). Cf. also the title of the publication *The Perquisite-Monger*, which appeared in March 1712.

3 See also the remarks in the chapter "The Main Genres of the Public Debate".

4 The latter was a hallmark of orthodox Whig rhetoric, with which Defoe was having to contend. Steele, for instance, concludes his pamphlet *The Crisis* (1714) by comparing "Her Majesty's Parliamentary Title, and the Succession in the Illustrious House of *Hanover*" to "the Ark of God to *Great Britain*": *Tracts and Pamphlets by Richard Steele*, ed. Rae Blanchard (Baltimore, Md., 1944), p. 181.

dicates that with the inclusion of natural science material Defoe wanted to incorporate the more secular side of the typical Dissenter's education. The use of commercial and maritime vocabulary to clarify political correlations is also a feature of the *Review* specific to its readership.

A linguistic examination of the *Review* confirms the educational level we have established. Of the four opinion-forming periodicals the *Review* has by far the smallest vocabulary, totalling only eighty per cent of that employed by the *Examiner*. There is a corresponding reduction in the proportion of foreign words, especially of hard words. Of course the incidence of foreign words in the *Review* is nowhere near as low as that in *Robinson Crusoe*, which shows that Defoe, despite special consideration for particular social strata, did not wish to impose any heavy readership restrictions on himself but was at pains to achieve a certain breadth of appeal. It is interesting to note that some pamphlets exactly share the *Review*'s approach in this respect; among them are *Reasons why this Nation Ought to Put a Speedy End to this Expensive War* (1711), *A Defence of the Allies and the Late Ministry* (1711) and *No Queen: Or, no General* (1712) in particular, while the later pamphlet *A Farther Search into the Conduct of the Allies* (1712), for instance, falls far short (Fig. 6). The fact that a large number of pamphlets are, along with the *Review*, on a much higher plane than Defoe's first novel in terms of vocabulary can be seen if we take a look at, for example, *Reasons Why*, so important for setting the course of the political debate; words like "Adjunct"[1], "eternize"[2], "Exigencies"[3], "Arbitrate"[4] and "expostulate"[5] are hard to imagine in *Robinson Crusoe*. In the use of imagery, too, the *Examiner* and the *Review* complemented each other. Whereas in Swift's periodical classical antiquity provided a relatively high proportion of the images and historical analogies, Defoe was at pains to use everyday language in the *Review*, in which - as has already been made clear in the treatment of the differences between Whig and Tory rhetoric - political metaphor played a not insignificant role. There is a good example in the *Review* of 9 August 1711, in which Defoe once more makes himself the advocate of "public credit" and clothes its possible disappearance in the following striking image: "[...] if it stops, the whole Circulation Stagnates, and the Body Politick must fall into Convulsions, and from thence into Death"[6].

Finally, an examination of the structure of the essays in the *Review* reveals uncomplicated syntax, which is easy to follow, offers ample opportunity for pauses and is marked by frequent repetition. Repetition is in effect the characteristic feature of Defoe's political didactics, a technique that he used out of consideration for an audience which, unlike Swift's, made modest demands intellectually and was evidently less well-read. In the *Review* of 5 June 1707, in which Defoe sketches his conception of himself as a journalist, the author had defended his repetitive

---

1 *Reasons why this Nation Ought to Put a Speedy End to this Expensive War*, p. 4.
2 *Ibid.*, p. 9.
3 *Ibid.*, p. 21.
4 *Ibid.*, p. 31.
5 *Ibid.*, p. 39.
6 *Defoe's Review*, VIII, 239.

style against his critics' frequent objections with the following sociological considerations: "For my part, I value the instructing and informing one honest meaning ignorant Person, more than the detecting and confronting a thousand Knaves, and 'tis for the sake of these I write; for their Sakes I dwell upon a Subject sometimes longer than the Rules of Language allow, for their Sakes I repeat and repeat, and quote my self over and over; and can with Ease bear the foolish Banters of the envious Critick and Reproacher; I had rather say the same thing over twenty times, than once omit, what may this Way be useful"[1]. This audience-consciousness again, with its resulting effects on the structure, links the *Review* with the pamphlets. Here are some typical examples. In *The Succession of Spain Consider'd* (1711) the danger of a concentration of Habsburg power in the event of an Austrian solution to the Spanish question is hammered into the reader by constant repetition[2]. The key-word 'Austrian greatness' achieves a similarly high frequency. *Reasons Why* is also characterized by a repetitive style. The material and economic draining of England is regularly invoked[3], and in addition casuistry of change, introduced by the sentence "*the Case is alter'd Now*", rings out through the entire pamphlet[4]. In *Armageddon* (1711) - a third example -, which is characterized by a rhetoric of concession addressed to the Opposition, attention is seized again and again by the idea, which flattered the Whigs, that the latter are by no means against peace so long as England's interests are preserved[5]. There is certainly a functional relationship between the repetitive style of the *Review* and the pamphlets on the one hand and the style that prevails in *Robinson Crusoe* on the other. Just as factuality is conveyed by regular repetition in the novel and, more importantly, repeated reflection on significant external events allows them to be grasped intellectually, the essays in the *Review* and the pamphlets signal the importance of a political subject through repetition. And just as the novel makes Robinson Crusoe's tenacious struggle with his environment comprehensible, the *Review* and the pamphlets employ this very technique of repetition in order to convey the intense struggle of the conscientious author with his delicate political topic. To this extent both genres were destined to be vehicles of their author's indefatigable propaganda efforts, which was consistent with Harley's approach of also determinedly canvassing a non-Tory clientele for support for his political line, a line which was to be presented as the only practical alternative given the particular demands of the time. That Defoe sought to accomplish this propagandistic task with inelegant, sometimes even ponderous syntax and eschewed any hint of flippancy at the same time was probably to his advantage given the fact that he was addressing a predominantly lower middle-class audience.

---

1 *Defoe's Review*, IV, 199.

2 See *The Succession of Spain Consider'd*, pp. 8, 18-19, 33, 35, 36, 38, 43, 44.

3 See *Reasons Why*, pp. 3, 5, 13, 19, 24, 31, 47.

4 See *ibid.*, pp. 5, 28, 29, 40, 42.

5 See *Armageddon*, pp. 5, 7, 27, 35, 40.

c) *The Medley*

In its function as a mere counter to the *Examiner* the *Medley* was also tied to a particular class of reader; at any rate it seems to have adopted the aim of demonstrating equality with Swift's periodical in every respect and under all circumstances. This probably explains its surprisingly frequent references to the classics, indeed sometimes more frequent than found in the *Examiner*, though Latin references generally take the form of paraphrases. In order to counter its opponent the *Medley* also takes up the *Examiner*'s classical orientation in order to secure a gain in prestige by means of an erudite refutation or perhaps an elaborate development of an historical analogy. Maynwaring's periodical is sometimes reminiscent of the competitive spirit of a schoolboy. The writer's aim in adapting classical references was to demonstrate his competence in this area in comparison with the obvious learning of the author of the *Examiner*. This led to a relative neglect of recent English history[1]. It is surprising that of the four opinion-forming periodicals the *Medley* has the lowest proportion of references to the Stuart age (Fig. 3), from an ideological point of view the Whigs' most fruitful period for their political polemics.

Lexically, the *Medley* steers a middle course. The *Medley*'s imagery clearly lacks the richness of the *Examiner*'s; here the approach is largely one of reaction without any individual emphases. Syntactically, the relatively high proportion of hypotactic constructions - the highest of the four periodicals - illustrates the pains to which the *Medley* always went to counter its opponent by means of the most logical analysis possible in order, as it were, to show him up. This method presupposes a certain ability of the reader to accept a challenge. Nevertheless it is difficult to make out any specific readership addressed by the *Medley* beyond the mimicry with respect to the *Examiner*. At any rate the vindication of the old Ministry or the Junto and the preference for the moneyed interest are not reflected in any corresponding linguistic idiosyncrasies or stylistic features.

d) *The Observator*

Being in competition with the *Review*, the *Observator* manifested a similar consciousness of its intended readership. In contrast to Defoe's periodical Ridpath's contains a comparatively high proportion of references to ancient history (Fig. 4) -

---

1 This was an area that proved particularly rich for political lessons; cf. - for the Seven Years' War - Marie Peters, "History and Political Propaganda in Mid-Eighteenth-Century England: The Case of the Essay Papers", *Eighteenth Century Life* 11 (1987), pp. 66-79, esp. p. 67. Peters' concluding generalisation, that the frequent use of historical references indicates a lack of concrete information in an author (p. 77), must however be contradicted; Swift, for instance, was much better informed than the average, and his historical examples were carefully chosen in the light of this knowledge.

presumably a consequence of the prestige enjoyed by classical studies at the time, even among the lower classes. At the same time it was clearly different in function from the other Whig periodical, the *Medley*, and correspondingly it was aimed at a different readership. While the *Medley* evidently desires to counter the impression that the *Examiner* is talking down to it like a schoolmaster, reprimanding it, as it were, with Latin slogans, and opposes Swift's conservatism with its own idea of the correct use of a classical education, the author of the *Observator* slips into the role of the teacher presenting the ignorant rural population with instruction applicable to real life but often having its source explicitly in the classics[1] . But it is true that even longer references to classical antiquity in the *Observator* tend less to become ends in themselves than those in the *Medley* with its cultural snobbery. The two issues of the *Observator* of 2-5 January 1712 and 5-9 January 1712, for example, which use the fate of Aristides in their reply to the accusations made against Marlborough by the Tories, directly follow the periodical's political and didactic line. Despite the relatively high proportion of classical references - almost half the historical references in the *Observator* are to ancient history - corresponding intellectual and linguistic demands are not made on the reader because, in response to Roger's request, the Latin passages are mostly translated or reduced to dog Latin. In references to the Stuart period, incidentally, the *Observator* comes closest to the *Review*, the leading periodical in this respect; this is an indicator of a certain polemical concentration on this period in competition with the *Review*. The *Review* and the *Observator* are about equal in their references to other periods of English history, too.

Compared with Defoe's periodical, however, Ridpath's journal is characterized by a marked lack of images, which in this respect puts it at the lower end of the scale among the four opinion-forming periodicals. This seems to indicate that the *Observator* was inclined to show even more consideration for a strongly dissenting readership distrustful of metaphorical illustration than was the case with Defoe. Moreover, it should not be forgotten that Ridpath's didactic medium was the continuous dialogue, in which rhetorical techniques such as the extensive use of images had no place but would rather have seemed artificial. The way in which this periodical presented its arguments was based on the idea of educational inequality, conveyed by the dialogue between the "Observator" and the "Countryman"; so any thought of intellectual equality between author and addressee, indispensable for successful metaphorical transfer, was not a part of the *Observator*'s didactic approach. In the case of the *Observator* there are further specific restrictions with regard to readership. The *Observator*, in contrast to the *Medley*, for example, makes hardly any reference to contemporary belles-lettres. The regular appearance of headlines summarising in advance the contents of an issue also indicates that the *Observator* sought to adapt to a public which was accustomed to comparatively plain modes of thought and preferred simple objectivity to brilliance of style. As far as vocabulary is concerned, the *Observator* ranges higher than the *Medley* mid-way between the two Tory organs. The relatively high level

1 See, for instance, the *Observator* of 2-6 December 1710 and its vindication of Marlborough's position by analogy with the Romans' treatment of Scipio.

of vocabulary employed by the *Observator* suggests that this peridiocal felt able to stretch its readers as far as the subject-matter was concerned, so long as the mode of presentation did not prove too much for them. At any rate the *Observator* was under no circumstances prepared to allow its vocabulary to descend to broadside level. However, the syntax underlines the intellectual consideration, characteristic of the *Observator*, for a public hungry for information but with limited linguistic and cultural experience. For instance, the relatively low proportion of carefully constructed complex sentences reveals the author's intention to keep the structures of his argument as simple as possible in order to enable his readers to concentrate entirely on the essential subject-matter.

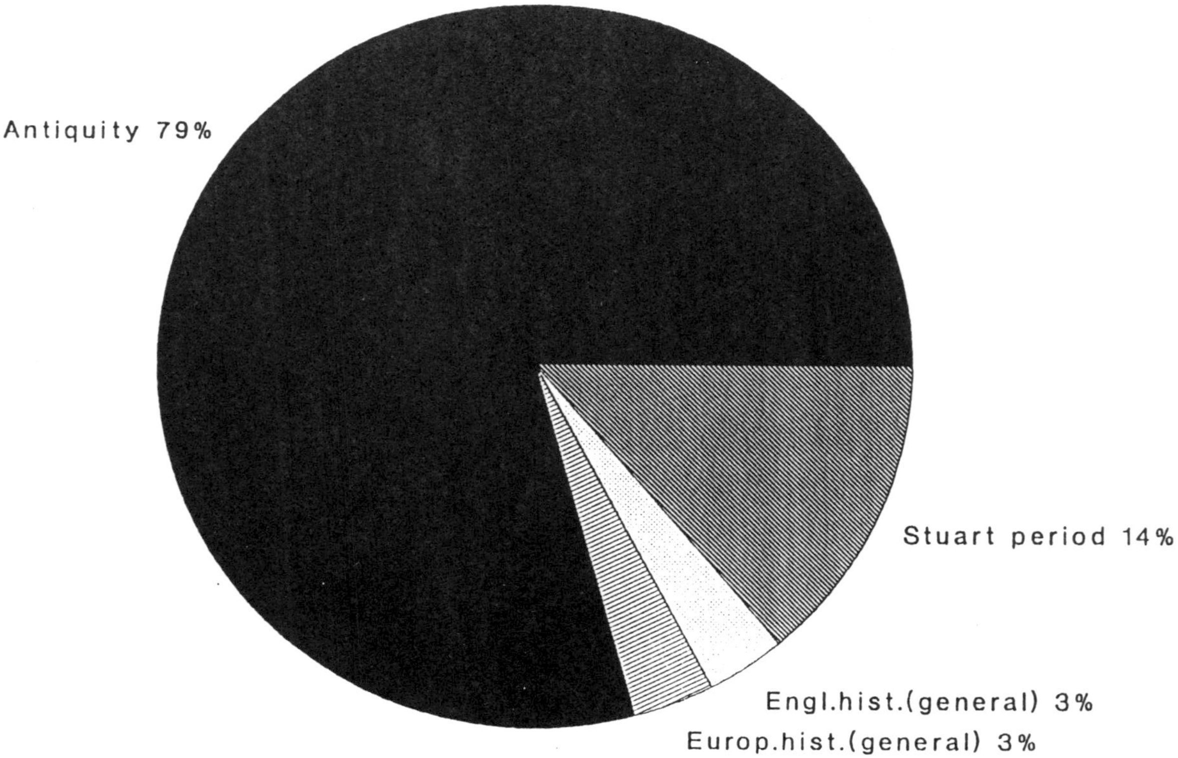

Fig. 1. Historical references in the *Examiner* (1710-1711).

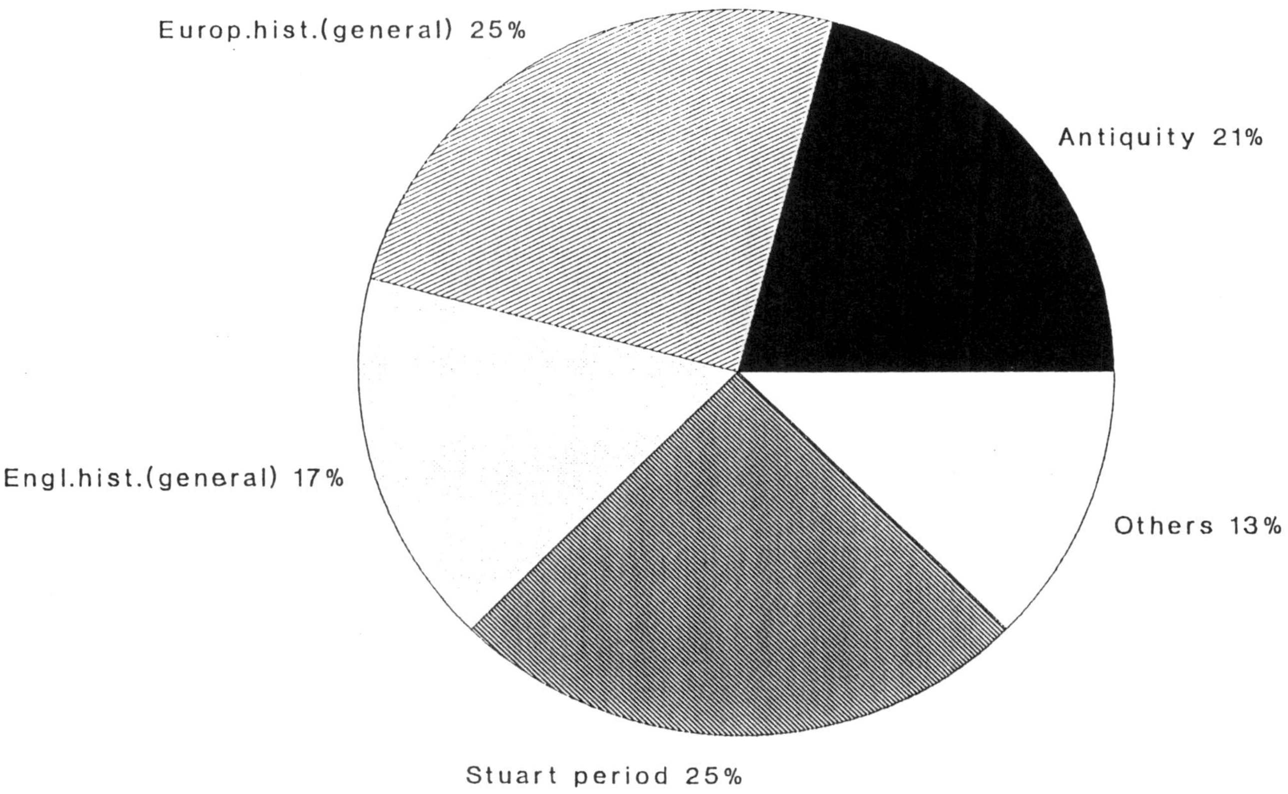

Fig. 2. Historical references in the *Review* (1710-1713).

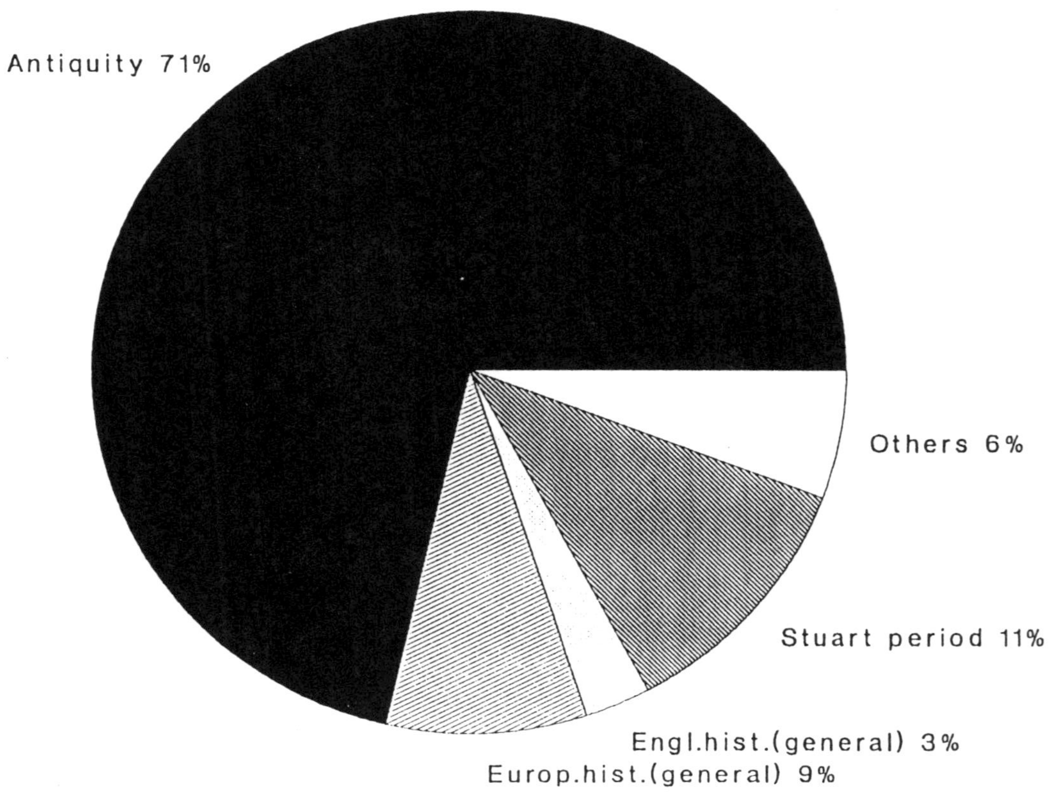

Fig. 3. Historical references in the *Medley* (1710-1711).

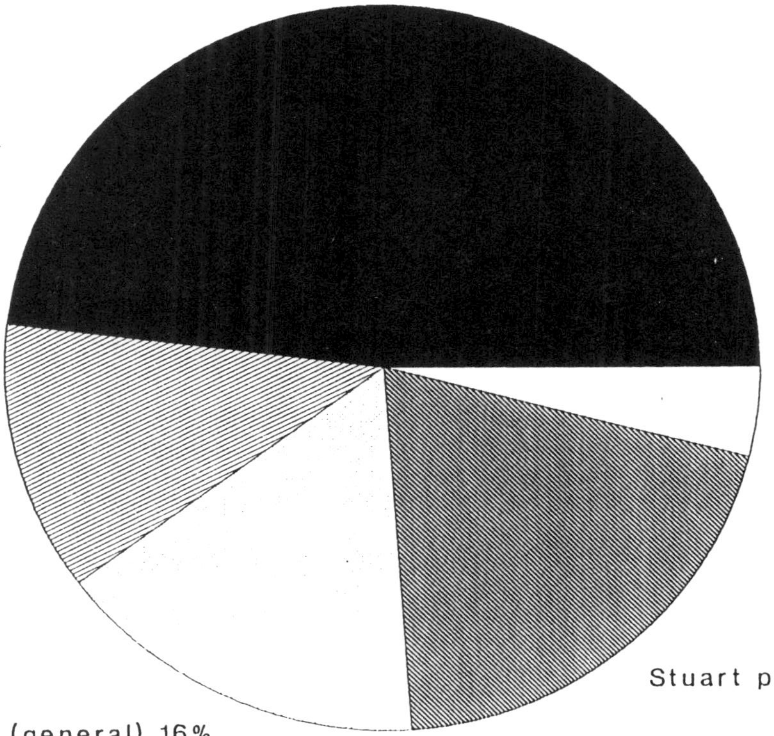

Fig. 4. Historical references in the *Observator* (1711).

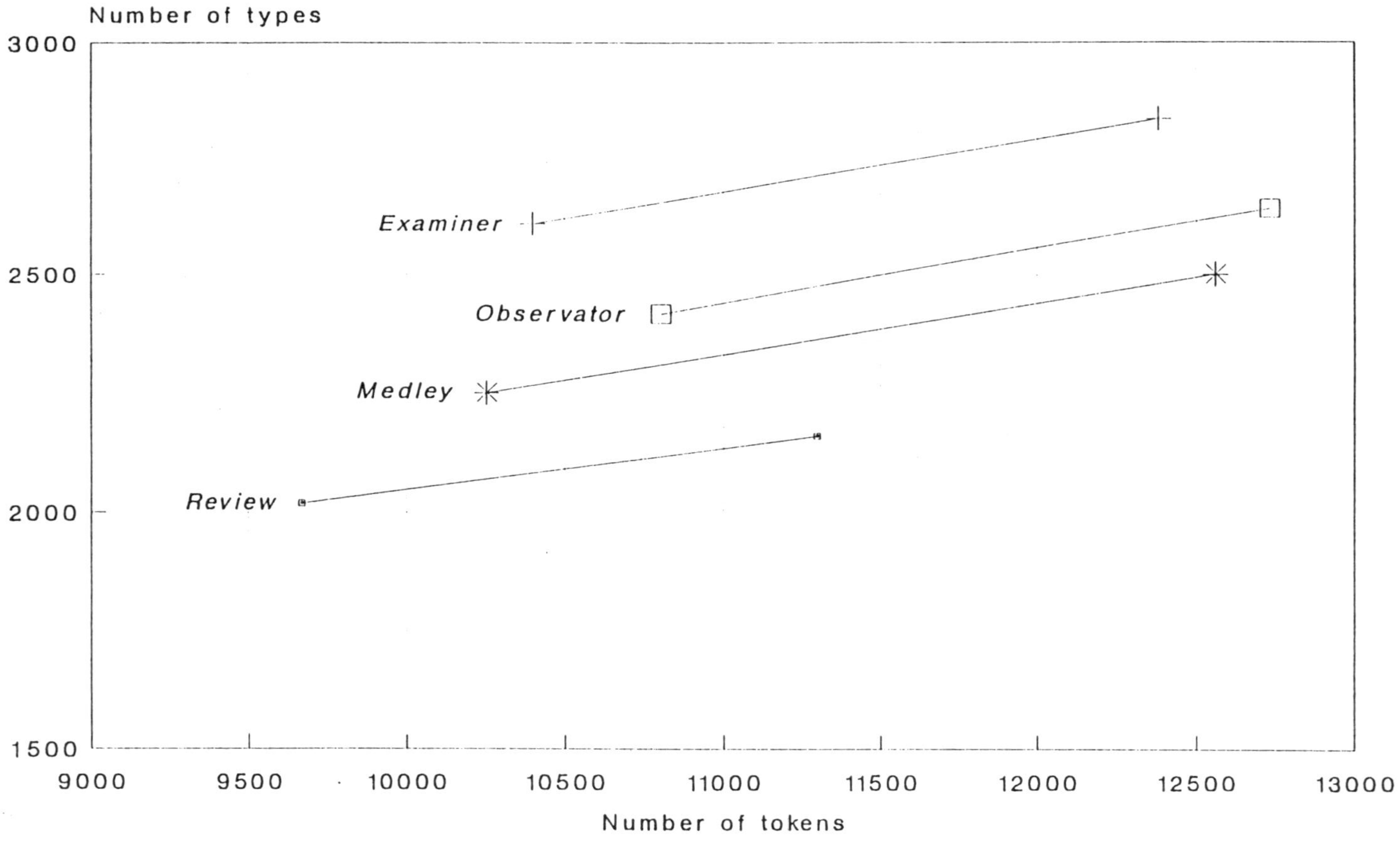

Fig. 5. Vocabulary diversity:
Type-token ratio of the periodicals
(1711-1712)

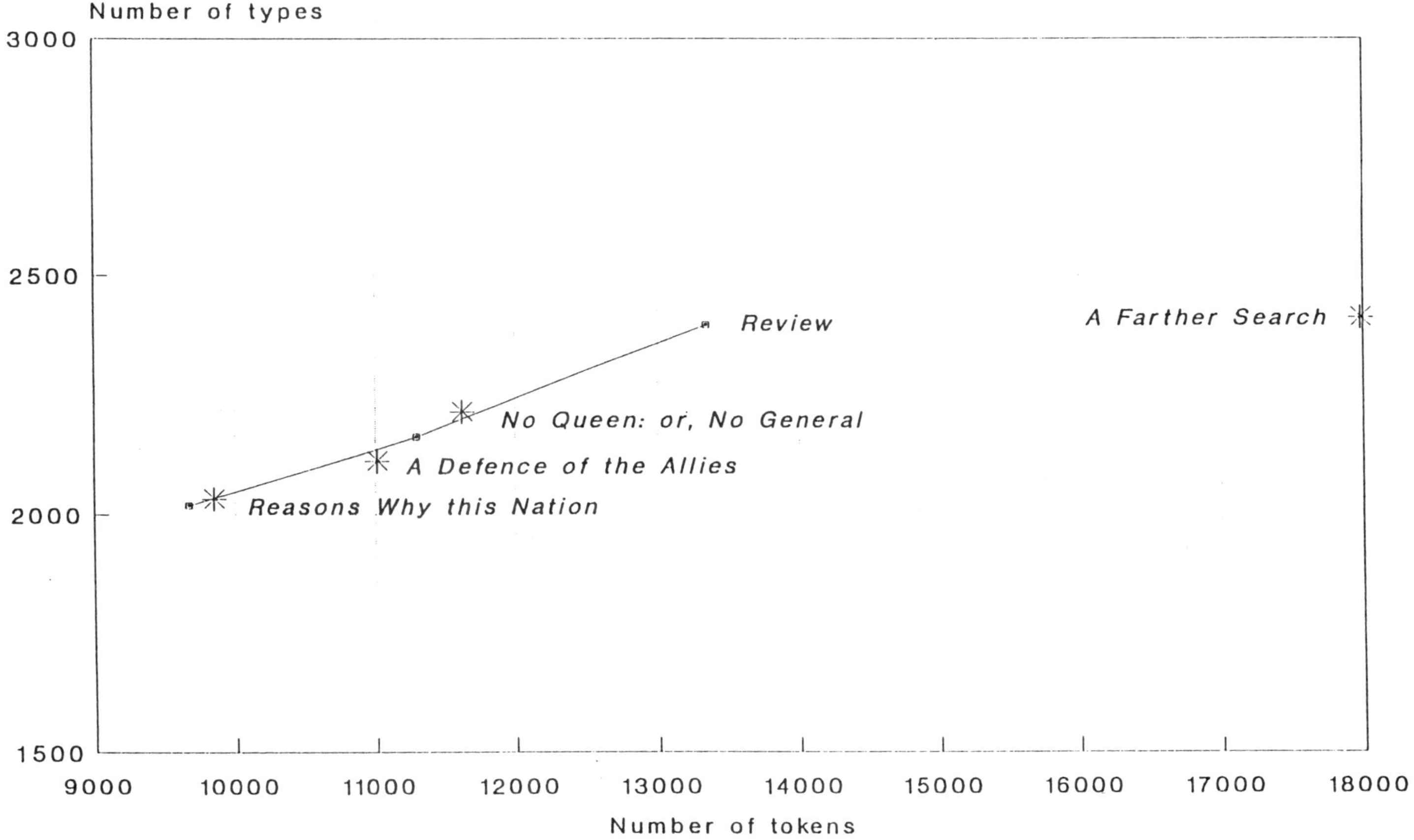

Fig. 6. Vocabulary diversity:
Type-token ratio of the *Review* and
some of Defoe's pamphlets (1711-1712)

CONCLUSION: PUBLIC POLITICAL CULTURE AND THE POLITICAL CLASS

In the light of the intensive as well as extensive interrelationship between public political culture and politics one is struck by the strange contrast between the sophistication of the public debate on the one hand and the well-nigh unanimity with which the political class distanced itself from the very process of the developing debate on the other. Under Queen Anne there was still a wide gap between theory and practice, between a fairly advanced and forward-moving culture of contention and a conservative and defensive school of political thought. This gives the period its Janus-faced character: it was a time when the public debate was taking root, but still lacked any theoretical foundation and acceptance in the collective consciousness of the political class.

The emerging opinion-forming process was widely ignored by Parliament, which still regarded itself as near-autonomous and in fact only took note of journalistic writings - to put it crudely - to the extent that they played a role in libel suits and similar measures of prosecution. Similarly, those who made the political decisions often kept aloof from the already fully developed public political culture, at least outwardly. If they were still deeply entrenched in more traditional ways of thinking, they did not quite know what to make of the new phenomenon[1], and even the more open-minded among the political Establishment adopted an attitude of cautiously distancing themselves morally as well as theoretically. Not even off the record did prominent politicians express their satisfaction at the new propaganda weapon that was now at their disposal; the few exceptions[2] were insignificant and never addressed matters of principle. Very few as yet were prepared to express their support for the institution of the press, something that was to become a matter of course in the Victorian age even for Conservative politicians[3]. A negative attitude prevailed towards everything connected with the press and with journalism[4], and the alleged licentiousness of the press frequently served as a justification for lashing out against it. Ironically, those politicians complained the most who had no scruples about using the press as an instrument in vigorously attacking their opponents[5]. And even Maynwaring, who kept Whig propaganda

---

1 See e.g. Godolphin's letter to Harley in September 1705: HMC, *Bath MSS*, I (London, 1904), 73.

2 Cf. Bolingbroke, *Letters and Correspondence*, I, 9.

3 Cf. - in connection with Lord Salisbury - Alan J. Lee, *The Origins of the Popular Press in England 1855-1914* (London and Totowa, N.J., 1976), p. 210.

4 See e.g. a remark of Marlborough's in this connection repeated in a letter written by H. Watkins to John Drummond dated July 1711: HMC, *Portland MSS*, V (Norwich, 1899), 50.

5 See Bolingbroke, *Letters and Correspondence*, I, 363-364.

on a tight rein, demanded in his correspondence with the Duchess of Marlborough, his benefactress, that the licentiousness of the press be curbed[1] ! And while in the face of looming repression leading writers - as illustrated in the introduction - argued in favour of a free press and described it as a necessary concomitant of the existence of political parties, those politicians who actually availed themselves of the press for their own ends failed to come out in its defence. This is all the more surprising as it was probably the politicians' support for the emerging culture of contention which encouraged writers in their own attitude. But frequent contacts between the two sides notwithstanding, the politicians retained their old-fashioned image of the press. Even Harley was no exception. Not only did he conspicuously keep his distance from Defoe, whom he regarded as socially inferior, but he did not publicly own up to his professional acquaintance with Swift, either, with whom he was on intimate terms socially. Whereas under Queen Anne politicians still assumed a defensive posture vis-à-vis the press, it was comparatively soon afterwards - during the Seven Years' War - that a representative of the political class like Lord Royston elevated freedom of the press to the rank of a constitutional freedom[2]. The outward distance between high politics and journalism was also demonstrated in the attitude of political authors towards Parliament. When Parliament was in session, this invariably led to a flood of political publications, something members regarded as interference and would have liked to stop by simply declaring both chambers out of bounds; writers, on the other hand, in spite of their relentless insistence on certain topics, were mostly quite respectful towards the political proceedings in Parliament in their comments, objective and matter-of-fact rather than critical and judgmental. Quite significantly the absence of any constructive and programmatic comment on the culture of contention by the Establishment was complemented by the reluctance of political writers to pass value judgments on politics as such. Thus Defoe, in his pamphlet *Eleven Opinions about Mr. H-y* (1711), dealt in great detail with the new phenomenon of a battle of opinions but abstained from voicing an abstract view on the business of politics.

Given the multiple and far-reaching links between high politics and journalism, it is not surprising that not all comments on the emergence of public political opinion were negative. For reasons of party-political expediency consecutive governments gave lucrative posts to journalists who in turn offered their services to politicians, like, for example, Boyer[3], Manley[4] and Toland[5] to Harley, thus demonstrating that those in power needed a good relationship with the media. Furthermore, both political parties distributed propaganda literature free, and the sheer number of responses produced at the instigation of high-ranking politicians

---

1 See *Private Correspondence of Sarah, Duchess of Marlborough*, I, 237.

2 See Royston's letter to Lord Hardwicke dated 16 October 1761: *Lord Bute: Essays in Re-interpretation*, ed. Karl W. Schweizer (Leicester Univ. Press, 1988), p. 93.

3 See a letter from Boyer dated 17 October 1710: HMC, *Portland MSS*, IV (London, 1897), 615.

4 See Mrs. Manley's letters dated 19 July and 2 October 1711: HMC, *Portland MSS*, V, 55 and 95-96.

5 See a letter of Toland's dated as late as 7 December 1711: HMC, *Portland MSS*, V, 127.

to political writings is a measure of the readiness among the political class to engage in the process of public debate. Not least the intensification of Tory propaganda at the beginning of 1712 indicated that decisions taken within doors against Marlborough were held to be in need of public support without doors. Such journalistic activity unmistakably demonstrated that what was still publicly denied and played down had in fact been silently accepted: the need to seek approval of political decisions beyond the traditional confines of Court and Parliament. The peculiar dichotomy, typical of Queen Anne's reign, between theoretical rejection and opportunistic acceptance of the public debate is epitomized by the two leading Tory politicians, who actually maintained particularly close links to the press. On the one hand Harley[1] and Bolingbroke availed themselves of the services of writers to propagate their political views, and on the other they did not hesitate to use the state apparatus to suppress journalists who had incurred their displeasure. In the case of Harley, who was a very cautious man, there is ample documentary evidence of this ambivalence, although no personal statements exist, whereas in the case of Bolingbroke there is even corroborating evidence in his personal correspondence. An especially revealing remark, for example, occurs in the postscript to his letter of 21 September 1711 to Mr. Harrison; referring to Whig journalists Bolingbroke writes: "They had best for their patron's sake, as well as their own, be quiet. I know how to set them in the pillory, and how to revive fellows that will write them to death"[2] ! The ambivalence is obvious. Bolingbroke did not shy away from threatening journalists with repression and at the same time was prepared to use them for his own ends. It is a striking example of the Janus-faced attitude of the Establishment towards public political culture. Politicians distanced themselves from, and at the same time took advantage of, the propaganda media. Bolingbroke's words in the above-mentioned letter show his - apparent - aversion but also his sensitivity to the potential usefulness of the printed word in the political process. A similar confidence in the power of the printed word prevailed among the Whigs, as a remark by Maynwaring[3] shows, who, of course, was also an active politician. In the final analysis, politicians under Queen Anne had not yet reconciled themselves unequivocally to the public debate, but they were fascinated by it and for pragmatic reasons actively supported it.

A public political culture had established itself even though the necessary theoretical foundation was still in its infancy. There was an impressive array of genres - with only the political print[4] still to come later[5] - that contributed, each in its

---

1 According to Oldmixon's allegations, he even approached Maynwaring for journalistic support after the change of ministry: *The Life and Posthumous Works of Arthur Maynwaring*, pp. 339-340.

2 Bolingbroke, *Letters and Correspondence*, I, 365.

3 See a letter of Maynwaring's dated July 1711: BL Add. MS 61461, fol. 137.

4 For its development since about 1720 see recently Jürgen Döring, *Eine Kunstgeschichte der frühen englischen Karikatur* (Hildesheim, 1991).

5 Painting, which had in the main kept aloof from the party-political arena during Queen Anne's reign - see Paul Monod, "Painters and Party Politics in England, 1714-1760", *Eighteenth-Century Studies* 26 (1993), pp. 368, 370, 382 -, was also a notable addition, but cannot compare in importance with the political print and its broader base.

own characteristic way, to the culture of contention, thus setting a pattern for future debates of great national issues. The gradually improving conditions for the press and the publishing trade, first during the Walpole era and subsequently during the Seven Years' War[1] - manifest in the availability of reprints, for example, - led to ever more intensive propaganda activities. There was, however, little of essence the later eighteenth century could add to the opinion-forming process that had so forcefully been ushered in during the early years, one notable exception being perhaps the heated constitutional dispute over the freedom of the press during the Wilkes era. The culture of contention under Queen Anne truly marks the beginning of the modern age as regards the participation of the public in the opinion-forming and policy-shaping processes. The interaction of print and politics characteristic of modern public life right up to our times was inaugurated in the reign of Queen Anne, more particularly during the Utrecht controversy. In many respects it was a brilliant beginning - all the more so because it took place in a constitutional void, in the twilight of uncertain and often disputed legitimacy.

---

1 On the later epoch see details in Brewer, *Party Ideology and Popular Politics at the Accession of George III.*

Secondary Works Quoted

Allen, Robert J., "William Oldisworth: 'the Author of *The Examiner*'", *Philological Quarterly* 26 (1947), pp. 159-180

Alsop, J.D., "The Detection of Matthew Prior's Peace Mission of 1711", *British Journal for Eighteenth-Century Studies* 7 (1984), pp. 61-67

Astbury, Raymond, "The Renewal of the Licensing Act in 1693 and its Lapse in 1695", *The Library*, Fifth Series, 33, no. 4 (December 1978), pp. 296-322

Backscheider, Paula R., *Daniel Defoe: His Life* (Baltimore and London, 1989)

Baker, Keith Michael, "Defining the Public Sphere in Eighteenth-Century France: Variations on a Theme by Habermas", *Habermas and the Public Sphere*, ed. Craig Calhoun (Cambridge, Mass., and London, 1992), pp. 181-211

Beljame, Alexandre, *Le Public et les Hommes de Lettres en Angleterre au Dix-Huitième Siècle, 1660-1744* (Paris, 1881)

Bennett, G.V., "Conflict in the Church", *Britain after the Glorious Revolution 1689-1714*, ed. Geoffrey Holmes (London and Basingstoke, 1969), pp. 155-175

Biddle, Sheila, *Bolingbroke and Harley* (New York, 1974)

Black, Jeremy, "The British Press and Europe in the Early Eighteenth Century", *The Press in English Society from the Seventeenth to Nineteenth Centuries*, ed. Michael Harris and Alan Lee (Rutherford, London and Toronto, 1986), pp. 64-79, 224-227

Black, Jeremy, *The English Press in the Eighteenth Century* (London and Sydney, 1987)

Black, Jeremy, and Jeremy Gregory (Eds.), *Culture, Politics and Society in Britain, 1660-1800* (Manchester and New York, 1991)

Bloom, Edward A., "Neoclassic 'Paper Wars' for a Free Press", *The Modern Language Review* 56 (1961), pp. 481-496

Bloom, Edward A., and Lillian D. Bloom, "Steele and his Answerers: May 1709 - February 1714", *The Dress of Words. Essays on Restoration and Eighteenth Century Literature in Honour of Richmond P. Bond*, ed. Robert B. White, Jr. (University of Kansas Libraries, 1978), pp. 167-197

Boucher, David, *Texts in Context. Revisionist Methods for Studying the History of Ideas* (Dordrecht/Boston, Lancaster, 1985)

Brewer, John, *Party Ideology and Popular Politics at the Accession of George III* (Cambridge, 1976)

Broich, Ulrich, *Studien zum komischen Epos. Ein Beitrag zur Deutung, Typologie und Geschichte des komischen Epos im englischen Klassizismus 1680-1800* (Tübingen, 1968)

Calhoun, Craig (Ed.), *Habermas and the Public Sphere* (Cambridge, Mass., and London, 1992)

Capraro, Rocco Lawrence, *Typographic Politics: The Impact of Printing on the Political Life of Eighteenth-Century England, 1714-1772* (doctoral dissertation, Washington University, 1984; Univ. Microfilms International, 1991)

Churchill, Winston, *Marlborough: His Life and Times*, VI (New York, 1938)

Cobbett, William, *The Parliamentary History of England*, VI (London, 1810)

Colley, Linda, *Britons. Forging the Nation 1707-1837* (New Haven and London, 1992)

Cook, Richard I., *Jonathan Swift as a Tory Pamphleteer* (Seattle, Wash., and London, 1967)

Coombs, Douglas S., *The Conduct of the Dutch: British Opinion and the Dutch Alliance during the War of the Spanish Succession* (The Hague and Achimota, 1958)

Corns, Thomas N. (Ed.), *The Literature of Controversy. Polemical Strategy from Milton to Junius* (London, 1987)

Cressy, David, *Literacy and the Social Order. Reading and Writing in Tudor and Stuart England* (Cambridge U.P., 1980)

Darnton, Robert, *The Literary Underground of the Old Regime* (Cambridge, Mass., 1982)

De Beer, E.S., "The English Newspapers from 1695 to 1702", Ragnhild Hatton and J.S. Bromley (Eds.), *William III and Louis XIV. Essays 1680-1720 by and for Mark A. Thomson* (Liverpool U.P., 1968), pp. 117-129

Deconinck-Brossard, Françoise, *Vie Politique, Sociale et Religieuse en Grande-Bretagne d'après les Sermons Prêchés ou Publiés dans le Nord de l'Angleterre 1738-1760* (Paris, 1984)

De Krey, Gary Stuart, *A Fractured Society. The Politics of London in the First Age of Party 1688-1715* (Oxford, 1985)

Demandt, Alexander, *Metaphern für Geschichte. Sprachbilder und Gleichnisse im historisch-politischen Denken* (Munich, 1978)

Denzer, Paul, *Ideologie und literarische Strategie. Die politische Flugblattlyrik der englischen Bürgerkriegszeit 1639-1661* (Tübingen, 1991)

Dickinson, H. T., "Party, Principle and Public Opinion in Eighteenth Century Politics", *History* 60 (1975), pp. 231-237

Dickinson, H.T., *Caricatures and the Constitution 1760-1832* (Cambridge, 1986)

Dickinson, William Calvin, *Sidney Godolphin, Lord Treasurer 1702-1710* (Lewiston, Queenston, Lampeter, 1990)

Döring, Jürgen, *Eine Kunstgeschichte der frühen englischen Karikatur* (Hildesheim, 1991)

Downie, J.A., "Mr. Review and His Scribbling Friends: Defoe and the Critics, 1705-1706", *The Huntington Library Quarterly* 41 (1977-78), pp. 345-366

Downie, J.A., "*The Conduct of the Allies*: The Question of Influence", *The Art of Jonathan Swift*, ed. Clive T. Probyn (London, 1978), pp. 108-128

Downie, J.A., *Robert Harley and the Press. Propaganda and Public Opinion in the Age of Swift and Defoe* (Cambridge, 1979)

Downie, J.A., "The Growth of Government Tolerance of the Press to 1790", *Development of the English Book Trade, 1700-1899*, ed. Robin Myers and Michael Harris (3rd impr., Oxford Polytechnic Press, 1982), pp. 36-65

Downie J.A., and David Woolley, "Swift, Oxford, and the Composition of Queen's Speeches, 1710-14", *The British Library Journal* 8 (1982), pp. 121-146

Downie, J.A., "Swift and the Oxford Ministry: New Evidence", *Swift Studies* 1 (1986), pp. 2-8

Downie, J.A., "The Development of the Political Press", *Britain in the First Age of Party, 1680-1750. Essays Presented to Geoffrey Holmes*, ed. Clyve Jones (London and Ronceverte, 1987), pp. 111-127

Downie, J.A., "Defoe's Early Writings", *The Review of English Studies*, N.S., XLVI (1995), pp. 225-230

Duchhardt, Heinz, "Die Glorious Revolution und das internationale System", *Francia* 16, 2 (1989), pp. 29-37

Duffy, Michael, *The Englishman and the Foreigner* (Cambridge, 1986)

Ehrenpreis, Irvin, *Swift: The Man, his Works, and the Age*, II: *Dr Swift* (London, 1967)

Eley, Geoffrey, "Re-Thinking the Political: Social History and Political Culture in 18th and 19th Century Britain", *Archiv für Sozialgeschichte* 21 (1981), pp. 427-457

Ellis, Frank H., "Arthur Mainwaring as Reader of Swift's *Examiner*", *The Yearbook of English Studies* 11 (1981), pp. 49-66

Ellis, Frank H. (Ed.), *Swift vs. Mainwaring: 'The Examiner' and 'The Medley'* (Oxford, 1985)

Feather, John, "The Book Trade in Politics: The Making of the Copyright Act of 1710", *Publishing History* 8 (1980), pp. 19-44

Feather, John, "The English Book Trade and the Law 1695-1799", *Publishing History* 12 (1982), pp. 51-75

Feather, John, "From Censorship to Copyright: Aspects of the Government's Role in the English Book Trade 1695-1775", *Books and Society in History. Papers of the Association of College and Research Libraries, Rare Books and Manuscripts Preconference, 24-28 June, 1980, Boston, Massachusetts*, ed. Kenneth E. Carpenter (New York and London, 1983), pp. 173-198

Feather, John, *A History of British Publishing* (London and New York, 1988)

Feiling, Keith, *A History of the Tory Party, 1640-1714* (Oxford, 1924, repr. 1965)

Fischer, John Irwin, "The Legal Response to Swift's *The Public Spirit of the Whigs*", *Swift and his Contexts*, ed. John Irwin Fischer, Hermann J. Real and James Woolley (New York, 1989), pp. 21-38

Foot, Michael, *The Pen and the Sword. A Year in the Life of Jonathan Swift* (3rd impr., London, 1966)

Furbank, P.N., and W.R. Owens, *The Canonisation of Daniel Defoe* (New Haven and London, 1988)

Furbank, P.N., and W.R. Owens, "Daniel Defoe and *A Letter from a Gentleman at the Court of St. Germains* (1710)", *Études Anglaises* 48 (1995), pp. 61-66.

Geikie, Roderick, and Isabel A. Montgomery, *The Dutch Barrier 1705-1719* (Cambridge, 1930)
George, Dorothy, *English Political Caricature to 1792. A Study of Opinion and Propaganda* (Oxford, 1959)
Grabes, Herbert, *Das englische Pamphlet I: Politische und religiöse Polemik am Beginn der Neuzeit (1521-1640)* (Tübingen, 1990)
Green, David, *Sarah Duchess of Marlborough* (London, 1967)
Greene, Donald J., "Is there a 'Tory' Prose Style?", *Bulletin of the New York Public Library* 66 (1962), pp. 449-463
Gunn, J.A.W., "Party before Burke: Shute Barrington", *Government and Opposition* III, no. 2 (Spring 1968), pp. 223-240
Gunn, J.A.W., *Beyond Liberty and Property. The Process of Self-Recognition in Eighteenth-Century Political Thought* (Kingston and Montreal, 1983)
Gunn, J.A.W., "Public interest", *Political Innovation and Conceptual Change*, ed. Terence Ball, James Farr, Russell L. Hanson (Cambridge U.P., 1989), pp. 194-210
Guskin, Phyllis J., "Political Implications of Thomas Swift's Sermon *Noah's Dove* (1710)", *Eighteenth Century Life* 1 (1974-75), pp. 46-50

Habermas, Jürgen, "The Public Sphere: An Encyclopedia Article (1964)", *new german critique* 1, no. 3 (Fall 1974), pp. 49-55
Habermas, Jürgen, *Strukturwandel der Öffentlichkeit. Untersuchungen zu einer Kategorie der bürgerlichen Gesellschaft* (17th ed., Darmstadt and Neuwied, 1987)
Habermas, Jürgen, *The Structural Transformation of the Public Sphere: An Inquiry into a Category of Bourgeois Society*, trans. T. Burger and F. Lawrence (Cambridge, Mass., 1989)
Habermas, Jürgen, "Further Reflections on the Public Sphere", *Habermas and the Public Sphere*, ed. Craig Calhoun (Cambridge, Mass., and London, 1992), pp. 421-461
Hanazaki, Tomoko, "A New Parliament of Birds: Aesop, Fiction, and Jacobite Rhetoric", *Eighteenth-Century Studies* 27 (1993-94), pp. 235-254
Hanson, Laurence, *Government and the Press, 1695-1763* (Oxford U.P., 1936)
Harms, Wolfgang *et al.* (Eds.), *Illustrierte Flugblätter des Barock. Eine Auswahl* (Tübingen, 1983)
Harris, Frances Marjorie, *A Study of the Paper War Relating to the Career of the 1st Duke of Marlborough, 1710-1712* (doctoral thesis, University of London, 1975)
Harris, Frances, "Paper-Round: The Distribution of Whig Propaganda in 1710", *Factotum* 9 (August 1980), pp. 12-13
Harris, Frances, *A Passion for Government: The Life of Sarah, Duchess of Marlborough* (Oxford, 1991)
Harris, Michael, "Newspaper Distribution during Queen Anne's Reign. Charles Delafaye and the Secretary of State's Office", *Studies in the Book Trade* (Oxford, 1975), pp. 139-151

Harris, Michael, *London Newspapers in the Age of Walpole. A Study of the Origins of the Modern English Press* (Rutherford, London and Toronto, 1987)
Hattendorf, John B., *England in the War of the Spanish Succession. A Study of the English View and Conduct of Grand Strategy, 1702-1712* (New York and London, 1987)
Hellmuth, Eckhart, *'Liberty' und 'Licentiousness'. Der Diskurs über Pressefreiheit im frühneuzeitlichen England (ca. 1660-ca. 1800)* (Habilitationsschrift, University of Trier, 1990)
Hellmuth, Eckhart (Ed.), *The Transformation of Political Culture. England and Germany in the Late Eighteenth Century* (The German Historical Institute London, 1990)
Hill, B.W., "The Change of Government and the 'Loss of the City', 1710-1711", *The Economic History Review* 24 (1971), pp. 395-413
Hill, B.W., "Oxford, Bolingbroke, and the Peace of Utrecht", *The Historical Journal* 16 (1973), pp. 241-263
Hill, B.W., *Robert Harley. Speaker, Secretary of State and Premier Minister* (New Haven and London, 1988)
Hinrichs, Ernst, "Wie viele Menschen konnten um 1800 lesen und schreiben?", Helmut Ottenjann and Günter Wiegelmann (Eds.), *Alte Tagebücher und Anschreibebücher* (Münster, 1982), pp. 85-103
Hölscher, Lucian, "'Öffentliche Meinung'", *Geschichtliche Grundbegriffe*, ed. Otto Brunner *et al.*, 4 (Stuttgart, 1978), pp. 448-450
Holmes, G.S., "The Commons' Division on 'No Peace without Spain', 7 December 1711", *Bulletin of the Institute of Historical Research* 33 (1960), pp. 223-234
Holmes, Geoffrey, *British Politics in the Age of Anne* (London and New York, 1967; rev. ed. 1987)
Holmes, Geoffrey, and W.A. Speck (Eds.), *The Divided Society: Party Conflict in England 1694-1716* (London, 1967, repr. 1970)
Holmes, Geoffrey (Ed.), *Britain after the Glorious Revolution 1689-1714* (London and Basingstoke, 1969)
Holmes, Geoffrey, *The Trial of Doctor Sacheverell* (London, 1973)
Holmes, Geoffrey, *Politics, Religion and Society in England 1679-1742* (London and Ronceverte, 1986)
Holstun, James (Ed.), *Pamphlet Wars. Prose in the English Revolution* (London, 1992)
Horn, Robert D., *Marlborough: A Survey. Panegyrics, Satires, and Biographical Writings, 1688-1788* (New York and London, 1975)
Horsley, L.S., "Rogues or Honest Gentlemen: The Public Characters of Queen Anne Journalists", *Texas Studies in Literature and Language* 18 (1976), pp. 198-228
Horwitz, Henry, "Parties, Connections, and Parliamentary Politics, 1689-1714: Review and Revision", *Journal of British Studies* 6, No. 1 (November 1966), pp. 45-69
Horwitz, Henry, *Parliament, Policy and Politics in the Reign of William III* (Newark, 1977)

Houston, R.A., *Scottish Literacy and the Scottish Identity. Illiteracy and Society in Scotland and Northern England 1600-1800* (Cambridge U.P., 1985)

Jäger, Wolfgang, *Öffentlichkeit und Parlamentarismus. Eine Kritik an Jürgen Habermas* (Stuttgart etc., 1973)

James, E. Anthony, *Daniel Defoe's Many Voices. A Rhetorical Study of Prose Style and Literary Method* (Amsterdam, 1972)

James, F.G., "The Bishops in Politics, 1688-1714", *Conflict in Stuart England. Essays in Honour of Wallace Notestein*, ed. William Appleton Aiken and Basil Duke Henning (London, 1960), pp. 229-257

Jensen, J. Vernon, "British Voices on the Eve of the American Revolution: Trapped by the Family Metaphor", *The Quarterly Journal of Speech* 63 (1977), pp. 43-50

Jones, Clyve, "The Division that never Was: New Evidence on the Aborted Vote in the Lords on 8 December 1711 on 'No Peace without Spain'", *Parliamentary History* 2 (1983), pp. 191-202

Klaits, Joseph, *Printed Propaganda under Louis XIV. Absolute Monarchy and Public Opinion* (Princeton U.P., 1976)

Laprevotte, Guy, "*Examiner* et *Medley*: La Référence à l'Antiquité dans le Débat Politique", *Bulletin de la Société d'Etudes Anglo-Américaines des XVIIe et XVIIIe Siècles* 27 (November 1988), pp. 123-140

Laprevotte, Guy, "*The Conduct of the Allies*: contexte et originalité", *Commerce(s) en Grande-Bretagne au XVIIIe Siècle*, ed. Suzy Halimi (Paris, 1990), pp. 239-260

Lee, Alan J., *The Origins of the Popular Press in England 1855-1914* (London and Totowa, N. J., 1976)

Legg, L.G. Wickham, "Torcy's Account of Matthew Prior's Negotiations at Fontainebleau in July 1711", *The English Historical Review* 29 (1914), pp. 525-532

Lessenich, Rolf P., *Elements of Pulpit Oratory in Eighteenth-Century England* (*1660-1800*) (Cologne and Vienna, 1972)

Lock, F.P., *Swift's Tory Politics* (London, 1983)

Loftis, John, *The Politics of Drama in Augustan England* (Oxford, 1963)

Lohrengel, Hans, *Politische Metaphorik in Defoes 'Review'* (Staatsexamensarbeit, University of Göttingen, 1992)

MacLachlan, A.D., "The Road to Peace 1710-13", *Britain after the Glorious Revolution 1689-1714*, ed. Geoffrey Holmes (London and Basingstoke, 1969), pp. 197-215

Madan, F.F., *A Critical Bibliography of Dr. Henry Sacheverell. Edited by W.A. Speck* (Lawrence, Kans., 1978)

Matchen, David, "Daniel Defoe's Rhetorical Art in the *Review*", *CLA Journal* 25 (1981-82), pp. 427-446

Metzdorf, Jens, "*The just and necessary War we are engag'd in*". *Marlboroughs Kaplan Francis Hare und die publizistische Debatte um die Beendigung des Spanischen Erbfolgekrieges in England* (Staatsexamensarbeit, University of Münster, 1993)

Mittag, Martina, *Nationale Identitätsbestrebungen und antispanische Polemik im englischen Pamphlet 1558-1630* (Frankfurt and Berne, 1992)

Monod, Paul, "Painters and Party Politics in England, 1714-1760", *Eighteenth-Century Studies* 26 (1993), pp. 367-398

Moore, John Robert, "Defoe, Steele, and the Demolition of Dunkirk", *The Huntington Library Quarterly* 27 (1963-64), pp. 279-302

Morley, William F.E., *Queen Anne Pamphlets. An Annotated Bibliographical Catalogue of Pamphlet Publications Spanning the Reign of Queen Anne, Held in the Eighteenth-Century British Pamphlet Collection, Douglas Library, Queen's University: 1701-1714* (Kingston, Ontario, 1987)

Müllenbrock, Heinz-Joachim, *Whigs kontra Tories. Studien zum Einfluß der Politik auf die englische Literatur des frühen 18. Jahrhunderts* (Heidelberg, 1974)

Müllenbrock, Heinz-Joachim (Ed.), *Europäische Aufklärung II*, Neues Handbuch der Literaturwissenschaft, 12 (Wiesbaden, 1984)

Müllenbrock, Heinz-Joachim, "Cicero und Quintilian als Mentoren britischer Publizistik: Die rhetorische Struktur von Swifts *The Conduct of the Allies* (1711)", *Antike und Abendland* 32 (1986), pp. 173-185

Müllenbrock, Heinz-Joachim, "Cicero and Quintilian as Mentors of British Journalism: The Rhetorical Structure of Swift's *The Conduct of the Allies*", *Swift Studies* 2 (1987), pp. 57-66

Müllenbrock, Heinz-Joachim, "Alexander Pope's *Windsor Forest* (1713): Genre and Political Propaganda", *Studi Settecenteschi* 11-12 (1988-89), pp. 9-15

Müllenbrock, Heinz-Joachim, "Swift as a Political Essayist: The Strained Medium", *Reading Swift: Papers from The Second Münster Symposium on Jonathan Swift*, ed. Richard H. Rodino and Hermann J. Real (Munich, 1993), pp. 151-158

Mulligan, Lotte, Judith Richards, and John Graham, "Intentions and Conventions: A Critique of Quentin Skinner's Method for the Study of the History of Ideas", *Political Studies* 27 (1979), pp. 84-98

Naphtine, D., and W.A. Speck, "Clergymen and Conflict 1660-1763", *The Church and War*, ed. W.J. Sheils (Oxford, 1983), pp. 231-251

Needham, Gwendolyn B., "Mary de la Rivière Manley, Tory Defender", *The Huntington Library Quarterly* 12 (1948-49), pp. 253-288

Neumann, Fritz-Wilhelm, "The Semantic Subsystems of ECCOP (The Eighteenth-Century Corpus of Pamphlets); or, the future of the toys for the boys critique", *Anglistentag 1992 Stuttgart: Proceedings*, ed. Hans-Ulrich Seeber and Walter Göbel (Tübingen 1993), pp. 418-426

Noelle-Neumann, Elisabeth, "Öffentliche Meinung", *Das Fischer Lexikon: Publizistik, Massenkommunikation*, ed. Elisabeth Noelle-Neumann, Winfried Schulz, Jürgen Wilke (Frankfurt a.M., 1989), pp. 255-266

O'Brien, John F., "The Character of Credit: Defoe's 'Lady Credit', *The Fortunate Mistress*, and the Resources of Inconsistency in Early Eighteenth-Century Britain", *ELH* 63 (1996), pp. 603-631

Owens, W.R., and P.N. Furbank, "Defoe and the Dutch Alliance: Some Attributions Examined", *British Journal for Eighteenth-Century Studies* 9 (1986), pp. 169-182

Ozouf, Mona, "'Public Opinion' at the End of the Old Regime", *Journal of Modern History* 60, Supplement (September 1988), pp. S1-S21

Patterson, Paul Baker, *Robert Harley and the Organisation of Political Propaganda* (Diss., University of Virginia, 1974)

Peil, Dietmar, *Untersuchungen zur Staats- und Herrschaftsmetaphorik in literarischen Zeugnissen von der Antike bis zur Gegenwart* (Munich, 1983)

Peters, Marie ,"History and Political Propaganda in Mid-Eighteenth-Century England: The Case of the Essay Papers", *Eighteenth Century Life* 11 (1987), pp. 66-79

Peters, Marie, *Pitt and Popularity. The Patriot Minister and London Opinion during the Seven Years' War* (Oxford, 1980)

Plumb, J.H., *The Growth of Political Stability in England, 1675-1725* (London, Melbourne, Toronto, 1967)

Porter, Roy, "Seeing the Past", *Past and Present* 119 (1988), pp. 186-205

Poston, Lawrence, III, "Defoe and the Peace Campaign, 1710-1713: A Reconsideration", *The Huntington Library Quarterly* 27 (1963), pp. 1-20

Price, J.M., " A Note on the Circulation of the London Press, 1704-1714", *Bulletin of the Institute of Historical Research* 31 (1958), pp. 215-224

Quinlan, Maurice J., "The Prosecution of Swift's *Public Spirit of the Whigs*", *Texas Studies in Literature and Language* 9 (1967-68), pp. 167-184

Ransome, Mary, "The Press in the General Election of 1710", *The Cambridge Historical Journal* 6 (1939), pp. 208-221

Rea, Robert R., "Introduction: The Mirror of Politics", *The English Press in Politics, 1760-1774* (Lincoln, Neb., 1963), pp. 1-11, 235-236

Richards, James O., *Party Propaganda under Queen Anne. The General Elections of 1702-1713* (Athens, Ga., 1972)

Richetti, John J., *Popular Fiction before Richardson. Narrative Patterns 1700-1739* (Oxford, 1969)

Richter, Melvin, "Zur Rekonstruktion der Geschichte der Politischen Sprachen: Pocock, Skinner und die *Geschichtlichen Grundbegriffe*", Hans Erich Bödeker and Ernst Hinrichs (Eds.), *Alteuropa - Ancien Régime - Frühe Neuzeit: Probleme und Methoden der Forschung* (Stuttgart-Bad Cannstatt, 1991), pp. 134-174

Rigotti, Francesca, *Die Macht und ihre Metaphern. Über die sprachlichen Bilder der Politik* (Frankfurt/New York, 1994)

Rogers, Pat, "Swift and Bolingbroke on Faction", *The Journal of British Studies* 9 (1970), pp. 71-101

Schenda, Rudolf, *Volk ohne Buch* (Frankfurt a.M., 1970)

Schlenke, Manfred, *England und das friderizianische Preussen 1740-1763. Ein Beitrag zum Verhältnis von Politik und öffentlicher Meinung im England des 18. Jahrhunderts* (Freiburg and Munich, 1963)

Schöffler, Herbert, *Protestantismus und Literatur. Neue Wege zur englischen Literatur des 18. Jahrhunderts* (2nd ed., Göttingen, 1958)

Schweizer, Karl W. (Ed.), *Lord Bute: Essays in Re-interpretation* (Leicester Univ. Press, 1988)

Schwoerer, Lois G., "Propaganda in the Revolution of 1688-89", *American Historical Review* 82 (1977), pp. 843-874

Scudi, A.T., *The Sacheverell Affair* (New York, 1939)

Sheehan, M., "The Development of British Theory and Practice of the Balance of Power before 1714", *History* 73 (1988), pp. 24-37

Sherburn, George, "Francis Hare and the Peace of Utrecht", *The Newberry Library Bulletin* VI, no. 3 (November 1963), pp. 65-73

Siebert, Frederick Seaton, *Freedom of the Press in England 1476-1776. The Rise and Decline of Government Controls* (Urbana, Ill., 1952)

Skerpan, Elizabeth, *The Rhetoric of Politics in the English Revolution 1642-1660* (Columbia and London, 1992)

Smith, Nigel, *Literature and Revolution in England 1640-1660* (New Haven and London, 1994)

Snyder, Henry L., "Daniel Defoe, The Duchess of Marlborough, and the 'Advice to the Electors of Great Britain'", *The Huntington Library Quarterly* 29 (1965-66), pp. 53-62

Snyder, Henry L., "The Reports of a Press Spy for Robert Harley: New Bibliographical Data for the Reign of Queen Anne", *The Library*, Fifth Series, 22, no. 4 (December 1967), pp. 326-345

Snyder, Henry L., "The Circulation of Newspapers in the Reign of Queen Anne", *The Library*, Fifth Series, 23, no. 3 (September 1968), pp. 206-235

Snyder, Henry L., "Daniel Defoe, Arthur Maynwaring, Robert Walpole, and Abel Boyer: Some Considerations of Authorship", *The Huntington Library Quarterly* 33 (1970), pp. 133-153

Snyder, Henry L., "The Prologues and Epilogues of Arthur Maynwaring", *Philological Quarterly* 50 (1971), pp. 610-629

Snyder, Henry L., "Arthur Maynwaring and the Whig Press, 1710-1712", *Literatur als Kritik des Lebens. Festschrift zum 65. Geburtstag von Ludwig Borinski*, ed. Rudolf Haas, Heinz-Joachim Müllenbrock and Claus Uhlig (Heidelberg, 1975), pp. 120-136

Snyder, Henry L., "A Further Note on the Circulation of Newspapers in the Reign of Queen Anne", *The Library*, Fifth Series, 31, no. 4 (December 1976), pp. 387-389

Snyder, Henry L., "The Authorship of *Faults on Both Sides* (1710)", *Philological Quarterly* 56 (1977), pp. 266-272

Snyder, Henry L., "Marlborough and the Reign of Queen Anne: The Status of Current Studies", *The British Studies Monitor* 8, 3 (1978), pp. 3-15

Späth, Eberhard, "Facts and Factions: Political Pamphlets of the Time of Queen Anne", *Zeitschrift für Anglistik und Amerikanistik* 40 (1992), pp. 130-140

Speck, W.A., and Geoffrey Holmes (Eds.), *The Divided Society: Party Conflict in England 1694-1716* (London, 1967, repr. 1970)

Speck W.A., "From Principles to Practice: Swift and Party Politics", *The World of Jonathan Swift. Essays for the Tercentenary*, ed. Brian Vickers (Oxford, 1968), pp. 69-86

Speck, W.A., *Tory and Whig: The Struggle in the Constituencies, 1701-1715* (London, 1970)

Speck, W.A., "*The Examiner* Examined: Swift's Tory Pamphleteering", *Focus: Swift*, ed. C.J. Rawson (London, 1971), pp. 138-154

Speck, W.A., "Political Propaganda in Augustan England", *Transactions of the Royal Historical Society*, Fifth Series, 22 (1972), pp. 17-32

Speck, William, "Politics and the Press", *The Press in English Society from the Seventeenth to Nineteenth Centuries*, ed. Michael Harris and Alan Lee (Rutherford, London and Toronto, 1986), pp. 17-63, 223-224

Spector, Robert D., *Political Controversy. A Study in Eighteenth-Century Propaganda* (New York: Greenwood Press, 1992)

Stephen, Leslie, *English Literature and Society in the Eighteenth Century* (London, 1910)

Stephens, John C., Jr., "Steele and the Bishop of St. Asaph's Preface", *PMLA* 67 (1952), pp. 1011-1023

Stevens, David Harrison, *Party Politics and English Journalism, 1702-1742* (Menasha, Wisconsin, 1916)

Stone, Lawrence, "Literacy and Education in England 1640-1900", *Past and Present* 42 (1969), pp. 69-139

Stratmann, Gerd, "'*Easy and Familiar*' - Zur klassizistischen Theorie des Prosastils", Rüdiger Ahrens and Erwin Wolff (Eds.), *Englische und amerikanische Literaturtheorie. Studien zu ihrer historischen Entwicklung*, I (Heidelberg, 1978), 237-251

Suerbaum, Ulrich, "'I Repeat and Repeat.': Repetition as Structure in Defoe's *Robinson Crusoe*", *Telling Stories. Studies in Honour of Ulrich Broich on the Occasion of his 60th Birthday*, ed. Elmar Lehmann and Bernd Lenz (Amsterdam/ Philadelphia, 1992), pp. 69-83

Sullivan, Robert E., *John Toland and the Deist Controversy. A Study in Adaptations* (Cambridge, Mass., and London, 1982)

Sutherland, James, *Daniel Defoe. A Critical Study* (Cambridge, Mass., 1971)

Sutherland, James R., "The Circulation of Newspapers and Literary Periodicals, 1700-30", *The Library*, Fourth Series, 15 (1934-35), pp. 110-124

Thomson, M.A., "Parliament and Foreign Policy 1689-1714", *History* 38 (1953), pp. 234-243

Treadwell, Michael, "London Trade Publishers 1675-1750", *The Library*, Sixth Series, 4, No. 2 (June 1982), pp. 99-134

Treadwell, Michael, "Swift's Relations with the London Book Trade to 1714", *Author/Publisher Relations during the Eighteenth and Nineteenth Centuries*, ed. Robin Myers and Michael Harris (Oxford Polytechnic Press, 1983), pp. 1-36

Treadwell, Michael, "On False and Misleading Imprints in the London Book Trade, 1660-1750", *Fakes and Frauds: Varieties of Deception in Print and Manuscript*, ed. Robin Myers and Michael Harris (Winchester: St. Paul's Bibliographies, 1989), pp. 29-46

Trevelyan, George Macaulay, *England under Queen Anne: Blenheim* (London, 1930)

Trevelyan, George Macaulay, *England under Queen Anne: The Peace and the Protestant Succession* (London, 1934)

Trevelyan, George Macaulay, "The 'Jersey' Period of the Negotiations Leading to the Peace of Utrecht", *The English Historical Review* 49 (1934), pp. 100-105

Tully, James H., "Review Article: The Pen is a Mighty Sword: Quentin Skinner's Analysis of Politics", *British Journal of Political Science* 13 (1983), pp. 489-509

Wackwitz, Beate, *Die Theorie des Prosastils im England des 18. Jahrhunderts* (Hamburg, 1962)

Wakeman, Mary K., *God's Battle with the Monster. A Study in Biblical Imagery* (Leiden, 1973)

Walcott, Robert, *English Politics in the Early Eighteenth Century* (Oxford, 1956)

Wasserman, Earl R., *The Subtler Language. Critical Readings of Neoclassic and Romantic Poems* (Baltimore, 1959)

Watson, George, "The Augustan Civil War", *The Review of English Studies*, N.S., XXXVI (1985), pp. 321-337

Watt, Ian, *The Rise of the Novel. Studies in Defoe, Richardson and Fielding* (5th impr., London, 1967)

Weber, Ottocar, *Der Friede von Utrecht. Verhandlungen zwischen England, Frankreich, dem Kaiser und den Generalstaaten 1710-1713* (Gotha, 1891)

Wellenreuther, Hermann, "Das spanische Reich in der englischen Diskussion während des Siebenjährigen Krieges. Überlegungen zum Habermas'schen Begriff der 'Bürgerlichen Öffentlichkeit'", *Iberische Welten. Festschrift zum 65. Geburtstag von Günter Kahle*, ed. Felix Becker, Holger M. Meding, Barbara Potthast-Jutkeit, Karin Schüller (Cologne, Weimar, Vienna, 1994), pp. 723-758

"What Is Intellectual History?", *History Today* 35 (1985), pp. 46-54

Woolley, David, "The Canon of Swift's Prose Pamphleteering, 1710-1714, and *The New Way of Selling Places at Court*", *Swift Studies* 3 (1988), pp. 96-117

Zaret, David, "Petitions and the 'Invention' of Public Opinion in the English Revolution", *American Journal of Sociology* 101 (1996), pp. 1497-1555

INDEX